JACK GROUT: A LEGACY IN GOLF

Pioneer Tour Pro and Teacher to Jack Nicklaus

DICK GROUT
with Bill Winter

Blue River Press
Indianapolis, IN

ISBN: 9781935628187
Library of Congress Control Number: 2012945453

Cover designed by Phil Velikan

Cover photo: Jack Grout working with Jack Nicklaus on the practice range at the 1974 U.S. Open at Winged Foot Golf Club in Mamaroneck, New York. (Bill Foley photo, used with permission.)

Editorial assistance provided by Dorothy Chambers
Packaged by Wish Publishing

Printed in the United States of America
10 9 8 7 6 5 4 3 2 1

Published by Blue River Press
Distributed by Cardinal Publishers Group
Tom Doherty Company, Inc.
www.cardinalpub.com

To the memory of my father.
Dad, you deserve so many more accolades
than you have received.

And to the love of my life, Denise;
our son, Tony; his wife, Vanessa; our daughter, Natalie; her husband,
Jim; and their precious children, Nolan and Quinn.
They sustain me.

Jack Grout image taken in 1939 during photo shoot for Better Golf Without Practice *by Alex J. Morrison. (Alex J. Morrison photo, used with permission)*

"Golf is a game that brings out both the best and worst aspects of a person's character. It rewards patience, self-control, and honest self-analysis. It penalizes anger and self-deception. It is a game that pits you alone against the course. And the course doesn't move around to block your shots, or try to knock you out-of-bounds, or throw you curve balls. It just sits there passively, waiting for you to challenge it – and yourself. In other words, the burden of proof in golf is solely on you, the player, which is one of the chief reasons why it is such a popular and, for many people, a lifelong game." – JACK GROUT

Author's Note: Jack Grout's advice and musings about golf and life are as true and valuable today as during his long and distinguished career as a playing and teaching professional. Look for them at the beginning of each chapter.

Table of Contents

1985: Jack Grout and Dick Grout in the main dining room at Muirfield Village Golf Club, Dublin, Ohio. (Grout family photo)

A Son's Tribute to a Hall of Fame Dad

"It is a game where men and women who are short in stature and slight of build can, and have, excelled. The ranks of great players, past and present, include far more Davids than Goliaths." – *JACK GROUT*

***

Honestly, sometimes I wish my father had been a self-centered, self-promoting publicity hound rather than the kind, humble, self-effacing person described by pro golfer Olin Browne (Page 273) as a man who "didn't look for accolades or recognition of any kind." Even as his straightforward, uncomplicated teaching guided Jack Nicklaus to 18 major golf titles and helped mold the games of major-title winners Raymond Floyd, Lanny Wadkins, and David Graham, Dad never sought the glare of public acclaim. There was no Golf Channel in his day. No ESPN. No Internet. No easy way for the full story of his amazing career as a golfer and golf instructor to be told to the world. So his story remained, for the most part, untold.

In 2015, important recognition finally came Dad's way via his induction into the World Golf Teachers Hall of Fame. He would have been proud, for sure, because whether it's Cooperstown, Canton or a shrine known only to the locals, selection to "the Hall of Fame" represents the pinnacle of achievement. It is recognition that an individual stands apart from the many who were notable in a particular sport or endeavor. To be in "the Hall of Fame," no matter where it is, distinguishes the performance and contributions of an inductee as exceptional.

In the game of golf, the ultimate honor is to be memorialized in St. Augustine, on the Atlantic coast of Florida, at the sport's hallowed ground, the World Golf Hall of Fame. By its own proclamation, "The World Golf Hall of Fame is home to the game's greatest players and contributors. Membership is, quite simply, golf's highest honor. Those recognized within the Hall of Fame represent individuals who have positively impacted the game of golf on the grandest scale." Among the unforgettables honored there are Hogan, Hagen, Jones, Ouimet, Vardon, Nelson, Sarazen, Snead, Palmer, Player...and Nicklaus. Jack Nicklaus. The Golden Bear. Arguably the greatest champion in the history of the game, it makes perfect sense that he would occupy a place of honor in his sport's Hall of Fame. Always, though, a Hall of

Fame is known, too, for those who are not included but should be. And that is an underlying point of this book.

My father – or as his star pupil Jack Nicklaus fondly called him, "J. Grout" – is recognized as the foremost golf teacher of his era...that time when the most skilled players among the club professionals were tour pros, too, and vice versa...when top players traveled long hours together by car from tournament to tournament, and often pooled their meager winnings to make ends meet...when club shafts were hickory and balls were tightly wound rubber bands encased in covers that would cut easily.

The accomplishments of these players pale in comparison with today's statistical measurements, and thus sometimes are underestimated.

Dad began working with Jack Nicklaus when little Jackie was a ten-year-old at Scioto Country Club in Columbus, Ohio. And after winning more major championships than any other player in golf history, Nicklaus would write: "Without him, I'm certain I would never have achieved the professional success I have enjoyed."

On Pages 272-273 of this book, World Golf Hall of Fame members Arnold Palmer, Ray Floyd, Gary Player, Lanny Wadkins, David Graham and other noted golfers and golf instructors offer similar tributes. And yet, Jack Grout's place in St. Augustine remains vacant, awaiting the day his unique excellence finally is fully recognized.

— Dick Grout, September, 2016

Jack Nicklaus Remembers Jack Grout

"Practice your mental skills as much as your physical ones. Use your brain as an asset to complement your techniques of play." – JACK GROUT

***

Through my adult years I've come to understand clearly that there is no greater gift in life than true friendship. Jack Grout was my unconditional friend for nearly four decades, serving as both my golf instructor and, after the premature death of my father in 1970, as a second father to me. Jack gave a great deal of himself to me as my only golf teacher from the day I first attended one of his junior golf classes at Scioto Country Club, right up through my final major championship victory in the 1986 Masters. Now I have the pleasure of giving something back to him by providing this foreword to what is a long-overdue book about the professional and personal life of one of my greatest friends.

During a recent interview I was asked for my favorite memory of Jack Grout, the man who taught me how to play golf. I responded that this was a tough one, that our friendship was so close, that we spent so much time just chatting as good friends on the lesson tee or in the clubhouse of one golf club or another through the years, that no single memory stood out. But as I pondered the answer, I came to something that has struck me many times as I've watched today's professional golfers go about their work in a way that Jack Grout would have perhaps found baffling. Many times I see today's pros out on the practice range with their swing gurus standing there behind them. And they've got their nutritionists, and they've got their strength coaches and their mental coaches, and I find it somewhat amusing. At the same time the memories flow of the thousands of hours I spent on the lesson tee with just one man beside me—a man who rarely stepped foot with me on the practice ground of a tournament, a man who felt that once I got to a tournament, it was mine to win or lose. (Of course, if I ever needed him, I knew he was there.) The fact is, I had only Jack Grout. No strength coaches, dieticians or psychologists. Just Jack Grout. And I was fortunate to enjoy a great deal of success, including the major championships that I deemed so important and the measuring stick of one's career.

If that suggests that Jack Grout was one tremendously effective teacher and mentor for me, not to mention the scores of other professional and amateur players he coached, well, indeed he was. And it seems to me that the key to Jack's teaching was that he wanted you to become so skilled at golf, to have such an understanding of your own golf swing, that you really wouldn't need him anymore. So, Jack pounded away on the fundamentals of the game—the grip, proper posture, the movement of the feet, tempo, the width and length of my swing (always preaching to me to reach back and get as high as I could). And even as he coaxed you gently into accepting and internalizing those fundamentals, he bombarded you with encouragement: never negative things, just positive.

That was Jack Grout's true genius, of course. He knew the golf swing probably as well as any instructor ever has. But I think his greatest gift to his students was his belief in them and his ability to get them to believe in themselves. He wanted you not only to be skilled technically, but also to be so confident of your skills that you could identify and fix your own swing flaws even in the heat of battle, even without him there by your side. In other words, Jack Grout worked to be *dispensable*. He wanted his students to be able to function at the highest level without him.

As reiterated in the following pages by a number of golf professionals and leading amateur players who studied under Jack Grout's expert eye, Jack never sought the public spotlight, never sought to take any of the credit for my career tournament victories or for those of any of the other successful players he mentored. As Dick Grout and others point out in the last section of this book, Jack's desire to not promote himself in the public eye seems a key reason why he hasn't yet taken his rightful place in any of the key golf halls of fame. But let me assure you that his absence from those halls—mystifying as it might be to those of us who knew him so well and benefited so much from his expertise on the lesson tee—wouldn't bother Jack Grout a bit. 'J. Grout,' as I called him, was just too humble and too comfortable in his own skin—and with what he accomplished in life—to spend even one minute worrying about such things.

Jack Grout has been gone for a couple of decades now, and I still think of him often, still chuckle at the story of how he gave me a final golf lesson even as he lay on his deathbed. Jack Grout never stopped teaching. Nor did he ever stop being my friend. I'm delighted that now, through this book, a wide range of people, golfers and nongolfers alike, will come to know the warm, often funny and always eventful story of this good man's life.

J.N.

A Day At Doral

"A good golf swing is a thing of beauty and a joy forever." – *JACK GROUT*

***

The Golden Bear was growling. Loudly.

Jack William Nicklaus, the greatest golfer in the history of the planet, had seen his unprecedented skills erode as he advanced through his forties, and was chagrined as even his friends in the media began writing him off as washed up, done, history. Now, Nicklaus reached out in his despair to his career-long coach and mentor. "I'd like for you to come down to Doral and watch me hit the ball," Nicklaus said in a telephone call seeking his old friend's help once more. "How about coming down for a day with Jackie?"

Soon thereafter, on a sunny March morning in 1986, young Jack Nicklaus II knocked on the front door of my father's home in Tequesta, Florida, north of Palm Beach. My mother, Bonnie, answered the door as my dad, Jack Grout, shuffled up behind her, sipping on a glass of orange juice. Dad was raring to go. Just three months earlier, he had undergone open-heart surgery, after which his doctors told him to go home and rest his seventy-five-year-old body for a while. But "a while" had passed and my father, the only golf teacher Jack Nicklaus had ever had, said good-bye to his revered Bonnie, stepped out the door, and got in Jackie's car for the ninety-minute drive down to Miami, where the Golden Bear waited.

Awash in the frustration of greatness gone sour, Nicklaus was playing that weekend in the annual PGA Tour event on the tough Blue Monster course at Doral. And, as had become routine for Nicklaus, things weren't going well. The burly, blond-haired intimidator was slogging through another in a long series of performances that fell far short of his lofty standards. In his disgruntlement over this state of affairs, he'd reached out to the man who had been his golf guru for thirty-six years.

Arriving at Doral, Jackie Nicklaus and my father headed for the course, walking in the gallery as the senior Nicklaus did yet again what he was doing far too often those days—shooting in the seventies on his way to a middle-of-the-pack finish. On the practice range after the round, Nicklaus asked his old friend for a diagnosis. And, true to the minimalist teaching style he'd exercised since he first began giving golf lessons at the age of fifteen, my dad got right to the point. He looked at his frustrated pupil and said, "Way too handsy."

Yes, it was as simple as that, Nicklaus quickly realized. His mighty swing, once powered by his arms and lower body, now relied far too much on manipulation of the golf club by his hands and wrists. He was over-cocking his wrists at the top of his backswing, robbing him of the downswing rhythm and control that for so long had resulted in shots both powerful and accurate.

Just a few weeks later, after intensive practice to correct the problem cited by my father—and with a bit of additional short-game advice advanced by fellow professionals Phil Rodgers and Chi Chi Rodriguez —Nicklaus did what most golf experts considered unthinkable: At forty-six years old he took the most gratifying victory of his long career. With son Jackie carrying his bag and with the Sunday afternoon gallery at Augusta National Golf Club shaking the grounds with the thunder of its roars, Jack Nicklaus shot a magnificent 30 on the final nine and rallied for his sixth Masters title, the eighteenth and last of his major-tournament wins.

My father watched all this from the comfort of his living room back in Tequesta, with my mother beside him in front of the family television. Nestled into his favorite chair, Dad could quietly exult as Nicklaus piled birdie on birdie through that last nine holes at Augusta National. I know that the pride Dad felt that day soothed his still-healing heart.

Nobody could have guessed at the time, and it really didn't matter then, that this was Nicklaus' last hurrah at the top of the golf world. What really mattered was that on an incredible afternoon on the steep hills and treacherous greens of Augusta National, the Nicklaus and Grout team had shown that it still had the magic. Even after all those years.

***

In retrospect, it was only fitting that the last great triumph of the Nicklaus-Grout pairing came in a major tournament. My dad's whole life, from the age of eight on, seemed destined for this kind of happy ending. From the day he discovered the game of golf, through his years of conscientious labors on the tough playing fields of the early PGA Tour alongside legendary players such as Ben Hogan, Byron Nelson, Jimmy Demaret and Sam Snead, then through more decades as a head club professional and renowned golf instructor, my father lived a purposeful life.

History perhaps will remember Jack Grout best for his molding of Jack Nicklaus into a classic golfing machine. The two men were, in fact, tightly bound together for nearly forty years by the sport they

Jack Grout and Jack Nicklaus at La Gorce Country Club's practice tee just prior to Nicklaus' victory in the 1962 U.S. Open at Oakmont Country Club. (From the Nicklaus family collection.)

both revered, and, in many ways, each man's life reflected that of the other. They both had their introduction to golf by the age of ten. They both saw action on the professional golf circuit by age twenty. And as adults, they both were devoted husbands and parents who led balanced lives, never letting their intense careers in golf overshadow their family responsibilities.

But while the pairing of the two Jacks *was* a key thread in the fabric of my father's life, it was only one thread in the rich tapestry of Jack Grout's experiences and achievements. In the following pages my father's full story unfolds. It is the story of a man who grew from humble roots into lofty status in a high-pressure sport, who was a favorite of rich, famous and powerful athletes, entertainers and business titans who sought his friendship and his help on the golf lesson tee, but whose head never was turned by their attentions. It's the story of the loving father I remember with such affection—a man who never really wanted much more than to be thought of as a true professional and a good person.

The story begins with my father's early discovery of the beautiful, exciting, demanding, exasperating but always alluring game called golf, and it ends with him on his deathbed, giving an impromptu final lesson to his dear friend and most accomplished student, the extraordinary Golden Bear.

In 1962, after joining Chick Evans and Bobby Jones as the only golfers to hold the U.S. Amateur and Open titles at the same time, Nicklaus thanked Jack Grout by writing this note on the photo above: "To Jack, the best friend and teacher a fellow could ever be lucky enough to have. Thank you for everything. Best wishes, Jack Nicklaus"

PART ONE: BEYOND THE WOODEN FENCE

Alex Thomas "Sandy" Baxter in 1941, Scotsman professional at Oklahoma City Golf and Country Club. (Grout family photo)

Chapter 1
The Golden Age of Caddies

"Golf is a learning experience, not something you just pick up."
– JACK GROUT

***

He felt like he was being *really bad.*

The little boy had sneaked out undetected, secretly following his three older brothers. Defying his mother's order that he stay close to home, he had set out to find where the three were going when they left the house early each summer morning, to be gone for the whole day.

Just what were they up to, these beloved older siblings?

Hiding behind trees and bushes, the little boy trailed his brothers for two miles and then watched as they stopped at a wooden fence, jumped over it, and disappeared.

Quietly, the eight-year-old crept up to the fence and peeked over.

What he saw took his breath away and changed his life forever.

***

The little boy who so boldly sought answers that day in 1918 was my father, Jack Grout. In his 1975 book, *Let Me Teach You Golf as I Taught Jack Nicklaus,* he recalled his discovery fifty-seven years earlier when he peered over that fence in suburban Oklahoma City:

"On the other side was the most beautiful sight I'd ever seen," my father wrote. "It looked like a huge pasture of lovely green grass and trees and lakes. People were strolling around, hitting little white balls with sticks. Fascinated, I stayed there drinking in the scene for many minutes before I realized that my mother would be looking for me. I ran all the way home.

"The next day I went back. I just had to see that pretty scene once again, because at my first sight of one I'd decided that a golf course was the nicest place in the world to be."

At that point my father not only knew where older brothers Duane, Dick and Herbert were going every day. He also had solved the mystery of how they were making all that money they were turning over to their parents at the family's evening meal: They were caddying at a golf course. Now Dad wanted a job there too, and his brothers convinced their mother that little Jack would do a fine job. Soon, with his big brothers close by to protect him, Dad would establish himself as one of the caddie-yard regulars.

The discovery of the beauties and special challenges of a golf course had, in an instant, changed my father's life. Even as an eight-year-old, Dad was sure that he had discovered the direction his life should take. First as a caddie, then as a successful player as early as the age of ten, Dad dove into the world of golf. Learning the game consumed him. By the time he was ten, his family members would hear him cheerily uttering golf-related declarations around the house. "Golf's going to be my career when I grow up," he would say. "I'm going to learn how to teach real good ... When my game gets a little better I'll play in all the big tournaments."

Dad's optimistic vision of the future fit well in the Oklahoma City of the early twentieth century. The city was incorporated in 1890 in the wake of the great "land rush" of April 22, 1889, in which thousands of citizens dashed into the territory that later became the state of Oklahoma to claim Indian land the U.S. government offered for free in 160-acre parcels. By the turn of the century, Oklahoma City had become a place of high energy and higher aspiration as local leadership emerged, businesses were developed, and the possibilities of a new town were turned into the realities of a growing city.

In 1910, its population having grown to about sixty-four thousand, the city petitioned to relocate the Oklahoma state capital from the town of Guthrie. Having won voter approval for the move, Governor Charles Haskell and his colleagues in government declared the Lee-Huckins Hotel in Oklahoma City the temporary state capitol building. A permanent structure was completed within a decade.

My father's parents—Herbert Duane Grout, an insurance adjuster and accomplished musician, and Eleanor Johanna "Nellie" Hickey, prominent in Oklahoma City's society circles—both were well known and thought of kindly in the booming little city. Married in 1899, Herbert and Nellie stayed true to their Catholic roots, quickly setting out on a robust regimen of procreation. By 1916 they were proud parents of eight children—a brood of five boys and three girls. Their first child, James (Duane), was born late in 1900. Dorothy came along in 1902, then Richard (Dick) in 1903, Herbert Jr. in 1907, John (Jack) in 1910, Raymond (Dutch) in 1911, Pauline in 1913, and the final child, Genevieve, in 1916. One can only imagine the beaming approval of their parish priest at Our Lady's Cathedral as this ever-expanding group appeared for Sunday Mass!

At the time of my father's birth—on March 24, 1910—the world was relatively calm yet brushed by the normal winds of change. The

Mexican revolution began that year, and the Union of South Africa was established. In the United States, the Boy Scouts of America was established; the cost of a first-class stamp was two cents, and, hard as it is to believe, the Chicago Cubs actually were in the World Series! (The Cubs lost to the Philadelphia A's, four games to one.) On the links that year, Alex Smith of the Philadelphia Cricket Club won the 16th U.S. Open golf championship, and the 27th President of the United States, William Howard Taft, became America's first chief executive to play recreational golf.

The Grout family home at 1035 NW 35th Street—several miles from the center of town—was a white, two-story, wood-frame structure with an inviting wide porch that spanned the front. Across the street a weed-filled green space called "Putnam Park" afforded the Grout children and their friends a comfortable place to roam as they went about their young lives. (The old Putnam Park later became Memorial Park, a recreation center with a playground, soccer fields, tennis and basketball courts and other diversions for all ages.)

Supplementing the house as a locus for family activities was the large downtown residence of my father's maternal grandparents, the Hickeys—said to be the first two-story house in the city. There was also the rural farmhouse of the paternal grandparents, the Grouts, on Britton Road about six miles north and west of downtown. The children could catch a streetcar near Putnam Park and ride to the home of either set of grandparents. Also, private ownership of automobiles became much more common as the 1910s gave way to the 1920s, and Herbert and Nellie purchased one for their family. So when weather or time considerations required it, Dad's mother or father could haul the children to their schools or afternoon jobs, or to their grandparents' homes.

The Oklahoma City of my father's youth was a safe place to live, yet Dad and his younger siblings were expected to stay pretty close to home. My grandmother's protectiveness may have been inspired by a story that young Jack and his little brother Raymond told of being out and about near their home one night when they heard the sound of horse hooves pounding the ground, and suddenly they saw a large group of white-robed men on horseback. "Get home right away because there is going to be trouble tonight," one of the Ku Klux Klansmen said in a deep voice.

***

Founded in 1888, St. Andrews Golf Club in suburban New York City is cited as this nation's oldest continually operating golf club. By

1900 there already were more than one thousand golf courses spread across the United States—evidence of just how quickly the game took hold here.

This boom in golf-course building led numerous talented European golf pros, and particularly those in Scotland, to move to the United States to take the very good jobs that were available for club professionals. Beginning in 1895, when the first U.S. Open golf championship was held, and extending through the 1900's first decade, twelve of the fifteen Opens were won by Scottish-born professionals and the other three by Englishmen. These successes heightened interest in the game in this country and also stimulated the development of U.S. golfing talent.

This growing tide of golf interest was given a huge boost in September 1913, when twenty-year-old American amateur Francis Ouimet defeated the British stars Harry Vardon and Ted Ray in a playoff for the Open title at The Country Club in Brookline, Massachusetts. Ouimet was not the typical well-to-do golfer of the day. He had grown up in humble circumstances across the street from The Country Club and learned the fine points of golf as one of the club's caddies. The young man's five-stroke victory over the great Vardon and six-stroke margin over Ray thus created a worldwide sensation. U.S. newspapers splashed it across their front pages, and Ouimet's fairytale story helped propel golf into the ranks of this country's most popular sports. At the time, only an estimated 350,000 Americans played golf. Just a decade later, in 1923, there were two million players in this country. American golf-course construction accelerated as well, with many of the new facilities being public courses rather than the members-only facilities that previously had dominated. Golf in the United States no longer was a sport just for the well-to-do.

In the spring of 1913, just months before Ouimet's incredible upset at Brookline, the oldest of the Grout children, my dad's brother, Duane, discovered that some of his school chums had jobs at a local golf course. Their task: carrying the clubs and balls for the rich people there. The twelve-year-old told his mother and father about this exciting new way of making money, and, with their parents' permission, Duane and his nine-year-old brother, Dick, made their way to the Oklahoma City Golf and Country Club for an introduction to the new game. Soon the two were serving as caddies at the nine-hole course, which opened in 1911 and is known today as Oklahoma City's oldest golfing institution. Younger brother Herbert had joined them by the time, five years later, my curious dad tracked his brothers to that idyllic spot.

The boys found within the club's pristine grounds a new world of intriguing, almost-addictive fun. Dick, a rollicking personality who over time would have his own very successful golf career and become my father's favorite brother, said that one of his best memories of caddying was when he carried the bag for a woman who was playing her first game of golf—without the benefit of any instruction. On the first hole alone, he recounted, she took 156 strokes, including an amazing number of misses! Failed golfer and incredulous caddie returned to the clubhouse soon after, and with her hands blistered from that first hole, the lady placed in the young caddie's hand a solitary nickel. Plainly, as the Grout boys discovered, caddying was not the route to quick wealth.

Francis Ouimet's shocking performance at Brookline had many beneficial and long-lasting effects on American golf, one of those being that caddies across the country stepped up a bit in status after it became known that Ouimet had started in that job. Instead of regarding the boys as cheap labor, golf clubs began to think of them as human beings, within whose ranks there might be another Ouimet. When the Grout brothers began toting golf bags, the typical caddie fee for eighteen holes was only twenty-five to thirty cents, with a tip of perhaps as much as a quarter for superior performance. Even at that modest pay, the boys earned what seemed to them a handsome income for a day's work. The older brothers were aglow with pride when they handed their earnings to their mother and father at the dinner table. The other Grout children, including my father, would watch and listen closely to the stories the older boys would tell and to the accolades they received from their parents.

Jack Grout's 1920 Silver Cup for winning the Caddie Championship at Oklahoma City Golf and Country Club — his first trophy. (Grout family photo)

In time, caddie conditions across the country improved considerably as golf became more popular. At the Oklahoma

City Golf and Country Club, caddie wages nearly doubled soon after Ouimet's victory. The club even decreed that the bag-toters should have a tournament of their own. Thus the club's first caddie championship was held in 1915, and soon a parade of young Grout brothers took turns winning the annual event. Duane won the title in 1916, and Dick was the champion in 1918. My father, Jack Grout, would win the caddie tourney in 1920, at the tender age of ten! Then, to show he was no fluke, he won it again the next year.

Besides having their very own tournament to compete in, and while appreciating the extra money they were able to make toting bags, the Grout boys derived real joy simply from being caddies and being on and around the beautiful, peaceful grounds. It was a great learning experience. For one thing, most of the people they caddied for were intelligent and reasonably refined; a boy could learn a lot about life and current events if he paid attention. Too, the club's members generally didn't exhibit poor sportsmanship or use bad language; these people shaped the young Grouts' early perception of the game in a positive way.

Duane's caddie championship in 1916 seemed to ignite his entire family's interest in golf. At ages fifteen, twelve and nine, the three oldest boys even decided that maybe they should have their own golf course to play and practice on. So, in the scraggly park across the street to the west of the Grout home, they designed a two-hole course. The vacant land had patches of long grass and areas with no grass at all. Rocks had to be cleared away to make room for two putting greens. The boys used empty tin cans for hole rims and a decrepit lawnmower to keep the "greens" in passable condition—though there really wasn't much grass to cut on those tiny greens, especially during the long, hot summer months.

When the older boys returned home from their caddying duties, they often would dominate the family's dinner-table conversation with stories of their golf-course labors. Dick always was the most animated when recounting his stories, and his often-humorous tales were the ones my father liked best. Once, for example, a member named Roy Finnerty shot nine consecutive 5s on the front nine, then nine straight 4s on the back nine. Afterward, when Mr. Finnerty was paying the lad his fifty-cent caddie fee, young Dick declared—in all seriousness—that he thought Finnerty did a better job on the back nine than he had done on the front. One can only assume that Mr. Finnerty agreed that a 36 for nine holes was better than a 45!

***

The caddie yard was home to a brotherhood of sorts. The caddies really were important to the club, after all; the motorized carts that are used to lug golfers and their bags around a course today didn't arrive on the scene until the early 1950s. The caddies who had established themselves were considered the leaders, and they were protective of their turf and their lofty position among the caddie rank and file. Since there were about two caddies for every golfer, the regulars considered it their right to run the new boys off by practically any means necessary. A kid had to prove himself quickly in order to stick around.

The standard procedure when a new caddie arrived was that the other boys had the opportunity to give him a hard time. If he could take the heat, the new caddie eventually would be accepted into the gang. A new caddie had to be particularly careful around Johnny "Pepper" Martin, the caddies' ringleader. Martin, who later would gain baseball fame as a player for the St. Louis Cardinals "Gashouse Gang" of the 1930s, could lick any caddie in town, no matter how big the other boy was. (It is worth noting, as proof of his aggressiveness, that at the age of forty-five, when he was manager of the Miami team in the Florida International League, Martin was fined and suspended for choking an umpire!)

In my father's later years, he would tell many stories about the rituals of the caddie yard. One of his favorites concerned a kid the caddies had nicknamed "Skeezicks." Supposedly when "Skeezicks" Mariner came back in from caddying one day, the older boys told him that the soda pop delivery man had mistakenly left behind a whole case of lemon soda, and that all of them got to drink it up for free. "All of the soda pop is gone except there's one left, and it's right over there," one caddie said, pointing to a bottle in the corner of the yard. What the boys didn't tell Skeezicks was that each of them had taken turns urinating into the bottle, and one of the bigger boys had put the cap back on it. When Skeezicks took a gulp he immediately spat it out and screamed "Peeeeeeeeeeeee!" Every time my father told us this story he would throw his head back and laugh.

While Dad appreciated the good times he had as a caddie, he also got more than just fun out of his early golf course labors. What Jack Grout did at the Oklahoma City Golf and Country Club and other golf venues in the city was establish what would be a lifelong pattern of watching, listening and learning about the game and the people in and around it. From other caddies, he learned the secrets of "getting along," of being accepted as a member of a competitive working group. From the educated adults he caddied for, he learned about the outside world. And, importantly, from those adults and from the club professionals and other excellent golfers with whom he began coming into contact at an early age, he learned the techniques and strategies of successful golf.

❋❋❋

The first money my dad earned was thirty-five cents for shagging balls on the practice range, tracking down the white missiles launched by the club's members and guests. As soon as he got paid, he'd run all the way home and present the cash to his mother. Dad told me the coins would be stuck in his sweaty little palm when he'd open up his hand to show his mother what he'd made. Dad was thrilled that he could bring home some money. Though the Grout family lived in a nice home and had plenty to eat, Dad would recall later that "money was hard to come by." The extra cash the boys provided helped pay for clothes, books and other necessities.

When my father wasn't picking up balls on the range, he would be getting lessons on the finer points of his craft from the caddie master, an Irishman named Kenny O'Brien. Around the club, O'Brien was called "The Irishman" by the members, but certainly not by the caddies. The man was a stern disciplinarian and demanded that the boys call him Mr. O'Brien. Dad was serious about learning the ways of a perfect caddie and thus always got along with O'Brien. Over time, The Irishman taught Dad how to take care of the clubs, how to carry the golf bag over his shoulder, how to find golf balls in the tall grass or the woods, and how to keep quiet and stay out of the way. My father's golf education had begun in earnest.

There were many things to learn, Dad discovered. In those days, for example, golf clubs weren't numbered, so it was decidedly more of a job than it is today for a novice to tell them apart. Dad got the lofter, the niblick, the jigger, the putter, the cleek, the baffy, the driver, the brassie and the spoon reasonably clear in his mind. What confused him, it seems, were the middle irons. Every one of them was some kind of a mashie, and the distinctions between the mid-mashie, the mashie-iron, the spade mashie and the mashie-niblick were difficult.

It took my father the better part of a week before he got his confidence. But by hanging around the caddie house every morning and listening to his older brothers, he finally became comfortable with the strange new vocabulary. About that time, The Irishman felt the "new Grout boy" was ready to caddie and assigned Dad his first "loop." Although my dad wasn't yet in his teens, it was physically possible for him to caddie because the golf bags of the day just didn't weigh very much. Although there was no limit at that time on the number of clubs a player could use during a round, it was common for golfers to have a little white bag that contained as few as six or seven clubs. When a player had a heavier bag with more clubs in it, the caddie master would assign one of the bigger boys.

As Dad became more skilled, he became a regular caddie at the Oklahoma City course. Caddie wages had continued to increase, and by the time he was working regularly he could bring home as much as $1.50 a day. His earnings always went toward the Grout family's bills. The money he made, the peaceful beauty of the golf course, and the seriousness required for mastery of the game all attracted my father. Even as a youngster, Dad was never much for "rough-housing" and carrying on like some caddies did. Golf seemed to him to be a substantive undertaking. It was more about being under control and using good technique, and that appealed to him. The game was played by impeccably dressed people in beautiful surroundings. In golf, the young Jack Grout saw all the good things he wanted for himself. It also didn't hurt that his family was gaining notoriety around the city. Quickly, the Grouts were becoming known as very good golfers, as exemplified by both Duane and Dick winning caddie championships in their midteens.

When spring chased away the chill of the Oklahoma winter in 1919, the Grout boys were back to the caddie yard. By this time, however, Duane was getting too old to caddie. He was about to graduate from high school and had begun making plans for college. There were more Grout children in the pipeline, though, and Duane quickly was succeeded by Dutch, the youngest brother. This seemed only natural; golf by now had become an important part of the family's life. Before they reached high school, the Grout boys normally were allowed to caddie only on the weekends. But by 1919, given his advanced age—fifteen—brother Dick sometimes was allowed to go to the club once his homework was completed, to see if a caddie job was available. Returning home, he'd often find his brothers practicing on their makeshift course across the street in Putnam Park. When one of them had a special trick or a new move that seemed to work, he would share it enthusiastically with the others. Each of the boys had a few clubs, and between them there might have been enough for a complete set.

As his knowledge of his chosen sport grew, my father came to appreciate that a golfer doesn't need another person playing along in order to fully enjoy the game. This aspect of the sport greatly appealed to him. Dad once told me about a special practice game he would play by himself. The game involved three golf balls, each with a different brand name such as Spalding Kro-Flite, MacGregor Diamond King or Cochrane Challenger. Dad named each ball after a famous player of the time—one Harry Vardon, another Walter Hagen, and the next perhaps Chick Evans. Playing them all himself, he determined who won by computing which ball had the lowest score at the end of the contest.

❊❊❊

In his prime teaching years, after 1950, my father displayed an amazing grasp of the fundamentals that were required of every good golfer—fundamentals he acquired growing up. He seemed to know intuitively from childhood that there were no "magic bullets" that could instill within a person's brain a clear understanding of golf's many nuances. Beginning early in his teenage years, Dad took advantage of continuing contacts with excellent players and golf teachers, and quietly but eagerly absorbed their knowledge of the game's key elements.

From 1920 through 1929, as he progressed through elementary and high school, Dad benefited greatly from contact with knowledgeable club pros in Oklahoma City, outstanding tour professionals who barnstormed through the city for exhibition matches, and even from his own brothers and sisters, a brood deeply talented in the game of golf. It was a living laboratory for my father, and he took it all in with an early and deep commitment to absorbing every bit of knowledge he could find that would help him achieve his dreams of a career in golf.

An important benefit for Dad was the presence at the Oklahoma City Golf and Country Club of a Scotsman named Sandy Baxter. A native of Carnoustie, Scotland, Baxter learned to play golf on Carnoustie Golf Links, a course generally considered one of the world's toughest. When he was twenty, Baxter sailed for America on the same ship as many other Scottish golf professionals, all determined to land jobs at top courses in a country in which golf's popularity was exploding. Baxter worked first at the Midlothian Golf Club in Chicago, then moved to a job in LaGrange, Illinois, then Rock Island, Illinois, then to one of the Southwest's best layouts, the Dallas Country Club. Baxter felt he had found a home in Dallas, but after six years there answered the call from members of the Oklahoma City Golf and Country Club. He became the head pro there in 1916, when my dad was just six years old.

When he began caddying a couple of years later, my father quickly came under Baxter's spell. Dad watched and listened as Baxter taught the game to others, and he decided at a very young age that it was what he wanted to do, too. Baxter would tell the caddies, "Laddies, if ye don't larn to keep your eye on the bloody ball, ye'll niver make a good player."

When Dad teed up balls for Baxter's pupils during their instruction sessions, he listened carefully as the pro made his comments. Once, when Baxter was asked about a golfer's swing, he was heard to say in his distinctive accent, "Aye, the lad has a good swing for sheep's turds and diezes (daisies), but he canna hit the ball."

Quiet and careful observation of Baxter's teaching gave my father a quick start in becoming a fine player, and once he got into the game Dad was hooked. His older brothers, especially Dick, gave Dad his first bits of actual hands-on golf instruction, and his keen eye for details and knack for imitation were helpful in learning to swing the club "pretty good," as he would say. From the very start my father had a fine, natural swing for which he received many compliments, and after he won his first caddie championship in 1920, his confidence in his game began to grow.

While my dad was just beginning to build his golf knowledge and skills, Dick graduated from high school and set his sights on becoming a professional in the golf business. It was his good fortune that in 1921, at age seventeen, he was hired by Sandy Baxter to be the caddie master for the Oklahoma City Golf and Country Club. The new job amounted to a formal golf apprenticeship. Under Baxter's guidance Dick learned about agronomy, teaching, the "care and feeding" of club members, and how to repair clubs. Often the kindly pro allowed his young apprentice to take home some of the secondhand woods and irons they repaired so that all of the Grout siblings could use them. Sandy Baxter epitomized the turn-of-the-century Scottish golf professionals who immigrated to this country in search of country-club jobs. He was honest, hardworking, proud and unfailingly forthright. He was a talented teacher and club maker, but he also could play the game. He proved that convincingly in June 1921 by winning the well-regarded Oklahoma Open.

Later that year, my father got his first chance to observe world-class players in action when Chick Evans and Bob MacDonald came to town. Evans, the best American amateur golfer until Bobby Jones came along later in the 1920s, and MacDonald, a fine Scottish professional, had been traveling across the United States staging exhibition matches. In November 1921 the two took on Sandy Baxter and James Kennedy, the Oklahoma amateur champion, in a two-day, thirty-six-hole exhibition match. Admission to such exhibitions featuring top professionals normally was $3 per person, but a group of the golf club's members underwrote the event so that spectators would be charged only $1 for the two days. The result was a large gallery, and the huge turnout proved to the club that other exhibitions should be scheduled.

Chapter 2
A Sucker's Game

"In order to make money, you must go where the money is."
– JACK GROUT

***

Playing on what passed as golf's pro-tournament circuit was not the route to financial security in those days. The colorful Gene Sarazen called pro golf "a sucker's game." Even the best players made little cash from tournament play, golf's purses of the day being far inferior to the pay offered the top athletes in, say, boxing and baseball. For example, the prestigious U.S. Open title carried a purse of only $500 in 1926. A golf champion's overall earnings, then, depended largely on his personal showmanship and ability to market his playing skills away from the scheduled tour. Exhibitions were where the money was in golf, and stars such as Walter Hagen and Gene Sarazen were among those who crisscrossed the country playing one- or two-day events for cash. These matches were a sure thing—no pressure and an automatic payoff. Once a player had established himself as one of the leading tour pros, the exhibitions offered an easy supplement to tournament winnings.

In 1922, Hagen shone a harsh spotlight on the importance of these good-paying exhibition matches to leading pros. After becoming the first American to win the British Open, he opted just a few weeks later not to defend his PGA Championship when the tourney was held at Oakmont Country Club in Pittsburgh. Hagen wasn't ill or injured. Rather, his schedule was full of more-lucrative engagements. During his career as a golf pro, Hagen played close to two thousand one-day stands. The man called "Sir Walter" played wherever cash was available—from Chatham, Massachusetts, to Salt Lake City, to the dusty fairways and sand-based greens of the Southwest.

In October 1922, the Hagen caravan pulled into Oklahoma City for an exhibition at the Oklahoma City Golf and Country Club. This one pitted club pro Sandy Baxter and caddie master Dick Grout against Hagen and fellow touring pro Joe Kirkwood Sr. Seven hundred people turned out to watch, and Hagen and Kirkwood were paid about $300 each. Baxter made $100, and my dad's brother, Dick, just eighteen years old but already playing in high-level company, took home $50. My dad also played a role in the club's big day. Having established himself by then as a first-rate caddie, even at age twelve, he was assigned to tote Hagen's bag, giving him yet another great learning opportunity. Hagen was at that time the most celebrated American professional golfer. Dad's big opportunity, then, would be comparable to a pre-teen caddying for Tiger Woods in his prime.

***

The barnstorming ways of many tour professionals, combined with the soaring popularity of golf in the United States, created something of a schism in the golf world. As top pros played exhibitions around the country, they not only thrilled spectators with their skills but also turned the heads of many key members of the private golf clubs where the matches were held. These influential individuals saw for the first time just how well the tournament professionals played and began insisting that their own club pros be high-caliber players, too. It didn't matter that their fully trained golf professional knew how to teach golf, fit members with proper clubs, and competently run a full schedule of golf events. Given a choice between a low-profile club pro who knew how to keep a golf operation running smoothly and a high-profile touring pro who could bring attention (and new members) to the club, more and more clubs began opting for the latter. The truth is that ordinary golfers enjoy being around "players."

In late 1923, Sandy Baxter was swept away by this tide of change. It was announced that he was leaving the Oklahoma City Golf and Country Club to seek other opportunities. In reality he had been caught in a tug-of-war between opposing factions within the club's board of directors. One group appreciated the fact that Baxter was an excellent teacher, dedicated to helping club members improve their golf games; another longed for the club to be represented by a man recognized as an excellent player, a pro who would bring attention to their club by shooting low numbers in golf tournaments. The latter faction won the argument. Baxter was out.

Over the next four years, my dad watched as Oklahoma City Golf and Country Club went through three new head pros, including Ed Dudley, a twenty-four-year-old who stayed for only one year, and Cyril Walker, the abrasive winner of the 1924 U.S. Open who left after just seven months. In the fall of 1927, the club decided it needed a professional who would stick to the job at hand by teaching and attending to the daily needs of the membership. That November, the club hired a fellow named Johnny Madden. With no irony intended, a member of the board said, "Madden is a wonderfully clever golfer and could fight his way well up among the playing pros, if he chose, but he prefers teaching the game."

The club had hired a professional who was just like Sandy Baxter.

***

While all of this was going on, my father continued to improve his golf game. He evolved technically and mentally and began to take seriously the idea of pursuing a career in golf. By 1926, he had won five caddie championships and finished as runner-up in the Oklahoma City Junior Championship. He also continued to learn from others. The club pros who rotated through the Oklahoma City Golf and Country Club in the middle of the decade, for example, all taught my father lessons about the techniques of golf and teaching the game. Dad was a sponge, soaking up the knowledge each of these professionals offered. My father was fortunate, too, in that he was surrounded by siblings who loved and were adept at golf. Brother Dick, the first family member to turn pro, competed in numerous important championships and eventually became known as an exceptional golf instructor. Jenny, the youngest of the Grout children, won dozens of tournaments and came to be regarded as one of Oklahoma's best-ever female golfers. Clearly, golf was in the Grout family genes.

Jack and Dick Grout with friend Bob Higgins in 1928 at Edgemere Country Club. (Grout family photo)

Before he began high school, Dad again found himself in position to rub elbows with another nationally prominent golfer, his caddying stint for Walter Hagen in 1922 being followed two years later by a chance to tote the bag of the extremely popular pro, Wee Bobby Cruickshank. The five-foot-four, 125-pound Cruickshank, like Hagen, came through Oklahoma City for an exhibition match, and fourteen-year-old Jack Grout was assigned to carry his bag. My dad enjoyed and admired the talented Cruickshank and caddied for him at every subsequent opportunity.

Writing later about Cruickshank, my father signaled

that he'd studied the golfer's technique and personal style carefully. He recalled that Cruickshank was the first "truly distinguished golfer" he was able to observe and wrote that the Scot was "a magnificent player with a beautiful style." Dad paid particular attention to the distinctive and artistic way in which Cruickshank played. From the time he first took up golf, Dad liked and emulated players who had smooth, graceful swings. It is no surprise that legendary players including Ben Hogan, Byron Nelson and many others would say that Jack Grout's swing as a professional golfer was flowing, effortless and beautiful to watch.

***

Had his school studies been as much a passion for my dad as the game of golf, he might have become a great scholar. But his studying, even before he entered his teens, was largely focused on golf. This devotion to his sport of choice came at the exclusion of many other normal youthful activities, including dating. Dad seems not to have had a clue about how to deal with women. So, he immersed himself in learning all he could about the game and the business of golf, and he found particular early inspiration within the career progress of his older brother, Dick. Having established himself as a solid player, Dick resigned as caddie master at Oklahoma City Golf and Country Club in May 1923 to take his first job as a club pro. He was only twenty when he was named assistant golf professional at Shawnee Country Club, located just southeast of Oklahoma City. Shawnee was experiencing a growth spurt tied largely to the discovery of oil in Oklahoma. The local chamber of commerce advertised the city as "The Hub of the World's Largest Oil Fields."

A year later, Dick would leave Shawnee to become the head professional at Dornick Hills Golf and Country Club in Ardmore, in southern Oklahoma. It was a good step up for him; the architect and builder of the beautiful Dornick Hills course was Perry Maxwell, who also designed such famous layouts as Southern Hills in Tulsa and Prairie Dunes in Hutchinson, Kansas, and did renovations of Augusta National and of Pine Valley in Camden, New Jersey. (Dornick Hills was Maxwell's first course design, and he is buried in the family cemetery on a ridge north of the course's seventh fairway.)

It couldn't have escaped my father's notice that his brother received a salary for his new job and was also paid about $1,000 monthly from pro-shop sales. "With astute promotion, maybe I'll double this figure," he told my father. The new job brought with it not only pretty good compensation, but also the beginning of a cache of wonderful golf stories that Dick would later tell to anyone who would listen. After finishing second to a fellow named Bill Creavy in the Oklahoma Open championship in 1924, for example, Dick relayed a story about a popular Dornick Hills member, Walter Critchlow, who had finished in a tie for tenth place. "After a bad round for him," Dick said, "(Critchlow) built a fire in back of the eighteenth green, burning all of his clubs, all with hickory shafts. The following day he brought me the iron heads for reshafting and purchased a new set of woods."

It was during this period that brothers Paul and Burt Blakeney, friends of my grandfather, H.D. Grout, opened a nine-hole golf course called Edgemere in the countryside outside Oklahoma City. Burt Blakeney had been a caddie at Oklahoma City Golf and Country Club and was impressed with my dad's play there in the city caddie championship in 1924 when he lost in the finals. So he brought Dad aboard as a caddie at Edgemere that year and soon gave him extra responsibilities making hot dogs, taking greens fees and selling golf balls and other goods. It was during this time that Dad also got his first substantive experience repairing golf clubs.

Even in his midteens, Jack Grout was a serious and responsible person. He felt increasingly drawn to a career in golf but also felt a need to help his parents finance the daily lives of their large family. So in 1925, he approached Blakeney with a bold suggestion: How about letting this young caddie and hot dog cooker begin giving golf lessons at Edgemere? Such a suggestion from a fifteen-year-old boy would be laughed off at any serious golf club today, but Blakeney had been impressed with the young Grout's work ethic and endless enthusiasm. So he agreed to let Dad give teaching a shot. The arrangement was that, on a trial basis, Dad would give instructions to beginning junior, senior and lady golfers. Dad was to receive a dollar an hour for this work and was thrilled and a bit surprised to learn that anyone would pay him such a sum for doing something he loved so much.

His deepening involvement in golf would bring my father new opportunities for watching top players, men from whom he continued to draw lessons that broadened his knowledge of the game. In August 1925, he watched as Wee Bobby Cruickshank, now the playing pro at the Twin Hills Club in Oklahoma City, won a spot in the annual PGA Championship through a two-day qualifying tourney contested over Edgemere's nine-hole layout. Later that year, Cruickshank returned to Edgemere for an exhibition match that marked his final days as a resident pro in Oklahoma City, his contract with Twin Hills being in its closing days and Cruickshank having decided to devote more time to playing the pro circuit. The outcome of that exhibition was a shocker.

Dad's brother Dick and his playing partner actually took a one-up victory (one hole ahead after the scheduled thirty-six holes) over Cruickshank and his partner, with Dick gaining most of the credit for the win because of his consistent ball striking.

His brother's growing success as a golfer had to be inspiring to my father. Dick was, by the mid-1920s, juggling roles as club pro and touring professional golfer. When he could get away from his club-pro job at Dornick Hills for a few days and a big tournament was within driving distance, he would seize the opportunity to test himself against quality players. It was his habit during this period, for instance, to drive the three hundred miles to Hot Springs, Arkansas, each year to play in the South Central Open, a big tournament that attracted many of the nation's best players. Dick would stay at the home of Jimmy Norton, the pro at the tournament site, the Hot Springs Golf and Country Club. It was at the Hot Springs tournament in 1926 that Dick's caddie was a high school kid named Paul Runyan, a smallish seventeen-year-old who knew the course well and helped Dick to a tie for ninth. This would not be my uncle's last contact with Runyan. The diminutive Arkansan went on to become one of the finest tournament players of his time, earning the nickname "Little Poison." He turned professional in 1930 and recorded twenty-six career victories, including two PGA Championships.

When Sandy Baxter was recruited away from Edgemere in 1926, Dick succeeded him—another good break for my dad. My father, already doing some teaching at Edgemere, became his brother's assistant at the club. He began teaching more and more, and over time also played a greater role in helping my uncle handle business matters in the pro shop. Dad would say later, "Oh, I wanted to play so much more than I did. But you couldn't make any money in those days playing. You could by teaching."

The summer of 1926 would be a big one for the golfing Grout family; Dad won the caddie tournament at Edgemere and finished second in the city's junior championship, and Dick won the Oklahoma PGA title, his win giving him a spot in the upcoming PGA Championship in Garden City, Long Island. It was a huge day for the family when Dick boarded a train on September 12 for the long trip east for his first appearance in one of golf's "major" tournaments, and the entire family gathered together on the wooden platform at the downtown Oklahoma City train station to see him off. Dick had a sleeper car for the trip but was so keyed up he used it little; rather, he talked all night long to other passengers who were kind enough to listen.

My uncle's introduction to the "big leagues" of golf turned out to be only a modest success. He made it through a thirty-six-hole stroke-play qualifying round and then managed a victory over Minnesota pro Jock Hendry in the first round of the championship's match-play tournament. Unfortunately, awaiting him in the second round was a vastly more experienced and confident pro, Walter Hagen. Recalling that his son had faced Hagen in an exhibition match four years earlier and that he thus should feel comfortable facing the great player, my grandfather sent Dick a telegram reminding him to stay calm. "Son, about all I can tell you," he said, "is go out there tomorrow and play your best, because if you do, you can't be beaten."

Unfortunately, my uncle did not play his best, and defending champion Hagen dispatched him from the tournament, seven-and-six. Hagen did a class thing after that match—he had lunch and drinks with Dick, then took him to the practice green for a putting lesson. My uncle was thrilled beyond measure and couldn't wait to practice what he'd learned. It's easy for me to imagine Dick recounting this story later at the Grout family dinner table, and his younger brother Jack filing away the details of the Hagen story as a lesson in real professionalism.

It seemed that so many of my father's early golf experiences and opportunities came to him courtesy of his older brothers. This was the case again in 1927, as Dick left the Edgemere Club for the head professional's post at a fine country club in Okmulgee, about one hundred miles east of Oklahoma City. Despite my father being only seventeen years old, Edgemere reached out to him to succeed his brother. Dad thus began his first job as a head club professional on April 1, 1927. He was paid a salary and received $1.50 per half-hour golf lesson. Inside the golf shop, Dad was responsible for overseeing the sale of food, golf balls, tees and greens fees. He also handled club repairs and supervised the caddie master and other golf employees. At seventeen and still in high school, Dad had become a golfer-businessman. He was gaining more knowledge about the golf business every day.

Dad watched and tucked away another lesson that summer, after his brother Dick birdied the final hole to win the Oklahoma Open title. That lesson came when Dick returned home to his head-pro job at Okmulgee, and club members gave him a hero's welcome. Dick discovered quickly the truth of the adage, "to the victor go the spoils." He sensed that his club's members were beginning to look at him differently; now, they seemed to want his opinion on everything. He mused that suddenly his jokes got bigger laughs, even his pro shop's sandwiches tasted better.

***

On December 4, 1928, oil was discovered under the area of S.E. 59th and Bryant in Oklahoma City. Oil would become the city's most important revenue source and make it the world's newest boomtown. In the twenty-seven days before the great gusher could be capped, it spewed more than one hundred thousand barrels of oil. The sprawling field became one of the world's major oil-producing areas. Discovery and development of the Oklahoma City oil field added great stability to the local economy and that of the state of Oklahoma, providing financial incentive for industrial and cultural progress. But in a day when top golfers always were looking for new sources of revenue, it also provided plenty of incentive for golf "hustlers" who preyed upon the egos and the mediocre playing skills of many well-to-do amateur players. The gushing oil had, among other things, provided huge new sums of disposable income for many in Oklahoma City. Golf "entrepreneurs" moved in to take advantage.

In the spring of 1929, the hot sports gossip in town was about a pair of strangers who'd come looking for high-stakes golf games. These outsiders were well known to the Grout clan. One of the men, Ky Laffoon, had become friends with my father in the fall of 1927 at an Oklahoma golf tournament. Laffoon, who later would share many good times with Dad on the professional circuit even as he won a reputation for erratic behavior, had by 1929 taken a job as a pro at the Miami (Oklahoma) Golf Club. When Laffoon and his buddy, the infamous golf hustler Titanic Thompson, swept into Oklahoma City in search of easy marks, they made a surprising tactical error: They engaged in a series of matches with the Grout brothers, Dick and Jack, who proceeded to dispatch the invading money-seekers. When the Grouts proved too tough, Laffoon and Thompson simply moved on to matches against easier foes, including wealthy oilmen who were members at other area clubs such as Lincoln Park, Shawnee and Lakeside.

Later that spring the Grout family added to its growing reputation for quality golf, and my father began to establish himself as a fine player. The venue was the Oklahoma Open at Dick's former place of employment, Dornick Hills in Ardmore. Dick won the tournament for the second time in three years, and his younger brother Jack finished just three strokes behind in a tie for second place. Much was written at the time about the two golfing brothers. An article by Bus Ham in

The Daily Oklahoman carried particularly strong praise for my father, saying, "Probably the most noteworthy performance in the state golf tourney ... was the tying for second by Jack Grout in the Open Saturday."

Dick Grout was quoted as saying that, given the choice, he would have preferred that his younger brother win the tournament. This and other things my uncle said at the time seemed to reveal his true feelings for the future of his own game: While he loved the challenges of competitive golf, he'd come to understand that his greatest opportunity to make money in the coming years was as an instructor rather than as a player. Jack Grout, on the other hand, had played superbly in just his third big-time golf championship and had launched himself toward what would be a very good, if not spectacular, career as a touring professional.

***

Eleven days after his runner-up finish in the state Open, my father graduated from high school. The fourth annual commencement of Classen High School in Oklahoma City began at 8:15 p.m. on May 29, 1929, in the school auditorium. Jack Grout was one of a graduating class of 388. My father was nineteen years old when he received his diploma. Compared to today's normal pattern he was in high school longer than most, but he usually attended classes for only half days and worked afternoons at Edgemere. It was common then for a person to work at least part-time while attending school, and Dad's salary of about $14 per week and the extra compensation he received for his golf lessons meant more money for the Grout household.

My father would learn much at an early age about the challenges of making a living. He surely learned just as much about human nature, though, given his early and frequent brushes with nationally prominent golfers and others who had many fascinating stories to tell and lessons to teach him. Even at Classen High School, my father would cross paths with a man who, while not yet famous, certainly would become so. Henry Payne "Hank" Iba, then a member of the school's faculty, would become one of this country's most successful college men's basketball coaches. Iba also is remembered as one of the toughest coaches in NCAA history. He was a methodical man, always expecting his charges to execute things perfectly. Once, as Dad and I watched the 1972 Olympics on television, a special feature came on concerning the USA basketball team and its legendary coach, Hank Iba. Dad listened for a minute, then turned to me and said, "Dickie, that's the sternest man I ever met."

As 1929 came to an end, Dad could look back at a year of accomplishment and of personal and family satisfactions. His older brother Dick had had his best success as a professional golfer, capping his excellent year by playing in the U.S. Open Championship—at that time also referred to as "The National Open"—at Winged Foot Golf Club in Mamaroneck, New York. My dad, for his part, had learned much about running a golf club's pro shop, had played well in several big tournaments, had gotten to know more big-name players as they barnstormed through Oklahoma City, and had graduated from high school.

The year also marked the beginning of the end for a cherished locale that had afforded my father his first awe-inspiring glance at the genteel world of golf. The 1929 Oklahoma City Open was contested at a brand new eighteen-hole course called Nichols Hills Country Club. The following year, Nichols Hills owner G.A. Nichols acquired the original, nine-hole Oklahoma City Golf and Country Club course in a trade for his new clubhouse and golf course, which took on the original course's name. The old Oklahoma City Golf and Country Club course, where Dad and his brothers and sisters grew up, where they first learned the beauties, frustrations and joys of golf, and where his labors convinced my father that golf would be his life's calling, was subdivided in 1930, and sales of a limited number of houses began.

Nichols called the new subdivision "Crown Heights."

I suspect that Dad felt some satisfaction in taking the final major step needed for his entry into the world of serious golf even as the old course was being vanquished. On October 30, 1929, my father was accepted into membership in the key organization of golf professionals, the Professional Golfers Association of America, known since its formation in 1916 as simply the PGA.

In retrospect, despite his new status in the golf community, that October 30 must have been a bittersweet day for my father. For years he had longed to be recognized as a serious practitioner of his chosen sport, and now he had achieved that. On the eve of this personal triumph, however, his country had absorbed a crushing blow that would stop the nation's economy in its tracks and slow the growth of tournament golf and the entire golf industry for years. October 29, 1929, had been the third and final day of the greatest stock market crash in history. Oklahoma, and the nation, had plunged into the Great Depression.

Chapter 3
Texas, Byron and Ben

"Every day you don't practice puts you a week behind in your preparations."
– JACK GROUT

***

Near the end of January 1930, a headline in the morning paper read, "Oklahoma Loses Dick and Jack Grout; Brother Pros Go to Fort Worth Club." Though most of the Grout family had known of the news long beforehand, it was a bit jarring when they actually saw the account in the *Daily Oklahoman*. The story read:

"Dick and Jack Grout, brother professionals who ranked topmost among Oklahoma's promising salaried golfers, will be lost to the state by Saturday, February 1st. The Grout brothers, both of whom are Oklahoma City products, announced ... that they had come to terms with the Glen Garden Club of Fort Worth, Texas. Dick Grout will become professional and Jack will become his assistant on February 1."

My father and his twenty-six-year-old brother had talked many times about working together at some point at a distinguished eighteen-hole country club, and the Fort Worth jobs offered a step up in both pay and responsibility. Dick already had tendered his resignation as professional at the Okmulgee Country Club, and Dad would do the same at Edgemere, where he had begun work as his brother's successor three years earlier.

As word spread of the Grout brothers' imminent departure, a number of people took note. The newspapers touted the pair's move from Oklahoma City as a major event, with articles such as:

"Two golfers of ability will be lost to Oklahoma links. Dick Grout had made it an almost annual habit to win either the Oklahoma Open or the state PGA Championship. He won the Open at Ardmore the summer of 1929. He won the State PGA title in 1926, the Open in 1927 and was just a few strokes away in 1928. He represented the state in both the National Open in 1929 at Winged Foot and in many professional tournaments ..."

And:

"Jack Grout, the popular Edgemere pro, though only 19 years old played his third major tourney this past summer and finished only three strokes behind his brother Dick, 153 to 150 in the Oklahoma Open. Jack has won numerous caddie and junior honors in the city and he has been coming along at a fast pace the last two years ... and ... his iron and wood games are equal to almost anybody. Dick maintains that his younger brother has the best collection of shots of any golfer in the state. Jack appears to have as big a future as Dick, the oldest and first one of this golfing family to turn to the links game as a profession."

When the brothers left Oklahoma City for Fort Worth, they ventured eagerly into a world of new experiences. A big-city life unlike anything they'd known had a lot of appeal, especially for Dad, who was fresh out of high school. The two stuffed their better clothing and golf gear into Dick's car and sped off in the direction of U.S.-77 on a drive of about four hours.

Their destination, the Glen Garden Club, was neither Fort Worth's oldest nor its finest golf facility. That distinction belonged to Rivercrest Country Club, which formed in 1910. Glen Garden, which organized three years later, was located three miles outside the city limits on the largely middle-class southeastern side of town, close to the interurban shuttle train that operated between Fort Worth and Dallas. Glen Garden's first clubhouse—a rustic structure with a large porch supported by open beams, rafters and fieldstone—opened in 1914 and served more than three hundred members, including many of Fort Worth's newest and most dedicated golfers.

Settling in for their Texas life, Dick and Dad found a nice place to stay for about $10 a week. Dick's starting salary was $500 a month, plus $2 to $2.50 for each half-hour lesson on the practice range. He also realized earnings from the sale of balls, clubs, golf bags and a small sampling of shirts and sweaters in the golf shop. The club paid my dad about $60 a week to be Dick's assistant.

Grout Brothers, Jack and Dick outside the clubhouse at Glen Garden Country Club in 1932. (Grout family photo)

Both Dick and my father dove happily into their new tasks, but the jobs were not without challenges. After the stock market crash of 1929, most golfers had to trim their playing expenses. They took fewer lessons, bought cheaper equipment, and otherwise cut down on spending for the pleasures of golf. And the introduction of steel shafts had closed the doors of a veritable gold mine for the club pro. When my uncle started as an assistant at the Shawnee Club in Oklahoma in 1923, he could earn $100 a month repairing clubs, primarily because the hickory shafts would bow and snap quite easily. In the average pro shop in the 1930s, though, club repairs scarcely totaled that much in a year once the wood shafts were pretty much gone.

As Dick's assistant, my father had a range of assignments around the club, but he also found a good deal of time to play and practice, sharpening his game for his burgeoning competitive career. It was just lucky for Dad that a couple of fellows named Ben Hogan and Byron Nelson were hanging around the club from early to late most days. Those two had first gotten to know one another during their nine-hole Glen Garden Caddie Championship match—won by Nelson—in December 1927. As one of their prizes for that match, they were allowed to play and practice at times when the club wasn't busy with member play. Hogan and Nelson took full advantage of their playing privileges, and Dad would say later that he and the future golfing legends "palled around together and played golf quite a lot." As it turned out, the friendship forged between the three men on the practice range and the nearly treeless course at Glen Garden would extend through their golfing lives, with Hogan and Nelson joining the ranks of the game's best-ever players and Dad being a very good player but eventually becoming recognized primarily as a great teacher of the game.

The three men's distinctive personalities and their approaches to the game of golf were displayed clearly in those days in Texas. Dad, the lifelong learner, focused on practicing and studying the game, but he was not fanatic about competing. Nelson and Hogan, meanwhile, already were showing the intense dedication to competitive golf that would characterize their brilliant playing careers. They spent countless hours practicing and playing, always with fierce determination to win.

Dad said that Hogan, even in those early days, displayed the go-it-alone posture that was characteristic of his golf life. He tended not, for example, to turn to my uncle Dick, the club's head pro, for advice. "Ben always was a loner," Dick told my father. "We would talk some about golf, but he didn't ask anyone for advice on his game. He worked things out himself. He had tremendous determination and concentration."

Byron Nelson took a different approach, reaching out eagerly for advice on his game and his future. Throughout the spring of 1930 Nelson consulted with Dick, who liked the young player right away and became more and more impressed with him as they interacted. "He was a good young player when I came to the club, just out of high school and trying to decide about his future," Dick said. Nelson asked him, "Do you think I can make it as a professional?" My uncle responded with encouragement, saying, "You have the tools and the temperament." During their rounds together at Glen Garden, Dick always was struck by Nelson's eagerness to learn.

Nelson had grown up not far from Glen Garden, while Hogan lived miles from the club, and my father said that both " ... would be out on the practice range just about every day, most of the day. They'd hit the balls off the practice tee, then go down and hit them back." Nelson would later recall that " ... back then there were plenty of caddies around, but I couldn't afford a caddie to shag my balls, so I would shag my own."

While his new buddies practiced maniacally, my dad continued to build what would be a lifelong approach to golf as a game of many physical and strategic nuances he often found more interesting than successes on the playing field. It didn't escape his notice, then, that in those marathon practice sessions that carried them to world-class status among professional golfers, Nelson and Hogan took distinctly different approaches, both of which worked well.

"Maybe Byron would practice with one club," Dad said. "He'd hit all day with, say, a two-iron. But ol' Bennie, he was out there using all the clubs. They were really determined to be good pro golfers. They both sure wanted it in the worst way."

My father turned twenty on March 24, 1930, and during that spring he and the eighteen-year-old Nelson regularly played together in Monday morning pro-ams in Fort Worth. Prize money was meager—maybe $25 to the winner—but even that small amount went a long way during the Great Depression. My father was widely considered the best pro player in the area, and Byron one of the top amateurs. They won those pro-ams so many times that the other pros instituted a rule that a professional could play with the same amateur only once a month. Years later, Dad and Byron would laugh together about their early successes as a golfing team.

***

Deep into the 1920s, what passed for a professional golf circuit was a loosely aligned set of tournaments stretching coast to coast, mostly in the southern half of the country. Efforts to formalize the circuit into a true pro "tour" were given a boost by the popularity of pros such as Walter Hagen, Gene Sarazen and Horton Smith, but it was Hagen's personal manager, Bob Harlow, who is given the most credit for finally getting a tournament circuit organized. Harlow was hired as the first full-time official PGA tournament manager in August 1929.

That early pro tour was a mere shadow of today's super-organized operation. To put it mildly, the tournaments usually were run in a very casual way, as illustrated by the case of Harry Cooper. Born in England, Cooper moved to Texas with his family when he was a youngster. He turned pro at age nineteen and won thirty-six tournaments in his career, leading the circuit in winnings and stroke average in 1937. A 1992 inductee into the World Golf Hall of Fame, Cooper recorded twenty top-ten finishes in majors—but never a first—and thus is widely considered the greatest player never to win a major championship.

In January 1930 Cooper made "special arrangements" with tournament officials that allowed him to participate in the Agua Caliente Open without postponing his wedding date. He was permitted to play twenty-seven holes on two different days and none on another, giving him a day free to "tie the knot." Such arrangements were not uncommon on the early tour, though. In March 1935, Hagen himself arrived a day late to the Charleston Open but still got to play the event; tournament officials simply allowed him to play thirty-six holes on his first day to catch up.

Adding further informality, tournaments back then were operated on a kind of "buddy system." The practice allowed certain players to more or less set their own starting times and decide with whom they would play, such things being determined when they showed up at the course on a given day. Over time, tour officials were able to change these customs without interference from the pros. Not only did this eliminate unfair and divisive practices, it also helped make the tour more popular. Spectators could know a day in advance who was playing with whom, and when so that they could plan their day and get excited about it.

When Bob Harlow took over as manager of the PGA Tournament Bureau, the pros were playing for their share of purses totaling $77,000 for the full year. That's $18,500 *less* than Tom Watson alone collected for finishing in a tie for eighteenth at the 2010 Masters. But between

1929 and 1932, the income of the average American family was reduced by thirty-five percent, from $2,300 to $1,500, and more than half of America's families were making $500 or less per year. In those terms, the fledgling tour offered a chance at some real money, particularly with the top players being able to pad their bank accounts with the take from exhibition matches across the land.

The winter tour through cities in California, Arizona, Texas, Louisiana, North Carolina and Georgia provided most of the action, along with late-fall tournaments in Florida and other southern points. There was also a new development on the horizon: In the early 1930s, a northern summer circuit of tournaments was beginning to take shape. In places such as St. Paul and St. Louis, important business leaders along with the chambers of commerce began pushing the creation of pro tournaments. By mid-decade, Harlow and his team had been able to add fourteen new tournaments to the summer schedule. Still, the powerful impact of the Great Depression reached into the golf profession as it did all others. After seeing total tournament purses climb to $130,000 in Harlow's first full year as tour manager, players on the pro circuit soon had to deal with prize money being cut substantially for many of their events.

My father competed in only a few professional tournaments in 1931 and didn't play particularly well. He managed only a middle-of-the-pack showing in the annual Texas Open at the popular Brackenridge Park golf course in San Antonio and finished twenty-third in the Oklahoma Open in Tulsa, where my Uncle Dick came in fourth. It was during this period that an important shift took place within the golfing Grout clan. Dick had made up his mind to travel and play a lot less and devote more time to being a club pro. Occasionally he'd play in a tournament if it was near his home club, but his time and efforts were focused mainly on golf instruction at Glen Garden. My uncle was leaving it to his younger brother to carry the Grout banner on the professional circuit.

By fall that year, Dad and others in his golf circle were feeling the itch to test themselves outside of Texas and Oklahoma. The tournaments in the two states were fine, but most were relatively low-paying compared to what was offered on the pro circuit. The real action was in the big pro tournaments around the country that sometimes paid as much as $1,500 for first place. So with visions of grandeur unimpeded even by the dismal Depression-era economic environment, twenty-one-year-old Jack Grout and nineteen-year-old Ben Hogan began to talk about going to the winter tour in California so they could "hit the big time."

Dad always thought that he was a pretty good player, and this was his chance to find out just what he was made of. In truth, his teenage pal was already beyond such self-questioning; Hogan knew he was tough enough to succeed. Hogan expected to win and win big. His heart told him he could be the best golfer in the world. In any case, to test themselves fully the two young pros had to challenge the very best players, and the best weren't all located in Texas.

As my father and Hogan made plans to join the winter tour in December 1931, another young pro named Ralph Hutchison decided to join them. Ralph R. Hutchison and my dad had been friends since the days when both were caddies and junior golfers in Oklahoma City. Hutchison was two years older than Dad and came from a golfing family, his older brother, Willard, having been the longtime professional at the Ponca City Country Club in Oklahoma. (Ralph later would follow his brother's path as a club pro, with long service at Saucon Valley in Bethlehem, Pennsylvania. He also had the pleasure of being the announcer for many years at the eighteenth green at the Masters Tournament.)

Dad and his friends faced formidable challenges as they planned their rookie campaigns on the winter tour. Many tournament sponsors from pre-Depression days either cut their purses drastically or pulled their support altogether and cancelled the tourneys. Furthermore, the three men were joining the pro circuit at a time when any tournament that offered a strong prize pool was approached very seriously by every veteran player. The tour dollars mattered even more to these men. There was, after all, no way of knowing whose home golf club would be next to fold. And when his club did shut down, a touring pro lost his home base and the income it provided.

In short, these three young men were about to take the plunge into the ultimate insecure job, touring professional golfer, at the precise moment when life on tour was at its toughest point. Things had gotten so bad that in December 1931 a key tour supporter, the Golf Ball and Golf Club Manufacturers Association (later the Athletic Institute, now the National Golf Foundation), put up $5,000 to support strapped sponsors of tournaments played throughout the Southwest.

On the modern PGA Tour, golfers are walking billboards, their hats, shirts and shoes plastered with corporate names and logos. By contrast, the pros of the 1930s mostly had to sponsor themselves. The concept of equipment manufacturers paying golfers to endorse and use their products had originated in a limited way in the early 1900s, and my father had a contract with A.G. Spalding and Brothers that provided him with annual updates of clubs, balls and shag bags and a bonus for any "top" finishes he had as a player. Other than that, though, he was on his own. He and other players of his early days on tour simply saved some cash or borrowed from a friend or parents, and took off to play the circuit, with a few of the best-known players also hauling in some easy money from special exhibition matches. No matter how it worked out, everyone took a chance. There were no guarantees. If the shots were working, the pro was in luck and he flourished accordingly. But if a pro played poorly, the money he'd accumulated through summer work as a club professional could be gone in a flash.

Putting his normal positive spin on what was for him and most of the other pros a frill-free lifestyle on the road, Dad told Columbus, Ohio, writer Paul Hornung that by spending wisely and pooling resources the touring pros of the 1930s could get by with only modest expenses. "You have to remember," Dad said, that "in those days gasoline was ten cents a gallon, you could get breakfast—two eggs, bacon, toast and coffee—for twenty cents, a real good lunch for thirty cents, and dinner for sixty to sixty-five cents, and in fine places. A decent hotel room was $1, the best hotel room in town, $2.50. We could go pretty good on $40 a week for everything." Dad once told me that he figured it took about $2,000 in prize money for a pro to break even if he played the entire winter schedule of tournaments. The problem was that there were eighty to ninety pros in most tournaments and purses averaged only about $3,500, dispersed among the first twelve or fifteen places. The last man "in the money" might get anywhere from $16.16 to $25 for his four rounds of golf. So, only a dozen or so players were able to make enough cash to come out ahead for the winter season.

Not just the tour, but the entire golf industry was hit hard by the Great Depression. As golf club memberships plummeted by half, more courses ceased operations than opened during this desolate period. My father and the other young golf pros had no choice but to do the best they could with the rough hand they were dealt. Many years later, Dad reflected on those days and talked philosophically about the choices he'd made. "I suppose it was a kind of reckless thing to do during the Great Depression, go out to California and play the tour," he acknowledged. "But, you see, when you're smack dab in the middle of something like that, you don't realize it. When you look back, brother you realize how tough it was, but at the time for some crazy reason, it didn't seem so bad. You know things are tight, but practically everybody's in the same boat, so you just keep going."

Dad said that when he, Hogan and Hutchison left Fort Worth for the West Coast, he thought that Ben was really hurting for money; he remembered Hogan having to borrow from family and friends almost as soon as they reached California. Actually Dad had made a pretty good guess about Hogan's finances; in an interview with CBS's Ken Venturi in 1983, Hogan recalled that when he went to the western tour for the first time, "I went broke. I left here with $75 in my pocket to go to the West Coast. Would you try that today?"

Hogan honestly didn't believe that money would be a problem for him once he got out on tour. While he hadn't won anything around Texas, he still expected to hit it big on an even larger stage and against much tougher competition. That was the level of confidence he had, and it would serve him well in the future. Hogan clearly demonstrated that deep self-belief as he and his pals prepared for their initial West Coast journey, using his share of a $1,600 golf bet he and a partner won over two amateurs to purchase a three-year-old Hudson Roadster. My dad had good memories of that Hudson, saying that "the three of us got into that Roadster and headed for the West Coast, but before we left, Bennie's mother (Clara) fixed us boys a whole mess of fried chicken to take along on our trip. And I'm telling you, was it ever good!"

Once their 1,250-mile journey was underway, they pushed hard to get to the coast as fast as possible. But with every passing mile, they realized they were leaving farther behind all those things familiar to them. My father remembered feeling both excited and lonely at the same time. But he also knew that those feelings were natural and that everything would turn out fine. Besides, all the way to California the three friends gabbed about golf, a subject that helped make the trip shorter.

Finally arriving in Los Angeles, the trio was stunned by the size of the place; Fort Worth hadn't been tiny, but it was nothing like this. Quickly though, they found their way to the site of the first tournament in their western adventure, the Pasadena Open. It was easy to find, actually; the tourney's host course, Brookside Park, sprawled in the shadow of Rose Bowl Stadium.

Over the coming weeks, five tournaments were to be held within a few hours drive of Los Angeles, so my father, Hogan and Hutchison found a group of rent-by-the-week roadside cabins to use as a base. They each paid just $15 a week for the rental and ate a lot of cafeteria food for about $1.50 a day. There was one more expensive necessity that none of the pros could avoid, though: While in California, each would have to shell out five bucks per round for a caddie. But even that drain on his meager resources couldn't dampen my father's excitement over this new stage of his golfing life. As he would say later, "We went for the experience, as we called it. And that's what we got, experience, a great experience."

1940 publicity photo of Rodney J. Munday; a great companion of Jack Grout. (Used with Permission)

Looking back on his initial foray onto the "big tour," Dad wrote that the purse for his first West Coast tournament was $3,500, with the winner getting $750. "That was a lot of money in those days," he said. "Heck, you could even buy a pretty good farm for $750 back then." The date was December 18, 1931 when Jack Grout, Ben Hogan and Ralph Hutchison teed off for the first time on the winter circuit. Because Pasadena was each man's first official event on the winter tour, they were required to join the "playing pros" organization, which they did for a nominal fee and a signature. My father's starting time that day was 7:40 a.m., and he was paired with Paul Cahill of Los Angeles and Fred Gordon of Santa Monica, definitely not a pair of household names. Ralph Hutchison teed off at 8:20 a.m., Ben Hogan at 1 p.m.

Pasadena was then, and remains today, a beautiful place with pleasant winter weather, and the Open tournament thus drew a large number of participants. After the first round, the field was pared to the low-ninety pros, with Dad and Hogan making that cut but Hutchison falling short. Hogan also made the thirty-six-hole cut, but my father played poorly and eventually "picked up" and posted no score for the second round, it being common in those days for a player to pick up his ball when he felt there was no chance to survive the cut or when he was destined to finish out of the money. Hogan played well the last day of the tournament, but not well enough to win any cash, so all that Dad and his two friends got from their first West Coast tournament was knowledge about the considerable challenges they were facing in the months ahead.

Tournaments weren't always scheduled from week to week back then; sometimes a couple of weeks would go by between events. As it was Christmas time, a number of the pros departed Pasadena to spend the holidays with family or friends, but my father and his two pals stayed in Los Angeles, already having determined that they'd be away from home for the holidays.

As luck would have it, staying in L.A. provided Dad and his friends a quick bonus. Richard Arlen, then a celebrated movie heartthrob renowned for his portrayal of a fighter pilot in the 1927 movie *Wings*, played in the Pasadena tournament. During the event several of the pros, including Dad, got to meet the famous actor, who invited them to play and practice at his Lakeside Golf Club in Burbank. On several occasions Dad, Ralph and Ben took advantage of Arlen's offer. For my father, Ralph and some of the other pros it was their opportunity to relax, have fun, meet some new people, and, of course, play golf and work on their games. But for Ben Hogan, it was all about going into seclusion on Lakeside's practice tee to concentrate on his golf swing. There he would hit balls all day, leaving his hands raw and sore. He'd just soak them in brine and practice more.

My father told me that it was darn near impossible in those days to get Hogan to venture out with them at all, unless it was for time on the range. Undaunted by Hogan's dedication to work, Dad and Ralph headed out to see what else was happening in the world. One day, for instance, they went to Grauman's Chinese Theatre on Hollywood Boulevard to see *Cimarron*, the movie that won the Academy Award for Best Picture of 1931. The film was of particular interest to both men because it was about the Oklahoma land rush of 1889 and thus gave them a soothing immersion in the recent history of their home turf.

Dad and his friends then somehow secured tickets for the Rose Bowl. On January 1, 1932, my father, Hutchison and another pro watched Southern Cal beat Tulane, 21-12, for the national collegiate football championship. Hogan skipped the game, saying he couldn't stand the distraction of watching football when he felt he should be working on his golf game. Much later, Hogan would explain the motivation for the intense dedication he'd shown in those early days of his career. "I would win twenty-five or fifty dollars" per tournament, he said in his 1983 interview with Ken Venturi. "I was always last if I got money at all. As I said, I was a terrible golfer." Eventually, he recalled of that first winter on the pro tour, "I wasn't in the money. I was broke and had to come home."

After Pasadena, Dad, Hogan and Hutchison moved on to the $2,500 Santa Monica Amateur-Professional tournament, where the highlight of my father's week of trudging through rain and cold wind was his first meeting with a man who would become one of his lifelong friends. Dad and fellow pro Rodney J. Munday struck up a conversation on the putting green shortly before they teed off on the tourney's first day, and they remained close for the rest of their lives.

It was Munday who later would relate a touching tale about eight-time tour winner Ed "Porky" Oliver to illustrate the dire financial situation facing many touring pros of the 1930s and early 1940s. Munday told the full story in an interview taped by his wife and daughter in December 1974, and made available for this book:

"On Sunday (in New Orleans) we're to play thirty-six holes as they did in all those tournaments in those days. And Porky Oliver came to me that morning and asked me if he could get a ride to Thomasville, Georgia (which was the next stop and about five hundred miles from New Orleans). At that time I had a Pontiac coupe. And, with all the baggage and all the clothes and all that I own in the back of that car, I didn't have any room for him. Well, about dark after we finished the tournament and everybody is getting ready to go, I see Ed Oliver. I said, 'Pork Chops, you got a ride yet?' When he told me that he didn't, I said, 'You goddamn dumbo, get your stuff and come with me.'

"So he came out with a suitcase that was about fourteen inches long. The guy traveled all over the United States and that was the biggest suitcase he had. Then, I asked him, 'Where are your clubs?' Porky said, 'I don't have any. I gave them to my caddie.' I said, 'How much do you owe your caddie?' He said, 'Three rounds.' At two dollars a round at the time, he owed the caddie six dollars, so he gave him his clubs.

"I said to him, 'If you had your money, could you get your clubs back?' Oliver said, 'I might, I don't know.' So I loaned him some money and he bought his golf clubs back. Well anyway, we head for Thomasville and, of course, I pay for his room and food for the next few days, which didn't amount to much. Once we got to Thomasville, Oliver said, 'If you'd loan me bus fare to Wilmington, Delaware, I'll go up there and get a job as a plumber. I am not going to play golf anymore. I'll give up golf and send you the money as soon as I get it.'

"As much as I hated to, I had to tell Porky that I couldn't afford to loan him that kind of money. I told him the best I could do was take him out to the club and maybe he could borrow money from someone else. About an hour after we got to the club, here comes Pork Chops and he tells me, 'I don't have the heart to ask any of these fellows.' At that point, I took him down to the bus depot and gave him $30 for his ticket to Wilmington. Also, I slipped him three more bucks so he could buy himself some candy bars on the way home. Now that was thirty-three dollars plus the extra it took to get his clubs out of hock and get him cleaned up. I figured he owed me a full fifty dollars!

"This happened in February. Well June comes along and I don't hear from Oliver. Don't forget, he said he was never going to play golf again and (would) work with his dad as a plumber. In July, I pick up *The New York Times* and notice they had a little tournament in Cornell, New York. It reads, Second Place—Ed Oliver, $120.

"I thought to myself, hmmm, that's pretty good for a plumber. Maybe, I might get my money now. Month later, I see another little tournament someplace, Ed Oliver $60. Anyway, I didn't see Pork Chops until the next December at Miami Springs in Florida. He came over and paid me the money he owed me. Wouldn't you know that winter the little son-of-a-gun won the Bing Crosby tournament and the Phoenix Open! Then, a few months later he did it again in St Paul! Think if I hadn't helped him ... "

***

Next for my dad was the Los Angeles Open at Hillcrest Country Club, where he failed to qualify for the main championship rounds but where the nineteen-year-old Hogan celebrated his first paycheck as a pro, a whopping $50 for a last-place finish. Not making the championship rounds in L.A. was a disappointment for Dad because of the tournament's great history as a top-flight event. But he was philosophical; he considered big-time tournament golf a learning experience, not something you could excel at automatically. He figured to be ready the next time.

It turned out, though, that the Pasadena and succeeding tournaments that winter demonstrated an unfortunate pattern in my father's work as a touring pro. He had many excellent rounds but tended to have too many high scores and finish, at best, in the middle of the pack. Overall, he found the life of a touring pro to be a real battle. I believe, though, that even if he'd known beforehand that the tour was going to be such a challenge, he still would have given it a go. Dad was an eager young pro looking for more of what life and golf had to offer.

The truth was that even though he struggled out there, my father greatly enjoyed the friendships he was developing with fellow golfers and found the tour to be a rich environment for his ongoing study of the game, its techniques and its strategies. Dad never received formal schooling beyond high school in Oklahoma City, but in his first year on the tour he was getting a graduate education in golf and in life. While the extensive travel, the endless series of hotels, and the modest food and frequent loneliness of the golf circuit of the 1930s eventually

Jack Grout and Ben Hogan in 1938 with musician and band leader Fred Waring, namesake of the Waring blender. (Grout family photo)

would weigh on him, Dad's early years as a tour pro found him excited and optimistic about his life and the long-term future.

The same couldn't have been said for Dad's friend Ben Hogan. Though he wasn't antisocial and could at times be warm and friendly, Hogan often came across as having a chip on his shoulder. Little Ben played the part of a tough guy, a distrustful loner who could be gruff, blunt and given to a sour disposition. When he didn't play well or things didn't go his way, he could be downright irascible. My father had to wonder, at one point or another while they traveled together, whether having a tough outlook like Hogan's was a requirement for tour success. Dad had to know that if it was, then fame and fortune as a player probably weren't in Jack Grout's future. As it turned out, of course, that was precisely the case; tournament golf was going to be a much better fit for the intensely focused Ben Hogan than for my gentle father.

***

Departing Los Angeles, the Grout-Hogan-Hutchison trio moved on with the tour to the third annual $15,000 Agua Caliente Open in Tijuana, Mexico, an event billed as the West's greatest money tournament. Dad and his two pals weren't close friends with the tournament's host, Leo Diegel, one of the finest players of the day; so they had to endure qualifying for the tournament. Dad and Hogan made it through that test, but Hutchison did not. Discouraged, he soon left the tour and headed off to Georgia for a job as assistant professional at Augusta National.

My father and Hogan were excited to get into the rich Tijuana tournament because they'd heard so much about it. Each remembered seeing the much-ballyhooed picture of Gene Sarazen admiring his $10,000 check for winning the event two years previously. Why not them? Unfortunately, Dad played just so-so that week. Hogan fared much better, taking home a nice check for $200 and achieving something else that would give his golf career a boost: For the first time he attracted national media attention, with sportswriters speculating about the taciturn Texan's long-term potential. Always an admirer of Hogan's obsessive work habits, Dad watched with interest. "Ben's fabulous success didn't come as a surprise to me," he would say later. "Everyone around Texas knew Hogan was a very promising young golfer, with determination and willingness to practice and sacrifice."

From Tijuana, Dad and Hogan drove to Phoenix for the Arizona Open, then back to Texas to wrap up their first winter tour at the Texas Open in San Antonio, where neither man would win a dime. From there it was back to Fort Worth and hard work getting their golf games in better shape.

Dad must have been somewhat disillusioned by how he handled himself on the golf course during his first winter tour, but I also think that, for the most part, he actually had the time of his life. It's likely that his expectations for success weren't too high to begin with. Knowing Dad, he probably looked upon his pro-circuit debut as a shiny glass that was half-full. The same could not be said for his good friend Hogan, of course. Ben felt that his first experience on tour had been a disaster. For Hogan, the glass wasn't half full at all; it was practically empty.

***

Ben Hogan's story is one of the most interesting in the history of golf. In a game that tends to be at least somewhat social, even at the highest levels, Hogan remained throughout his life a standoffish, intimidating figure. He had a terrible "hook" that flung his shots far to the left through his early life on the tour, and he worked endlessly but without apparent joy to improve his golf game.

Tough luck, it seemed, was the only luck the young Ben Hogan had. His thirty-seven-year-old blacksmith father, Chester, committed suicide as nine-year-old Ben watched. And with a brother, Royal, and a sister named Princess in the family, too, there was no money for the comforts of life. Certainly there was no money for new golf clubs. Ben's clubs were a mixed bag of left-handed and right-handed models because he used whatever clubs he could acquire on the cheap. My father remembered that "Ben's mother was a seamstress and a wonderful woman. She had a hard time ... the family had it real tough. Ben sold papers on the corner and then he took to caddying. That's how he got started in golf."

After school little Bennie, even at age nine, would hustle straight from the school yard to the train-station platform to peddle the late edition of the *Fort Worth Star-Telegram*. "That station was where I learned to take pretty good care of myself," Hogan mused later. Sometimes it was necessary for him to fight other newsboys in order to defend his paper-selling territory on the platform.

Frustrating Hogan's early efforts to learn the golf swing was that he was neither a natural right-hander nor a natural left-hander. Dad said that when he and Ben met in 1930, Hogan was, in effect, ambidextrous. He had great strength on both sides of his body and seemed to do things equally well right- or left-handed. "First time I saw Ben he was playing cross-handed, right-handed or cow-handed, as they say in Texas, or orthodox left-handed," Dad said. "He was all mixed up, but he got that all straightened out, and I guess you'd say he mastered the right way pretty well." Dad added that, "Ben carried seven clubs in his bag then. And not only were they not a matched set—three were left-handed and four were right-handed clubs! Well, Ben would hook when he hit left-handed and hook when he hit right-handed, so he couldn't decide which way to play. My brother gave him three more hickory-shafted, right-handed clubs, and we persuaded him to play right-handed."

Hogan practiced with a fury. "Sometimes he wouldn't even go out with us to play," said Matty Reed, a good Fort Worth amateur who was five years older than Ben. Young Hogan's diligence was all the more amazing because he had no model for it and he got almost no immediate rewards from his work. To keep his game sharp and bring in a few extra bucks, Hogan counted on his afternoon matches at a course called Katy Lake, a nine-hole layout on the south side of Fort Worth, and at a course called Z-Boaz (pronounced "Zee-boze"). "One time in '29 or '30," Reed recalls, "Smiley Rowland (a local pro) and I played Hogan and Jack Grout at Z-Boaz. You talk about the birdies flying. Smiley and I shot 62, and they shot 61. But I still never dreamed that Ben would get that good. He had such a lousy hook."

Despite his so-so performance during his first winter on tour, Hogan remained steadfast, playing the winter tournaments again in 1932-33. But once more his results were disappointing. He'd play in a few tournaments, finish out of the money, go broke and have to return home. My father took a different path. After playing the '31-'32 winter circuit, he chose to spend most of the next three years working in Fort Worth and saving his money. Dad didn't pick up the pro-golf circuit again until December 1934.

Chapter 4
"The Hawk" Takes Flight in Texas

"Remember that sometimes the ability to hit a ball correctly comes suddenly, without warning, after a series of setbacks." – JACK GROUT

❊❊❊

When my father and his friend Bennie returned to Fort Worth in early 1932 after better than two months on tour, they both were physically exhausted and down to their last few dollars. Dad actually looked forward to getting off the road and back to work with his older brother at Glen Garden, the daily routine of his club job being more suited to his way of living. Unfortunately for Hogan, he didn't have a job waiting for him, and he was in dire need of something that would provide him some money. His desperate situation made it necessary for him to sell his car for a few hundred dollars and take the only golf job he could find—as the pro at Nolan River Country Club, a public course located about a half-hour's drive south of Fort Worth in Cleburne, Texas. The new job, which he reached in an old car borrowed from his mother, really wasn't much, even for those days. But considering that it was the worst year of the Great Depression, he was lucky to find any job at all.

At Nolan River Hogan had the typical club pro's job, putting in long hours for short pay. He got the golf bags out of storage in the morning and put them away at night; cleaned the dirt from the faces of the golfer's clubs and did his best to keep their irons looking polished; kept the pro shop clean and orderly and sold balls, tees and some clubs and bags. He also gave as many lessons as he could, but just for the cash; he would say later that he didn't enjoy teaching the game to others.

As the 1932 golf season wound down at Nolan River, Hogan returned to Fort Worth for the pro job at a new nine-hole layout near downtown, called Oakhurst. The job paid the struggling pro about $60 a week, which was considered meager even then. "Not much of a job," Hogan recalled in the late 1940s. "Practically all of my revenue came from selling golf balls by the dozen to one rich foursome and by winning bets from them."

On the positive side, though, being back in Fort Worth afforded the opportunity for additional nighttime jobs to help with the finances. In that aspect, Hogan was just like my dad—always looking for additional income. And it would turn out that both found some of that extra income through activity that is taboo for professional athletes today—involvement in professional gambling.

***

Dallas-Fort Worth and environs had become known as a "Sportin' Town" in the early '30s. In those days, people who wanted gambling action had no problem finding all they could handle in north Texas. In the small town of Arlington alone, there was a choice selection of gambling sites, including a famous (and infamous) gambling casino called Top O' Hill Terrace, where well-heeled patrons entertained themselves betting on cards and dice in luxurious surroundings, and Arlington Downs, where anyone could bet the horses. Both establishments had national reputations and attracted gamblers from all over the Southwest and beyond.

Arlington Downs was owned by W.T. Waggoner, and the casino by C. Fred Browning. Both were high rollers and self-anointed sportsmen, and both basked in the notoriety their exploits brought them.

Arlington Downs opened just after the stock market crashed, in November 1929, a few months before my father and uncle moved to Fort Worth to start work at Glen Garden. W.T. Waggoner's horse-racing operation was located halfway between Dallas and Fort Worth and was reachable by the electric trolley that linked Fort Worth, Dallas and several smaller towns. It cost Waggoner nearly $3 million—equal to $38.8 million in 2011 dollars—to construct the 1 1/4-mile track, which had a grandstand seating more than six thousand. For its day, Arlington Downs was a fine racing facility.

Waggoner found in north Texas a strong public appetite for horse racing and the attendant wagering action, but he was confronted with one particularly thorny problem: Pari-mutuel betting (the largest income-producing aspect of horse racing) was illegal at the time of the track's opening. Waggoner had influential friends, however, and while he was spending thousands of dollars lobbying the legislature in Austin for legalization of pari-mutuel wagering, he gained community support by allowing the use of his facility for a variety of events, including local civic activities.

In 1933 the Texas legislature legalized pari-mutuels and issued the first permit to Arlington Downs. The entire place had just been expanded and remodeled when Dad went there looking for work in the fall of that year. With things at Glen Garden not exactly hectic, Dad knew he could take a job at the track and still handle his primary job at the golf club. Like most people those days, he was scraping to make enough money just to survive. And not to be minimized, my father always liked the horses. The thoroughbred track thus was a place where he could supplement his meager income while enjoying the atmosphere immensely.

My father was twenty-three years old that October of 1933 when he started working at Arlington Downs, sitting behind a window and selling pari-mutuel tickets to bettors. The excitement of the crowd as the race drew nearer was something Dad always liked. "The pace of everything quickens and it can make your head kind of dizzy," he said. Even in his later years, Dad still felt that tingle of excitement when the track announcer called for "post time."

Horse-racing historians say that during the track's first year of full operation under the new wagering laws, more than six hundred horses ran there, and average daily attendance was nearly nine thousand. Happily for Waggoner, after payment of daily purse distributions and other expenses, he was left with a tidy profit. The income and excitement generated by now-legal pari-mutuel betting breathed new life into the racetrack, and as Arlington Downs' financial health improved, so, too, did the size of Dad's paycheck. It was during this time that he adopted what would become his favorite axiom: "In order to make money, you must go where the money is."

Once during a particularly busy afternoon at the track, Dad received an unexpected bonus, the event causing him some consternation but in the end making for a terrific payday. It happened after a long-shot horse won one of the featured races of the day in an exciting photo finish. One fellow came to Dad's pay window with a number of winning tickets to cash. Dad took his time precisely counting out the man's money, but as the fellow gathered up his winnings and walked away, a $100 bill was left behind.

When Dad noticed the bill lying there, he glanced up just in time to see the man disappearing into the crowd. My father didn't reach for the money right away, thinking that surely the man would return for it, because in those days nobody ever left a tip that large. Dad's mind suddenly went in every direction with questions: "Did he mean to leave the cash as a tip for me? Did the chaos and his haste cause him to forget to take all the money that he had won?" Eventually Dad grabbed the big bill and stuffed it into his jacket pocket. Once he did, he kept quiet about it, never mentioning his bonanza to any of the other ticket-takers. He always remembered that the whole episode made him excited, scared and happy all at the same time.

My father continued working at Arlington Downs during the track's spring and fall racing seasons over several years, even after the death of the 82-year-old Waggoner in late 1934. With the powerful Waggoner gone, though, the state legislature moved again to ban pari-mutuel gambling. The 1937 racing season was the last one for Arlington Downs. The site of rodeos and other events for twenty years, the racetrack complex was torn down in 1958.

Many years later when I heard my father speak so fondly about working at the racetrack, it was obvious to me that he really loved those days. Even in his glory years as head golf pro at Scioto Country Club in Ohio in the 1950s, and later when he worked in Florida, Dad periodically would gather up friends and club staff for afternoons at the racetrack. In truth, he seemed as comfortable there as he ever was anywhere.

***

While Dad was earning extra bucks at Arlington Downs, Ben Hogan started working as a "stick man"—a croupier on dice and roulette tables—in the evenings at some of C. Fred Browning's betting parlors. The future winner of nine major championships and a total of sixty-eight professional golf tournaments either dealt cards in a back room at the Blackstone Hotel or ran a craps game in a basement on Ninth Street in Fort Worth. It was during this time that Hogan became an expert card mechanic and earned the nickname "The Hawk," which also would be used later to describe his ability to study and then conquer a golf course. "I tell you, when Hogan dealt the cards he did it so fast they just spilled out of his hands," said his pal and fellow golfer Paul Runyan. "It didn't look like he was doing what we were doing. He not only had fast hands, he had fast eyes. When anybody else was dealing, he would say, 'Deal your cards lower, I know what you've all got.' "

Over the first six months of his new employment, Hogan proved to be such an adroit card dealer and croupier that he was offered broader opportunities at a magnificent gambling house Browning opened in nearby Arlington. To create this home for illegal wagering, Browning had bought and extensively remodeled a rambling stone home and popular restaurant called Top O' Hill Terrace, located on a thousand-foot-high ridgeline that was the highest point in Tarrant County.

Thanks to a scholarly paper written by Gloria Jean Van Zandt as a student at the University of Texas at Arlington in 1969, we know that the gambling emporium Browning built was an extraordinary structure. Browning moved the original house off its foundations and built a huge underground structure, then moved the house back over it. The expanded structure was not apparent from the highway, the only part located above ground being its modestly sized first floor that housed a restaurant, lounge, guest rooms, and living quarters for Browning and his wife. An inner floor and the basement buried deep inside the main building were much larger than the original house and were built expressly for casino operations.

The whole operation was lavishly guarded; to gain access, invited customers had to pass through the large iron gates of a stone entrance and ascend a winding paved road. Transported in the luxury vehicles that crowded the club's parking lot were famous guests including Howard Hughes, Bonnie and Clyde, Frank Sinatra, Will Rogers, Lana Turner, Mae West, Walter Winchell, Dean Martin, John Wayne, Ginger Rogers, Buster Keaton, Hedy Lamaar, Bugsy Siegel, W. C. Fields, Gene Autry and even Jack Ruby, the man who decades later would slay President Kennedy's assassin, Lee Harvey Oswald.

Top O' Hill Terrace was officially billed as a dining resort, but it was written that "the only thing money could buy there was chips" for illegal gambling. Entering customers had to pass through a series of monitored doors, the final one leading to a hat-check stand above which was a sign reading, "Park your revolver here." Inside the casino there were three pool tables with low-hanging lights above each, two roulette wheels, two blackjack tables and two craps tables. At first, Ben Hogan was employed as one of the nineteen paid dealers operating the tables, but later on he did other jobs for Browning such as barkeeper and part-time casino manager. Bootlegged whiskey and the occasional big-name dance band were all part of the fast action at "The Top."

The building was so ingeniously constructed for its purpose as a gambling casino that it remains a wonder that a raid by the police ever could be successful. In the event of an ambush by lawmen intent on shutting down the illegal wagering, there was a tunnel about ten feet tall, four feet wide and nearly fifty feet long that served as a route for gamblers to hustle outside to the tea garden. In this peaceful area, densely populated with shrubbery, there already would be drinks and food set up to make it appear that nothing out of the ordinary—and certainly not illegal gambling—was going on.

The fun and games at Top O' Hill Terrace finally came to an end on August 13, 1947, when Captain Manuel Trazazas "Lone Wolf" Gonzaullas and his fellow Texas Rangers came calling, crawling several hundred yards through the woods to avoid the casino's guards. The Rangers made an aggressive assault on the gambling den, kicking down doors and coming in through the escape tunnel. About $25,000 worth of gaming equipment was smashed and confiscated. Fifty patrons, eight employees and Mr. Browning were arrested.

Ben Hogan, of course, was not among the casino employees scooped up that night. By the time Gonzaullas and his colleagues swooped down on Top O' Hill Terrace in 1947, Hogan was plying his trade with extraordinary success at distant and varied sites, having firmly established himself as one of the finest golfers in the world. He had moved far beyond the need to moonlight in a second job.

***

It's easy to question my father and Ben Hogan taking jobs with gambling organizations, given the dangers of mixing gambling and competitive sports. But this was, after all, in the middle of the worst economic crisis in our nation's history. The reality is that when you're hurting for money and looking for that one break that'll help you get ahead, influential people often can make all the difference in your life. Back then was no exception, and men such as Fred Browning and W.T. Waggoner had the money, power and influence to make things happen for Dad and for Hogan.

The Great Depression years were incredibly traumatic for the United States and brought cause for worry about whether the country had a future at all. On July 7, 1932, the stock market hit bottom at 33.98, the lowest it had been since the 1800s. Vast numbers of Americans were living below the poverty line. Yet some industries—not including golf, for sure—avoided the steepest sales declines for a time in the early 1930s as the public looked for ways to escape the national gloom. If Americans couldn't find work, some at least could use their modest resources to go for a drive, have a cigarette, or go to a movie. Reports of such consumer spending inspired humorist Will Rogers' memorable one-liner: "We're the first nation in the history of the world to go to the poorhouse in an automobile."

Gambling was another activity that maintained its audience, and Ben Hogan would turn this fact to his advantage, not only at Top O' Hill Terrace but also on the golf course. While the golfing activity at Glen Garden remained reasonably steady during this period and kept the Grout brothers busy throughout the day, Hogan's Oakhurst course tended to be pretty much deserted most mornings. That allowed Hogan to get in hours of practice before noon and then prepare for the frequent afternoon visits of Fred Browning, his gambling buddies and other bettors who had made Oakhurst their unofficial headquarters.

1935 Texas Cup pro team. Kneeling: Francis McGonagill, Larry Nabholtz, Willie McGuire Sr., Jack Burke Sr., George Aulbach. Standing: Tom Sockwell, Jack Grout, Graham Ross, Jimmy Demaret, Harvey Penick, Bryan Winters. (Photo used with permission)

The little nine-hole Oakhurst course on the west side of Fort Worth had become a place to hang out if you wanted some real action, and as Hogan's game improved he could count on a number of fellows from the club to back him (financially) against anyone who wanted a match. Hogan seldom disappointed his backers, and one of the gamblers—it is said to have been Browning—loaned Ben the money to try the professional tour again in the winter of 1932-1933.

***

Golf began as a diversion for people living in harbor towns along the east coast of Scotland, but when the ancient game finally reached our shores in the 1880s, it quickly gained popularity as a pastime for the elite. Its reach, however, remained mostly along the Atlantic seaboard, and because of this stagnation it got a relatively late start in the vast American South and Southwest. Once the game hit the hardpan of Texas and Oklahoma, it produced many of the finest players that ever lived. Beginning in the 1920s, outstanding golfers such as Byron Nelson, Ben Hogan, Jimmy Demaret, Ky Laffoon and Dick and Jack Grout began streaming out of Oklahoma City, Houston, Fort Worth, Dallas and Miami to make their marks on the pro circuit. Even the tiny burg of Arkansas City, Kansas, fed this migration onto the tour, producing ten-time tournament winner Dick Metz, one of the outstanding players of the '30s and '40s.

Why was it that so many wonderful players came from this swath of the country? Many believe that the prime factor was the changeable weather in the region—considerable sunshine but also lots of wind, rain and extremes of heat and cold, conditions that forced players to develop solid swing mechanics. From the moment he started playing with the Texas pros, Dad saw a wealth of excellent golf swings, most of which were carefully constructed to be adaptable to all kinds of weather. Although Dad lived in Oklahoma City until he was nineteen, it was the talented group of Texas pro golfers of the day—Hogan, Nelson, Demaret, Ralph Guldahl, the Mangrum brothers (Lloyd and Ray), Henry Ransom and others—with whom he felt the closest kinship. It was only after he got away from home and into the circle of these players as assistant to his brother Dick in Fort Worth that Dad began to come into his own as a golfer.

Facilitating Dad's contacts with the great Texas players was an unusual and highly popular series of matches between Fort Worth and Dallas professionals in the early 1930s. The tournaments were held all over the two cities at courses such as Rivercrest, Z-Boaz, Glen Garden and Brook Hollow. Dad and Hogan would travel over to Dallas in Ben's mother's car. My father said, "I can still see it—an old Buick, I think it was. Every time you'd go over twenty miles an hour it would start to smoke, so you had to ride with the windows down no matter how cold the weather was."

Among the regulars who played for Fort Worth in these matches were Hogan and my dad. Byron Nelson played some, too, but by April 1933 he had gone off to be a club pro in Texarkana, Texas. Jimmy Demaret even came up from Houston to play in some of those tournaments. Dad recalled that "Jimmy would bum over on Sunday, play in a tournament Monday, and hitch a ride back with somebody driving to Houston, or on a freight car. He'd usually stay with us overnight, so I got to know Jimmy pretty well."

Also making appearances were Lloyd and Ray Mangrum, who between them won forty tour events and one major. Ralph Guldahl, who would win sixteen pro tournaments, including three majors during his career, played in the matches for a short time but moved out of Texas in 1933. Guldahl's golf talents would be missed by the Texans, but perhaps not his on-course personality, which was cool to the point of being frigid. Sam Snead once said that "if Guldahl gave someone a blood transfusion, the patient would freeze to death."

The truth is that the pro circuit then was a tighter-knit fraternity than its successor, the modern PGA Tour. The camaraderie among the players was strong, and my father particularly enjoyed the constant give-and-take about the golf swing. Tour pros today, four-time major championship winner Raymond Floyd said in an interview for this book, "sit around and chat about the next jet they're going to buy or whether Dubai is going to offer a half million here or a million there" to have them come over and play.

Chapter 5
Too Nice a Guy

"You fool no one when you overestimate your abilities, least of all yourself."
– JACK GROUT

***

My father's key tournament during the summer of 1932 was the PGA Championship stroke-play qualifier in St. Paul, Minnesota, where he failed to make the championship proper. Other local tournaments and exhibitions helped fill his playing schedule. Then, before calling it quits for the year, Dad and his younger brother Dutch played in the $500 Texarkana Open, an obscure event remembered today as the place where Byron Nelson declared himself a golf professional.

The next two years found Dad sharply reducing his playing commitments. He played in a number of local exhibition matches with his brother Dick, and participated in the Inaugural Texas Cup matches in 1933 that pitted top Texas pros against the state's best amateurs. In 1934, Dad's only professional tournaments of note were the U.S. Open at the Merion Golf Club in Ardmore, Pennsylvania, where he missed the 36-hole cut and a qualifier for the PGA Championship. Dad was co-medalist in the PGA qualifier but then failed to advance through the stroke-play qualifying rounds for the match-play championship proper at the Park Country Club in Williamsville, New York.

During this period, Dad's golf game and money supply just didn't give him the comfort level needed by a touring pro. He continued banking his money whenever possible, working most days with Uncle Dick at Glen Garden and evenings at Arlington Downs, but he found himself challenged by some of the tougher realities of tour golf. The professional golf tournament circuit of the 1930s offered neither an easy-going nor a high-paying environment. Perhaps the toughest barrier for my father was the quality of the competition. Playing against veterans such as Hagen, Sarazen, Cooper, Cruickshank and Tommy Armour, he had to feel he was surrounded by a pack of hungry wolves. Compounding his challenge was the emergence of a number of new stars on the tour such as Guldahl, Nelson, Paul Runyan, Johnny Revolta and Ky Laffoon. And then there was Ben Hogan. The talented Texan wasn't even listed among the can't-miss players as the 1934-35 winter circuit began, although once he solved his money issues and swing problems he would win sixty-four PGA Tour events.

Despite the somewhat gloomy outlook for his playing career, my father headed to California in December 1934 to dive again into the challenging winter tour. This time he traveled with Byron and Louise Nelson, who at that time had been married for only about six months. The three of them traveled in Nelson's 1932 Ford Roadster, a royal blue convertible with cream wheels and top. The car had just a single seat across the front and a little rumble seat in the back—not exactly a roomy vehicle. There were no glass roll-up windows in Nelson's roadster; the car had curtains that flopped in the wind. And like many cars of the day, this one had no heating system. Drivers of such cars often would heat bricks in the oven and wrap them in bags before leaving home, placing them near their feet in the car to provide some warmth. Every so often they'd stop to heat the bricks again.

1939 U.S. Open champion Byron Nelson (used with permission)

Nelson would write much later that the lack of room in his roadster led to an awkward situation. "Jack Grout traveled with us by car, and I remember his golf clubs wouldn't stand up in the back seat and kept falling on one or the other of us," Nelson wrote. "By the time we'd reached L.A., Louise had had enough and said, 'Either the clubs go, or I go.' So Jack had to find another way home, but he was very understanding about it."

As Dad and the Nelsons made the long drive to California, he had plenty of time to think about what he'd accomplished and where his career was headed. It had been three years since he first ventured west with Ralph Hutchison and Ben Hogan; it had taken him that long to save enough money to take another crack at the tour. My father worked hard on his golf game during those three years, and I know that as he and the Nelsons headed west, Dad felt better prepared than ever and even more determined to succeed. Once he got to the West Coast and began competing, though, reality hit home quickly: It was tough out there.

Dad played five events in California, Mexico and Arizona during the 1934-35 winter season, and a fifteenth-place finish at the Phoenix Open was his best result. He was seeing more clearly now how different the winter tour with the "big boys" was from playing the circuit back in the Southwest.

Still, Dad had that long, languid golf swing that was the envy of his fellow pros. He was single and could afford to get by on light earnings. And he loved the game of golf and hungered to master it.

So Jack Grout pushed on.

***

Back in Fort Worth in the spring of 1935, my father mulled his up-and-down performance on the pro-golf circuit and considered what he'd need to do to perform at a higher level. The answer wasn't that hard to find. He needed to look no farther than his friend Byron Nelson to see the difference between a laid-back competitor and a fiercely determined one.

Good friends as young men, the two remained friends for life and were alike in a number of ways. Both were six-foot-two, slim and rangy. Each grew up in a good family and came of age in the Southwest during the Great Depression. They were warm, kind-hearted gentlemen. And each made his livelihood and reputation in golf: Dad as a renowned teacher and respected player, Nelson as a renowned player and respected teacher. Despite all their similarities, though, it's clear the two really had very little in common when it came to their inner drive and personal sense of what was important.

My father was only moderately competitive, although he could hold his own when things got tough. His disposition was mostly serious, but he enjoyed having fun, too. He made friends easily and loved to laugh. In practically every old golf photograph I have of my father, he has a smile on his face; you can sense his joy and the pleasure he received from the game. Dad truly loved golf but was not consumed by it.

Byron Nelson, on the other hand, was the personification of a goal-oriented competitor. He had a mild and reserved personality but, particularly on the golf course, a deadly serious disposition. In many pictures of him taken on the golf course, he appears either expressionless or somewhat agitated. Sam Snead has been quoted as saying about Nelson, "While he was always polite, friendly and professional, he didn't seem to be having any fun." When Nelson heard this he replied, "Tell Snead I had a lot of fun winning all those tournaments."

It was clear that to survive on the pro circuit, Dad would have to learn to fight as hard as the elite players did. His friends on tour told him that to win tournaments, he'd have to become single-minded, egotistical and selfish, and look after only himself. But the reality was that these were traits that just didn't jibe with his personality. Byron Nelson would reflect on this many years later, saying, "Jack (Grout) had a wonderfully long, fluid, smooth swing and good rhythm, but he was too nice a guy, not a tough enough competitor ... "

Throughout the summer and fall of 1935, my father played well enough around Texas and Oklahoma to feel more confident about his chances on the upcoming California winter circuit. In fact, just before he and Jimmy Demaret left Fort Worth in December, Dad established the Edgemere course record with a 65.

As Dad and Demaret made their way to the West Coast, both were realistic about the money to be made on tour; with the country still struggling financially, the pro circuit offered modest purses at best. So as a hedge against either of them going broke, they agreed to share expenses as much as possible and to split their individual winnings. In the end, though, there wasn't much to divide between them. "There was so damn little money around, we didn't really take ourselves too seriously," said their fellow pro, Paul Runyan. "We fought like cats and dogs for titles, you better believe it, but the money didn't seem to make much of a difference then. You had a little one week, none the next. Somehow, though, you kept going."

Interviewed later about those days, Dad recalled how he had "saved up my money for a couple of years and decided to join the tour again ... I had a beat-up old Ford, and Jimmy (Demaret) ... had a set of clubs, a few bucks in his pocket and, of all things, a personal caddie—Charley Schwartz, who had caddied for him around Houston."

"You know," Dad continued, "Jimmy and I are just about the same age ... and back then Jimmy wanted to be a singer more than he wanted to be a golf pro. I remember him buying sheet music and learning all the words to popular songs. He sang all the time, especially when we were riding along in the car."

It turned out Dad needed Demaret's singing to keep his spirits up that winter. He missed the cut in the Pasadena Open and then tied for thirty-seventh in Riverside, was thirty-sixth at the L.A. Open, then tied for fifty-first in Sacramento. A tie for twenty-fifth in the rainy Catalina Open completed his less-than-outstanding California play.

It was the kind of start that had to be discouraging. Luckily, though, there were others around Dad whose even worse play or off-course antics helped keep him from falling into a funk. There was, for example, a fellow named Bill Mehlhorn, a talented tour veteran who had tied for first at Sacramento but set tongues wagging during the third round at Catalina when he required eight putts on the par-three eighteenth. Twice "Wild Bill" hit the ball while it was moving, this rules violation costing him two strokes each time. Dad said that during a weather delay at this tournament, "all hell broke loose" as Demaret and Mehlhorn squared off in a game of checkers. "It was a bad, rainy day," Dad said, "and this Mehlhorn was a whale of a checkers player. But ol' Jimmy beat him bad. I remember one game where Mehlhorn sat back and just said, 'It can't be done,' but Jimmy had him all right." It was a good thing, too, because Demaret won enough money from Mehlhorn to pay the hotel bill for himself and my father.

During Dad's final nine holes at Catalina, Demaret came out to check on him. "Yeah," Dad said later, "I remember ol' Jimmy walking around with me. He'd been shooting those 80s and 82s and he was giving me that, 'Come on, Jack boy, we don't want to walk home, let's get some gas money, boy' stuff." In the 1954 Demaret book titled, *My Partner, Ben Hogan*, Demaret wrote that Dad didn't seem to realize he was playing for cash in Catalina, and that when he was apprised of the fact, Dad blew himself right out of a chance to collect some meal money. Asked later about Demaret's reminiscence, Dad was amused. "I knew I was playing for money," he assured, "but I was just a kid from Texas ... and I didn't think I had a chance."

My father was deeply disappointed by his poor finish at Catalina, a 72 on a short par-66 course. His 269 total left him three shots out of the money, and he thought if that was the best he could do in a tough situation, maybe he didn't belong on the tour. So while Demaret moved on to the winter circuit's Arizona leg, Dad got into his aging Ford and struck out across the desert toward Fort Worth.

It was a lonely trip, with plenty of time for Dad to reflect on where he'd been and where his career was headed. He'd made the pro circuit three times by 1936, but there were some realities that he needed to deal with. The primary one, of course, was that if he wanted to remain a tour player, he was going to have to play better.

One thing eating at Dad was that golfers with swings much less classic than his own—some of them, in fact, downright strange—were winning tournaments, while he finished down in the pack. Some of these players just didn't look to Dad as if they belonged out there. There were even times when he would look at the pros who had beaten him and wonder how they got into the tournament in the first place! It eventually became evident to my father that the real secret to tour success was not the look of a golf swing but the desire and determination of the man using it. In most cases the players who shot the lowest scores weren't any more knowledgeable or talented than he was. The winners didn't always have the best technique or necessarily the most skill. Rather, they often were simply the toughest competitors.

The problem was how does a quiet, humble man make himself over so that he is comfortable in an everything-goes, take-care-of-yourself-first atmosphere? Even his best friends out there would run over him without a second thought if he stood between them and a golf title. And off the course, Dad just wasn't a good fit with most of the other players. He was a conservative fellow, neither a drinker nor a skirt chaser. The after-hours carousing indulged in by many of his fellow pros just didn't fit his style.

Jimmy Demaret, winner of thirty-one tournaments including three Masters in his great career, typified the free-spirited tour pro of the day. The outgoing Demaret seemed to relish every single moment of every day and night on the tour, no matter how his golf game was going. In 1938, after a victory in San Francisco, he even managed to find financial backers, two men who owned a nightclub in Galveston. They liked the potential of the stylish singer/golfer and decided to sponsor him.

Over the years, the unofficial goodwill ambassador from Texas made multitudes of friends everywhere he traveled. He related to the galleries who followed the golf tournaments like few before or since. Jimmy popularized colorful golf garb, from two-tone shoes to rainbow sweaters to loud caps and tasseled tams. Jimmy said he got the color idea from his father, who was a house painter.

But Jimmy Demaret was much more than a sideshow on the traveling PGA circuit. He could flat-out play the game. He was strong and straight off the tee, efficient on and around the greens, and tenacious in competition. He played his shots from a narrow stance, and quite possibly was the finest wind player there ever was.

Despite their shared love of golf, though, there is little doubt about the mismatch of personalities when Dad and Demaret traveled together in 1935-36. My father certainly wasn't a somber man. He liked to have fun. It's just that his social disposition had its clear limits; being around people for too long just plain wore him out, and once a long day of serious-minded golf was over, he wanted to go home and rest. Not Demaret. "You going home, Jimmy?" someone once asked Demaret as he left the locker room after a tournament in Houston. "Nah," said Demaret. "I haven't gone straight home in thirty years. Why should I start now?"

My father probably didn't realize it as he was driving across the desert in early 1936, heading back to Texas, but a key factor in creating a higher comfort level for himself as a touring pro was finding the right traveling companion. Having a pal alongside to help ease him through the rough patches, a chum right there to share the good times, was what he lacked. In each of Dad's previous winter excursions he paired himself with friends who would become exceptional players. As great as Hogan, Nelson and Demaret were on the golf course, though, all three were emotionally tough guys to be around on a daily basis, at least for my father. All three were, in a sense, lone wolves.

***

Although Dad played the winter tour and occasional summer tournaments through the coming years, he had come to understand

Claude Whalen, Craig Wood, Henry Picard and Dick Grout in 1936 at Colonial Golf Club. (Photo used with the permission of the Colonial Country Club)

by the late '30s that he was not going to be an elite touring professional. He had begun to accept that he lacked the sheer single-mindedness that made great champions of players such as Nelson, Hogan or Demaret—the kind of winning-is-the-only-thing determination shown much later by Arnold Palmer, Jack Nicklaus, Tiger Woods, Ray Floyd and other great champions. Dad was realizing that Byron Nelson had been right when he said his friend Jack Grout was just "too nice a guy" to be an elite player in the demanding world of professional golf.

As he held a series of club jobs from 1937 through the early 1940s, my father experienced an intense period of learning about the golf swing. He spent hundreds of hours refining his personal theories about the game and how to teach it. The serious-minded Henry Picard was one from whom he learned a great deal during this period, but he also sought out some of the game's other great thinkers such as Alex Morrison and Jack Burke Sr., both of whom had studied the golf swing in great detail and shared their swing theories with all who would listen.

Dad's inquiries also were welcomed by the tour's seasoned campaigners—Hagen, Sarazen, Leo Diegel, Joe Turnesa, Johnny Farrell, Willie MacFarlane and many others. He learned from each of these men, and he also had the advantage of playing alongside Nelson, Hogan, Demaret and many others who, in the close-knit fraternity of the nascent PGA Tour, willingly shared their knowledge with their golfing pals. If his early caddying and teaching days in Oklahoma City had been his K-12 schooling in golf, and his days at Glen Garden were his collegiate years of golf study, then his time on the pro tour and in jobs at places such as Hershey (PA) Country Club and other fine clubs constituted my father's graduate school.

World Golf Hall of Famer Raymond Floyd, one of my father's students in the 1970s and 1980s, talked of the rich learning environment in which Dad and his golfing colleagues toiled during the pro tour's early decades and the culture of shared knowledge in which they willingly participated. "You've got to remember that in this era, all of those guys ... there was no such thing as a pure touring pro then," Floyd said. "They were all (club) golf professionals, so they taught as much as they played. Even the top players, they were all teachers. They had club jobs somewhere, so that was a part of their life ... Today, your touring professional never teaches, never gets involved with it ... but that's why Jack Grout was a guru; he grew up in an era where great players were great teachers."

My father approached the game of golf the way a botanist would approach the study of plants: He wanted to know not only the mechanics of the golf swing, but also why a certain type of swing action seemed to work better than another. He wanted to know not only the results that good teaching brought, but also the finite elements of competent teaching. So he dug deeper and deeper into the well of knowledge about the game he loved, and he came to understand its mechanics, ethics, pitfalls and rewards as well as a man could learn them.

In essence, when he arrived back in Fort Worth after his early-1936 stint on the winter tour, my father went back to school, with golf as his field of study. It was a period of learning from which he would emerge as one of the most knowledgeable professionals in and around the game of golf, and one of its most effective teachers.

Dad would continue to labor on the professional golf circuit and win frequent praise for the grace of his golf swing but would achieve only inconsistent results in tournament play. From 1936 through 1941 he managed a respectable sixteen top-ten finishes in nearly sixty professional tournaments, and he won once, in 1938 at the Mid-South Professional Four-Ball at Pinehurst, North Carolina, with Henry Picard as his partner. Too often, though, Dad would be in contention early, then falter under the demands of weekend play.

Chapter 6
The Perfect Partner

"Just like there are no gimmicks in the swing, there are no magic clubs. Some clubs are better suited for your size, your strength and your game than others. Find them and stick with them." – JACK GROUT

❋❋❋

My father's search for a supportive tour traveling companion came to a happy conclusion in 1936 in the person of one of the game's most accomplished players, Massachusetts' own Henry Picard. Picard liked Dad's strong character and businesslike approach to the game, and a close and lasting friendship developed. As they traveled the circuit together and eventually worked side by side as club professionals, Picard became one of my father's key mentors, teachers and colleagues.

Dad and Picard had met in 1935 while playing the California tour. Picard won seven tournaments that year, and was the circuit's leading money winner. Dad later was quoted saying, "The fancy golf the 'Hershey Hurricane' was playing ... made him the top player in America at that time."

During the 1935-1936 winter campaign, Picard was traveling and rooming with his pal Johnny Revolta, an excellent player who would win nineteen pro tournaments, including the 1935 PGA Championship. But there was a problem. When my sister Ronnie and her husband visited Picard at his South Carolina home late in 1995, the aging pro reminisced how Revolta was "out on the town every night." While Picard enjoyed Revolta's company, rooming with him was difficult because Picard was a staunch family man. Picard said that in the evenings, he didn't want to party with Revolta, Demaret and other pros. He didn't begrudge these men their nighttime fun; he just preferred to have calm and restful evenings, better to prepare himself for the next day's golf.

Picard and his wife, Sunny, had married in 1930 and by 1936 were parents of a pair of young sons, Bill and Larry, my dad the latter's godfather. It was disquieting to family-man Picard during his West Coast golf tour of 1935-36 that Revolta sometimes was returning to their shared hotel room just as Picard was leaving for his morning round. It was a happy coincidence that Picard began to notice my father's purposeful ways and quiet work ethic at about the same time.

1937: Jack Grout and Henry Picard at Hershey Country Club. Picard's father once advised him, "You'll always be rated by the people you choose as friends." (Photo courtesy of Hershey Country Club)

Soon the two men began palling around away from the golf course, and later in 1936 they began traveling together.

My dad would find no greater ally, confidante and roommate in all of golf than Henry Picard. In retrospect, the Picard-Grout pairing seems such a natural. Their playing styles were similar; each had a long, rhythmic swing and could hit the ball a long way. More importantly, the two also were like-minded, with many similarities in the way they approached life. Honesty, hard work and modesty were attributes they shared. Picard was more serious-natured than my father and a tougher individual both physically and competitively. With his lighter personality, Dad generally was more fun to be around. In many ways these contrasting traits tended to attract one to the other.

My father had a distinctive voice; Texas and Oklahoma still lingered in his accent. Henry had a strong voice and spoke with a crisp northeastern accent left from his youth in Massachusetts. Dad had firm beliefs but often kept them to himself. Picard, on the other hand, was opinionated and tended to let others know how he felt. Sometimes what he said and how he said it could be ill-received. Picard's own son, Larry, admitted that his father could be "a mean, nasty, tough individual" when pursuing something he really wanted. Picard also believed deeply in his own abilities. Before the 1938 Masters, for example, Picard simply said to himself, "It's my turn to win this thing." (And he did just that!) I can't imagine my dad ever having been that absolute about something like a golf tournament.

In December 1936, Dad and Picard began the long drive to catch the tour's winter swing through California. Following Route 66, the two passed Shamrock and Amarillo, Texas, then Tucumcari, Santa Rosa, Albuquerque and Gallup, New Mexico, and Holbrook, Winslow, Flagstaff and Kingman, Arizona. Finally with Barstow, California, in the rear view mirror, they pulled into Santa Monica, which would be a base of sorts for their winter play. The routine now was familiar to my father. This time, his winter playing schedule included tournaments in Santa Rosa, Oakland, Sacramento, San Francisco and other cities as December dissolved into January and January into February.

A highlight of that winter's tour was the January stop in Oakland that turned out to be a coming-out party for Dad's friend, the West Virginia country boy, Sam Snead. With his booming drives and gallery-pleasing demeanor in full force, Snead won in Oakland and then followed with three more wins during 1937, then another eight during 1938, establishing him firmly as one of the tour's top attractions. On the eve of this great stretch, Snead provided Dad with one of his favorite golf memories—and one of golf's great inside stories.

Dad and Picard were standing on the driving range at the Presidio Golf Club in San Francisco, watching Snead struggle mightily with his tee shots. "Sam couldn't play any driver he had or find any club he liked," my father recalled. Then Dad described a fateful exchange between "Pic," as he called his friend, and the man who soon would come to be known as The Slammer, mainly for his prodigious drives:

"Hey Sam, I got a driver I think you'd like."

"Where is it?"

"It's in my car."

"Where's your car?"

(Snead was sounding a little desperate.)

"Right over there."

(Picard calmly pointed toward the parking lot.)

"Well get it out and let's have a look at it before I hurt myself!"

The club was too big for Picard, even though he had made it for himself. It was a persimmon-headed driver, stained brown and with a leather grip and stiff shaft that gave Snead good control of his shots. "Snead swung the club with that great rhythm of his and ripped it down the middle," my dad reported. "Then he swung it again and again with the same wonderful result. He turned to Picard and with a big grin said, 'God, this is good.' He then asked Henry, 'How much?' 'Five dollars and fifty cents,' Picard said. 'That's about what I've got into it.' "

Whatever the source of its magic, the club was a real find for Snead, who used it constantly from 1937 through the '60s. He had it refinished and refaced, and he had the sole plate put back on even after it started falling out from rot and old age. The club fit him, and he stuck with it. The story goes that he never let another man hit with that club. It was even said that he sometimes slept with it!

***

While the tour moved on through its early-1937 California swing and Snead used his new driver to great effect, Henry Picard began focusing on his own increasingly busy work schedule and how my father could help him deal with his obligations as head pro at Hershey Country Club. Picard would be out of the country for much of the summer and fall of 1937, participating in the Ryder Cup matches in Southport, England, and the British Open, then playing a series of exhibition matches in South America. His travels would pull him away from his head-pro duties in Hershey for so long a time that it was essential to secure a suitable replacement. Picard had decided back in April 1936—after a pair of exhibitions that pitted him and professional Craig Wood against teams including first Dick Grout, then my father, at the new Colonial Golf Club in Fort Worth—that my dad would make an ideal assistant for him in Hershey. He said nothing to Dad, though, until the two men reached San Francisco in January 1937. There the job offer was made and accepted.

My father appreciated such a tangible demonstration of Picard's respect for him. He was well aware of his friend's lofty standards and considered the offer a great compliment. Particularly appealing was that the Hershey assistant's position offered him greater financial security, plus the opportunity to continue improving his game while also learning more about the golf business at one of the nation's premier country clubs. Dad also knew that Hershey CC's strong reputation and Picard's wide network of friends in the business would help advance his own career. Besides that, this new job would broaden his perspectives by getting him out of the Southwest, which was something he had looked forward to.

Energized by the career boost Picard provided, Dad happily looked forward to playing in that February's inaugural Bing Crosby National Pro-Amateur Golf Championship in Rancho Santa Fe, California. The Crosby "Clambake" paired celebrities and businessmen with a pro for a thirty-six-hole weekend of golf and fun that would become a much-anticipated annual event on the pro circuit. While the fellowship was memorable in that first Crosby tourney and through many that followed, one major problem seemed to intervene with regularity: the event was cursed through the years by truly horrid weather. That certainly was the case during the 1937 event; rain was so intense that small streams around the course overflowed and tournament officials were forced to travel the layout in a small boat. Unfortunately for my dad, the wet, loose footing caused him to slip so violently on one tee shot that he seriously wrenched his back. Dad later would maintain that it was during this Crosby tournament that he added a career-limiting back injury to a laundry list of personal physical ailments that included poor eyesight and sore feet.

Chapter 7
Learning from Each Other

"The only way to play consistently good golf is through the mastery of a set of basics that the great players of the past have proven to be integral to the swing." – *JACK GROUT*

***

As the 1937 winter tour drifted out of California, through Arizona and on to Texas, my dad and his friend Picard looked forward to one of their favorite treats. Every time they passed through Houston they would visit with the great golf teacher Jack Burke Sr. By the spring of 1937, Burke, the pro at the River Oaks Country Club in Houston, had been my father's friend for six or seven years. He always welcomed to his home the younger pros such as my dad, Picard, Ben Hogan and Byron Nelson, and great golf instructors such as Harvey Penick. Penick later became famous as an author of inspirational books about playing better golf and as the teacher of outstanding pros such as major tournament winners Ben Crenshaw and Tom Kite.

My father knew he and the others would get a good meal, hot coffee and some insightful golf instruction at the Burke house. "When I was a boy, the dinner table at the Burke home was an informal classroom where well-known players would stop by to talk golf with my father," said Jackie Burke Jr., himself an excellent tour player with a record that included two victories in majors and, in 2000, induction into the World Golf Hall of Fame.

The sharing of golf knowledge by talented players was, by the 1930s, an established practice in the United States. When golf was relatively new in America, there were few teachers and professionals who knew much about the intricacies of the golf swing. As a result, thousands of people learned to play by experimenting. Even the best golfers at that time were more or less self-taught. Most of them, however, enjoyed the certain advantage of starting out as young caddies and thus were able to gain understanding of the game's subtleties by observing and talking with the better players they caddied for. Great champions such as Hagen, Sarazen, Nelson, Hogan and Snead served apprenticeships in the caddie yard where all this sharing of golf knowledge took place, yet many of these men have been quoted as saying that they "never learned from anyone." While this might technically be true, they indisputably all learned from one another.

Johnny Revolta, Henry Picard, Jack Grout and Sam Snead in 1938 at Colonial Golf Club. (Photo used with permission of the Colonial Country Club)

When my father played the tournament circuit in the 1930s and 1940s, there was no such thing as a full-time teaching pro. A few fellows such as Seymour Dunn, Ernest Jones, Alex Morrison and Percy Boomer specialized in studying the golf swing and wrote about it. But mostly, it seemed that golf instruction was just a jumble of theory and conjecture. Dad's golfing buddy, Ky Laffoon, put it this way: "There was nobody around who knew much." That may have been an exaggeration, but it also helps explain why golf's "secrets" increasingly were becoming hot commodities with pros, fans and sportswriters alike. Lessons from the tour became the foundation for instruction by the era's combination tour-club pros, and the teaching pros that came along later.

As more and more young players joined the tour, so grew the number of players who were difficult to beat. Accordingly, the established pros searched constantly for new ways to improve their games. Shaving off just one stroke per round often meant survival, so whenever one pro found a way to improve his score, others were quick to scrutinize the innovation and, maybe, copy it. If a good player made a small change in any part of his swing, his grip, or his set-up, it would open the door to any number of adjustments by the others. Each new idea would be thoroughly vetted and either accepted as a better way to do things or thrown on the scrap heap of yesterday's so-called miracles.

Discussions about playing and scoring better dominated the interactions among the pros. When Dad, Picard, Hogan, Demaret, Laffoon, Nelson and others needed help, they turned to one another. They consulted on the driving range and during practice rounds, and they gabbed about their favorite subject for hours on end during the long drives from tournament to tournament.

Another boon to conversation in general, and for golf talk specifically, was the lack of air conditioning or television in hotel rooms, which tended to push the players toward better-ventilated parts of the hotels. Said Jackie Burke Jr., "I remember being about ten years old, traveling with my father, in some hotel lobby out on the circuit. There was Hogan, Ky Laffoon, Henry Picard, Jack Grout—all swapping ideas to beat the band, trying this or that, trying to get some edge up. These guys were all club pros, remember, who made their money giving lessons, so sharing ideas wasn't the least bit unusual for them. The Tour was a laboratory for them."

During their dinner-table visits with Jack Burke Sr. in Houston, my father listened carefully to the elder Burke, absorbing his knowledge and integrating the Texan's theories into his own convictions about the golf swing. "Jack Burke Sr. would inspire us young pros during our visits," Dad said. "(He) was a wonderful man, one of the finest that ever lived. If he wasn't the greatest teacher that ever lived, he was easily among the top two or three.

"He was a great man with the young pros," Dad continued. "If any of them needed help, he helped them. He gave hundreds of lessons free to young pros. He just loved kids—had nine of his own. Young Jackie (Burke) is exactly like his daddy, a real gentleman, a wonderful guy all around." Dad believed that Burke Sr. was responsible more than any other man for the crop of great golfers coming out of Texas during the 1920s and '30s. "He gave lessons to most of the boys at one time or another, and he inspired all the young pros in Texas at that time," Dad said. "He had a beautiful swing and we all copied it."

"Jack Burke ... was an outstanding player, but also developed into a wonderful teacher and club pro," said Texan Ben Crenshaw, a student of Harvey Penick and great admirer of the senior Burke and his teaching principles. "He was very much a fundamentalist, and he made a lot of teachers think about how they were going to treat a pupil." Burke's emphasis on fundamentals and on showing respect for his pupils had great impact on my father, who is recalled by all of his golf pupils as a quiet, respectful teacher who focused again and again on the core elements of the golf swing.

Sometime back in the 1930s, Jack Burke Sr. gave my father a bit of advice—not about golf mechanics, but about life—that resonated deeply with him. "I suppose Jackie Burke felt I had promise as a player," Dad recalled, "because he told me, 'There is a lot more to golf than hitting a ball—sportsmanship, friends, a whole way of life.' I can honestly say that I never forgot what he said. It had an impact on how I thought about the game in its entirety." It's probably worth noting that in 1988, my father wrote about "sportsmanship" in a congratulatory letter to Jack Nicklaus after Nicklaus was honored as "Golfer of the Century." Some forty-six years after the senior Burke's death, my father still was feeling the influence of his famous friend's advice.

***

Dad began working at Hershey Country Club on March 6, 1937, living within a driver and five-iron of the club, first at the Hershey Community Center and later in an apartment in a lumbering four-story, red-brick hotel called the Cocoa Inn. Dad liked the city and became a regular at Lucy's restaurant, at the Hershey Theatre where he indulged his taste for the movies of the day, and at St. Joan of Arc Roman Catholic Church. The impeccably maintained Hershey Country Club—established in 1930 by Milton S. Hershey, founder of both the Hershey Chocolate Company and the company town of Hershey, Pennsylvania, just after the turn of the century—offered him a comfortable and classy place to work. Its rolling fairways shone with natural beauty, and Dad rated the Hershey layout the most beautiful he'd ever seen.

At this point, Dad could see things finally beginning to fall into place for him. As the decade of the 1930s reached its later stages, not only was the national economy steadily improving, but so too was my father's personal well-being. Thanks to increasing responsibilities and all the traveling he had done, Dad had become a mature man. Now closing in on thirty years old, he had become more self-reliant and was more confident than ever before about his ability to take care of himself. While he loved his extended family, he now was fully independent, making it on his own. Working at a fine private country club in the East and no longer living in Oklahoma and Texas, he regarded himself as a true professional.

During Dad's three years at Hershey, his aptitude for playing the game increased. His day-to-day association with Henry Picard had a lot to do with that. That is, Picard and Dad worked together on the golf swing for countless hours. It was during those practice sessions that my father, for the first time in an intensive way, was exposed to the thinking of another great student of the swing. Picard began passing along "secrets" shared with him by one of the best golf teachers of the day, Alex Morrison. Henry had been learning from the respected West Coast swing doctor since the summer of 1935.

Morrison, who began his studies and analysis of the golf swing as a caddie at the Los Angeles Country Club back in 1912, two years after my dad's birth, was known for his belief that golf was ninety percent mental, eight percent physical and only two percent mechanical. Based in Los Angeles, he fit right in with the Hollywood crowd—given that he favored multi-patterned sweaters and bright argyle socks and had the nervy showmanship to try stunts such as smashing golf balls off a man's head. Still, Morrison was a serious instructor who prided himself on using "impersonal, scientific" principles and state-of-the-art films of famous golfers to demonstrate technique. Morrison was the first person to make extensive use of the motion picture camera for golf instruction. His clientele included Charley Chaplin and Douglas Fairbanks, and a driving range he owned in New York City was frequented by Bob Hope and Bing Crosby.

By the time my father became acquainted with Morrison, the swing theorist already had written his first book, *A New Way to Better Golf.* During Dad's time at Hershey, Morrison began formulating certain "keys" to the proper golf swing and would make those the basis for his second book, *Better Golf Without Practice*. My father, ever hungry for new knowledge about the golf swing, considered Morrison "a really great teacher" and absorbed all he could from the man's theories. Typical of my father, though, he accepted some of Morrison's teachings but rejected others. Dad always was willing to listen to new thinking about the golf swing, but he also had confidence in his own knowledge and would not blindly follow others into new ways of thinking.

***

Through the spring of 1937, Dad worked long hours at Hershey Country Club, getting acquainted as quickly as possible with the membership and all aspects of the golf operation. There was time for fun, for sure, typified by Dad's card games with the members, but there was also a sense of urgency attached to his work, because Picard often was called away for one reason or another. Dad quickly took responsibility for making sure the golf operation was running smoothly, and his education in the club's operations thus was fast and thorough. By the time Picard departed for the Ryder Cup matches in June at the Southport and Ainsdale Golf Club in England, he knew he was leaving the club in good hands.

It turned out that Picard's winning foray with Sarazen, Snead, Nelson and other great U.S. pros in the Ryder Cup—the American team's first win on British soil!—and his entry the next week in the British Open at Carnoustie gave my father a welcome opportunity to establish himself in his Hershey job. While Picard was away, club members got a thorough look at Dad's way of doing things, and they liked what they saw. Dad enjoyed that he was appreciated so much by the membership, but he never allowed the positive attention to cause him or the members to forget that Picard was the boss.

Later that year Dad once again was called upon for solo duty at Hershey when Picard, Nelson and Denny Shute traveled to Argentina for a series of exhibitions and to play in the Argentine Open. Pan American Airways financed the whole trip, the pioneering airline having just opened a number of new routes and seeing golf exhibitions as a good way to demonstrate the ease of South American travel. Though it's hard to believe by today's standards, it took the men seven full days to fly to Argentina, using a combination of DC-3s and PBY Catalinas—planes that could land and take off on water. All the pros agreed that the worst part of the trip was going through the Andes Mountains at high altitude in a nonpressurized cabin. The wind whipping through the mountain passes caused heavy turbulence, and Denny Shute became terribly sick from all the dipping and shifting.

Safely on land for their exhibition matches, the American party confronted a challenge of another type in the form of a full-scale plague of locusts! Picard told my father the sky was thick with bugs, and every time he swung a club, he'd literally whack a cluster of them. When he walked, he crunched dozens of the large insects under his shoes. The pros actually played three or four holes before officials finally called a halt to things. Play was resumed after several days when the wind switched directions and the bugs flew off.

***

The United States may have been distancing itself from the Great Depression as 1937 drew to a close, but touring golf pros felt little economic benefit. For most of them, sharing travel expenses still was the smart thing to do. The tour's weekly prize money still was modest and, for most players, would cover only expenses. Thus it meant at least a bit of welcome savings for the players when, beginning with the 1937-38 season-opening Miami Biltmore Open, the United States Golf Association (USGA) introduced a new rule limiting a player to fourteen clubs. A special "checker" was on duty at the first tee to count the clubs, and several of the players had to deposit excess sticks with the starter.

The fourteen-club rule was a smart one. Famed course architect Donald Ross had been a prominent critic of the policy that allowed an unlimited number of clubs, contending that "if a golfer gets the notion the more clubs he carries, the better golf he is going to play, there never would be a limit. In due time, pack mules would have replaced caddies. As it was, the caddies of the nation were all getting humpbacked, staggering along under freight car loads."

My uncle Dick, still the head pro at Glen Garden when the club-limit rule was instituted, agreed with Ross. "It was high time that somebody did something about putting the screws on the number of clubs carried by tournament golfers," he said. "Most of the guys were warping the backs of their caddies with the tons of clubs they carried. And half of the sticks generally were pets and good luck charms. I've seen pros and amateurs, too, for that matter, carry as many as twenty-five clubs in a tournament."

The new limit was hardly the lone issue facing many of the pros as the 1937-38 winter tour got underway. The endless travel by car from one part of the country to another remained difficult. There still were long stretches of separation from family. And as always, there was the challenge of making a living.

Ben Hogan was one of those who seemed to have the toughest financial woes. Hogan had joined the pro circuit toward the end of 1931 but still had not broken through as a big money winner nearly a decade later. He continued to battle that horrid hook. My father recalled an encounter when he and Picard were playing exhibition matches in Fort Worth that showed the extent of Hogan's financial issues. On New Year's Eve, 1937, Dad and Picard ran into Ben and Valerie Hogan in the dining room of the Blackstone Hotel and joined them for a drink. It soon became apparent that the Hogans were having a difference of opinion. Ben appeared relieved to see an old friend like Dad and to meet Picard, who arguably was the tour's best player at the moment. He politely asked the two men to join them for a few minutes, because he needed to hear what they thought about the predicament he and his wife were facing. The Hogans' disagreement was over whether they had enough money to go on tour together.

Hogan was very discouraged. "I've got to quit," he told his tablemates. "If I go back on the tour, we don't have the money for her to go with me." That said, the Hogans eyed each other silently as Dad and Henry did their best to encourage them that it was in their best interest for Ben to play and for Valerie to be there with him. Finally Picard told Ben, "I'm not the richest man in the world, but go ahead and play. If you run out of money, I'll take care of it." Both my dad and Picard knew that Hogan was a determined and talented little guy who was much too stubborn not to succeed.

Hogan did hang in there for the 1938 season and at the Hershey Four-Ball tournament finally took the first of his sixty-four wins as a professional. It's amazing to think how close this great player came to chucking the game before even his first win. Dad, Picard and a number of other players had to feel proud as Hogan compiled win after win in the 1940s and '50s and won Player of the Year honors four times, knowing that they'd played a role in keeping him going during his darkest days.

***

My father continued his perplexing pattern of earlier years on the 1938 winter tour. He played well and finished sixth in Pasadena, then weeks later during the tour's southern swing finished ninth in New Orleans. But in his final seven tournaments Dad had only one particularly encouraging performance: He and Picard teamed to tie Tommy Armour and Bobby Cruickshank for first in the well-regarded Mid-South Professional Four-Ball at Pinehurst No. 2. Disappointingly for Dad, he failed to qualify for both the U.S. Open and the PGA Championship. Still, there was something to celebrate during the year. His great friend, Picard, elevated himself to the top of the day's golfers by winning the Masters, the first of his two major tourney victories and one of twenty-six wins he achieved in a hall-of-fame career.

Picard's return to a hero's welcome at the Hershey Country Club following his 1938 Masters victory marked the beginning of the heavy golf season there. Dad had the pro shop in top condition, fully stocked and ready for a busy year. But with all the golf-shop hours that had to be covered, especially during the summertime, Dad found himself confined to indoor work more than he wanted. He preferred being outdoors where he could practice, play and teach. Besides, he needed the revenue from his time on the lesson tee. My father's employment contract at Hershey gave him four weeks off for vacation, and he wanted to use that time, and more, to play events on the summer tour.

The pro circuit was offering a record $185,500 in prize money in 1938, and the summer season of events was better than ever. A few of the leading pros such as Snead, Demaret and Horton Smith could participate in all the tour events, but the vast majority of the pros—such as my father—had seasonal club jobs and were forced to juggle those jobs and tournament appearances.

As it turned out, Dad would have to stay close to his home club in the '38 summer season, but this time the term "home" didn't apply to Hershey CC. Late that spring, Picard heard from another of Dad's friends, Ky Laffoon, who was head pro at the Northmoor Country Club in suburban Chicago. Laffoon had decided to play tournaments full time that summer and told Picard, "I need Jack up here to look after things while I'm gone. Whaddya' think?" Picard thought it over and then gave his reluctant approval. He knew that exposure to a new club would be good for Dad's career and, not unimportantly, for his short-term finances, given that he would have much more time for teaching. While Picard couldn't have foretold it, there would be yet another important bonus in store for Dad that summer: He would make a new friend in Chicago who, within a couple of years, would introduce him to the young woman who would be the most important person in his life.

***

Dad quickly found the Chicago golf market more energetic than those he'd experienced in northeastern Pennsylvania. The Northmoor Club, with its Donald Ross-designed golf course, was a bustling place six days a week. It compounded Dad's workload that Bill Laffoon, the club's second in command, was traveling and caddying for his big brother. Fortunately for Dad, though, Ky Laffoon's youngest brother, Woody, stayed in Chicago to help out, and the kid was a whiz at running the pro shop. Dad thus quickly immersed himself in a heavy load of teaching. He'd never seen members so eager for instruction and many days spent six to eight hours on Northmoor's lesson tee.

His busy teaching schedule notwithstanding, Dad still managed to play in a few area tournaments, and in one of those events, a pro-am at North Shore Country Club, he struck up one of his most significant personal friendships. Edward Warren Bradley, Dad's playing partner in the tournament, was born in Boston in 1900. A tall, sturdy man who spoke with a crisp New England accent, Bradley was a traveling salesman for Reefer-Galler moth preventatives. He was a golf member at two Chicago clubs, North Shore and Tam O'Shanter. By 1938, when Dad played with him for the first time, Bradley had been married to Vera Fox for three years. My dad and

Bradley quickly became friends, occasionally complementing a round of golf with evening card games. Eventually Dad met Vera—the oldest sister of the young woman who within a few years would become my father's bride.

All in all, it was a productive summer for Dad. But after Labor Day, he headed back to Hershey to finish out the fall golf season. Then, with Picard, he picked up the second stage of the 1939 winter tour in Arizona. The two men had decided to skip the California circuit to avoid the usual bad weather there, only to encounter a snowstorm in Phoenix! Dad managed some good stretches of play after the weather surprise, though. He finished twelfth in New Orleans and tied eventual hall of famer Ralph Guldahl for third in the St. Augustine Pro-Am before returning to Hershey to prepare for what he knew would be a busy golf season.

Dad may as well have been Hershey's head pro at that point, as Picard frequently was gone from the club, enjoying a stretch of excellent play that included a win at the 1939 PGA Championship. That PGA, held at Pomonok Country Club in Long Island, New York, was the first tournament ever broadcast on radio, and Picard did his part to make the broadcast interesting. On the thirty-seventh hole of the final match, a short par four, he hit his drive under a radio truck. Byron Nelson, who was tied with Picard at that point, powered his drive down the middle. Nelson was first from the fairway and hit a great shot, just five feet from the pin. Then, after Picard got relief from the obstruction, one of the radio trucks actually ran over his ball! Still, he eventually knocked his second shot seven feet from the pin, made the putt, then watched as Nelson missed his, giving Picard the championship.

***

By the fall of 1939, my father decided it was time to end his work at Hershey. He'd had three solid years there, gaining in-depth knowledge about how a first-rate club was operated and sharpening his teaching and playing skills. By that point, also, he'd been closely associated with Picard for several years, and it felt like time to establish his own identity by running his own show.

That fall, Dad drove to Mamaroneck, New York, to spend time with his friend Craig Wood, the pro at Winged Foot Golf Club. Before leaving Hershey, though, Dad accepted a job as the teaching and playing professional at Irem Temple Country Club in the community of Dallas, Pennsylvania, for the 1940 season. The club was owned and operated by the local Masonic Lodge, and its pro at the time was an older gentleman. The members wanted a younger pro to complement the head pro's work by teaching, playing and representing the club in tournaments around the country.

Dad spent a full month at Winged Foot, reenergizing and working on his golf game. Craig Wood had been the pro there for a number of years and was a great player in his own right, winning twenty-one PGA titles, including two major championships. This was a time of rapid innovations in the golf swing and in equipment and golf course design, so as Wood and my father played and practiced together, they shared advice and instruction on the many new ideas sweeping through the game.

This was a welcome period of reflection and reassessment for my dad. The professional golf circuit had drawn more than half a million spectators in 1939. However, with the threat of World War II lingering in the air, the 1940 pro tour would not be as rich in attendance or prize money, and there were approximately five fewer tournaments on the schedule. Also, by the beginning of the 1940s the golfing careers of a number of my father's contemporaries had passed him by.

Dad had performed well through the 1930s against the likes of Demaret, Hogan, Picard, Snead and Nelson. Now, though, as a new decade loomed, most of these men were consistent money winners, but he wasn't. Many of his friends already had secured high-profile positions as head professionals, but he hadn't. A few of the leading golfers also had found a brand new way of enriching themselves, signing on as playing representatives of resort hotels that paid generously for the privilege of boasting about their big-name golf pros. On top of all that, the new decade would bring another thought-provoking change for Dad. On March 24, 1940, he would turn thirty.

Dad was a realist, and he had to know as he looked back in that fall of 1939 that his real future in professional golf resided on the lesson tee, not on the fairways and greens of the professional circuit. He was a studier, a learner, a natural teacher. He was not ready to abandon competitive golf, and in fact would continue tournament play with sporadic success into the 1950s. But it was becoming evident that he simply was not cut out for high-level success in the cutthroat milieu of the tour.

There was much for my father to think about. Was the game passing him by? After all, at nearly thirty he no longer was a young man. There were moments when he even began to feel old and tired. He wasn't hurting financially; he'd always been thrifty, so money was not a critical issue. But that one great job opportunity that might really have empowered his professional life hadn't come along yet. Also, despite his love of home and family, Dad still was a bachelor, with no serious romantic relationship on the horizon.

Dad would have laughed at this somewhat pessimistic recounting of his personal outlook at age twenty-nine. While he did face his share of obstacles, my father was wise enough to keep them in perspective. He figured that all he could do was give his best effort, which is exactly what he did as the teaching and playing professional at the Irem Temple club during the summer of 1940. The club, located not far from Wilkes-Barre and the Susquehanna River, had a beautiful, rolling golf course that was designed in the 1920s by A.W. Tillinghast. My father enjoyed his work with Irem Temple's members and also kept his game in tune through tournament play. Still, his second-banana position at the club did not offer him the higher visibility and stretching responsibilities he now craved. Soon he began to ponder his next move.

Dad didn't have to ponder for very long. When he visited a nearby country club, Fox Hill, that summer for an exhibition match featuring members of a commercial golf venture called the Spalding Tour, several of the club's officials sidled up and began talking with him. It turned out they knew about Dad's good work both as a player and an assistant pro and were sufficiently impressed that they eventually offered him the job as their head professional.

This would be a big step up for my father. His career thus far had consisted of a logical series of learning experiences, both on the golf course and in various golf club pro shops where he'd had increasing levels of responsibility but not the top job. Dad was delighted by the job offer and signed on to become Fox Hill's new head professional effective in April 1941.

My father thus achieved one of his primary goals—a chance to run the golf operation at a well-respected club. And while he didn't know it as he accepted the new post, he was about to begin the pursuit of a second major goal: Soon he would fall into the unyielding grasp of deep and lasting love for the young and lovely Bonnie Fox.

1941-1942: Jack Grout, golf professional at Fox Hill Country Club in West Pittston, PA. (Photo courtesy of Fox Hill Country Club)

PART TWO: "THE VERY THOUGHT OF YOU"

Much anticipated and requested (by Jack Grout) photograph of Bonnie Fox in 1941. (Grout family photo)

Chapter 8
The Babysitter and the Golf Pro

"Golf is a game that entices you to try to play better and better but always leaves room for advancement. The more you play and the better you play, the more you will see areas for improvement and will want to respond to them." — JACK GROUT

***

At the end of Irem Temple Country Club's 1940 golfing season, my father headed for South Carolina on what had become an annual trek to Henry Picard's Charleston home. The two would spend a few weeks playing and practicing at the Country Club of Charleston, where Henry's younger brother, George, was the professional. The club made a welcoming headquarters for Dad and Picard as they prepared for a new golf season.

In early December my father left his car in Charleston and rode down to Miami with Picard. By then, both pros felt their golf games to be in good condition and they were itching to play the circuit again. It was a good cycle, this rotation of labor as touring golf professionals through the winter and early spring, then as club pros and part-time players through the summer and fall. It was a blending of club and tour life that provided welcome variety.

My father enjoyed playing in Miami because of its warm climate, and because he could count on seeing many of his best pals there. In 1940, players in the $10,000 Miami Open included such friends as Ben Loving from Springfield, Massachusetts, the unpredictable Arkansan Ky Laffoon and the sophisticated Martin Pose from Buenos Aires, Argentina. There were many backs to slap and stories to tell as the pros renewed their friendships.

Dad thus entered this first week of his 1940-41 winter golf schedule as excited as always about the tournaments, the new friendships and the learning that lay ahead. What he had no way to know, though, was that he eventually would look back at this week in Miami as one of the most important of his life, and not because of the golf—he would finish fortieth in the tournament, a whopping eighteen strokes behind the winner, Byron Nelson.

During the week of the tournament, Dad got a call from Ed Bradley, whom he'd befriended during the summer of 1938 while filling in for Ky Laffoon at Chicago's Northmoor Country Club. Bradley was vacationing in South Florida and saw in *The Miami Herald* that his friend Jack Grout was there for the Miami Open. On Thursday evening, after his first round in the tournament, Dad borrowed Picard's car and drove to Miami Beach, where the Bradleys had rented an apartment. Ed and Vera greeted my father warmly, then introduced him to their two baby daughters: Joan, who was three, and Barbie, about fourteen months. Finally, Dad turned to meet Vera's youngest sister, who was there as the babysitter.

When Dad entered the apartment that December night, young Bonnie Fox was sitting on the carpet, playing with the toddlers. When she looked up to catch her first glimpse of my father, she saw a tall, slender man with black wavy hair who was as handsome as a matinee idol. His dark, suntanned face, neck and arms gave him the athletic appearance of someone who spends a great deal of time outdoors.

It's doubtful that Vera's sister, at nineteen years old, was accustomed to being in the presence of men who fit that description. She almost certainly was physically attracted at her first sight of him, but I think it's also safe to say that Dad was immediately smitten, as well. Bonnie was sweet, kind and vivacious. She had just come back from a day at the beach with Vera and the kids, and Dad was struck by her beauty.

No question, Bonnie Fox had caught my father's eye, and he decided to act on the attraction he was feeling. The next day he asked her to join him for an evening out, and she agreed. That night Dad again borrowed Picard's car and drove off for his first date with this young woman who had so impressed him.

Dad and his date had a quiet dinner at the site of the golf tournament, the Miami Springs Country Club, and then wandered to the club's pool area, where a water ballet show was scheduled. During the synchronized swimming, a loudspeaker blanketed them with the song, "The Very Thought of You." Dad came up behind Bonnie, slipped his arms around her waist, and softly mouthed the words of the hit song—a ballad that, as things turned out, would be "their song" for nearly five decades. Bonnie would talk about that evening with her children many years later, recalling that on their drive back to the Bradley's apartment, my father said something that might not have been a marriage proposal but strongly hinted at his hope that their new relationship would be an enduring one.

In truth, while the young lady may have found Dad intriguing when they met, she may not have been overly interested in him at that point. She had just broken off her engagement back in St. Louis, and it's likely that she was not yet ready for another serious boyfriend. Also, my father was thirty years old—eleven years older than she was; Bonnie surely wondered how much they possibly could have in common. Unlike her sister, however, Vera Bradley and her husband had been thrilled when Bonnie's engagement ended; they wanted her to meet a different man, someone mature and dependable—a man such as Jack Grout.

The evening after his date with Bonnie, my father returned to the Bradley apartment to play cards. "Eddie," as Dad referred to Bradley, had invited several fellows over for a poker game. Dad always enjoyed a good card game, like most of the pro golfers, but the real reason he wanted to play was so he could see that "babysitter" again.

During the evening, Vera cleverly decided to send Dad out for something she needed at the store, and she directed her sister to go along to show him where the store was. My Aunt Vera took great pains that evening to be the perfect hostess/matchmaker, and she also took some snapshots of everybody there, especially Bonnie and Jack. Dad recalled later that when he was "sittin' in" at the poker table, the cards were treating him kindly. But he admitted that his best moments were the ones he was able to spend with the vivacious Bonnie Fox.

When it came time for them to say good-bye, the girl and the golf pro exchanged addresses and agreed to write one another and stay in contact. My father cautioned that he would be on the road and moving around a lot, so he would be hard to reach. He gave Bonnie the address of his parents' house in Oklahoma City, explaining that any letters she sent him there would be forwarded to him at one of his tour stops. Bonnie gave Dad her address in St. Louis, where she lived with her parents. Then, in parting, Dad said that he hoped the next time they met he wouldn't be in such a darn hurry!

As Dad, Picard and the other pros headed their separate ways for the 1940 Christmas holidays, it's safe to guess that both my father and Bonnie were feeling a tingle of anticipation over their budding relationship. Despite their respective ages, they had at least one important thing in common: Both were the products of solid and large Midwestern families. While Dad was one of eight children of Herbert Duane and Eleanor Johanna Grout of Oklahoma City, Bonnie was the last of seven children in the home of Harmon Harrison Fox and his wife Anna of St. Louis.

But just how would this romance work, with Bonnie ensconced in St. Louis and Dad traveling half the year and working full-time in a distant golf club the other months? Without the convenience of cell phones and email, and with air travel limited and expensive, Jack Grout and Bonnie Fox built and maintained their relationship the same way soldiers in the 1940s kept in touch with their wives and girlfriends back home. As 1940 rolled into 1941, what would keep the fire that had been lit in their hearts as their Miami flirtation turned into a serious courtship through the next two years was a set of very basic communication tools: pen, paper and ink.

The romance of Jack Grout and Bonnie Fox was built on letters.

***

The year that ended with the Japanese attack on Pearl Harbor and America's entry into World War II also proved to be my father's busiest and most successful on the professional golf tour. Dad played in eighteen events, more than in any other year of his pro career. He won one tournament, had five top-five finishes and eight top-tens, and took home more than $4,200 in tour prize money and winnings from exhibitions and other "unofficial" events. The pro tour's official statistics listed him twenty-fifth in the player rankings for the year.

Dad and Picard left Miami on December 16, 1940, heading back to Charleston for a month or so of practice and conditioning, then driving the sixteen hundred miles to the Grout home in Oklahoma City for a short stay. Through those weeks of practice and travel, Dad seemed to slip into a physical and mental funk. Then on January 17, something happened that snapped him back to life: He received his first letter from Bonnie. Dad later would recall that "As far as I was concerned it (the letter) came in the nick of time."

Her letter clearly touched my dad, triggering from this quiet Oklahoman a virtual rainstorm of communications that over the next twenty-plus months would include 113 letters! Those missives, all of which Bonnie saved, and scores of letters from her that Dad destroyed because he felt they should be kept private, would form the foundation for their courtship and a marriage of more than forty-six years.

***

Dad's first letter to Bonnie, written in a hotel room in Fort Worth on the evening of January 18, 1941, was typical for the warmth and simplicity with which he addressed his future wife:

> *Dear Bonnie,*
>
> *Thanks for your nice letter. It came when I had a bad case of influenza and I must say it made me very happy ... I am just now starting on the Tour again, will meet the pros in Phoenix, Arizona. We play also at San Antonio and New Orleans ...*
>
> *I would very much like to hear from you again Bonnie and may I say I am sorry that I didn't get to see more of you in Miami. I*

hope next summer when I am in Chicago during June I can see you again ...

You can write me, if you wish, before Feb. 2 at Phoenix Arizona c/o Golf Tournament or at the Jung Hotel New Orleans before Feb. 12th ...

Adios, Jack

With that initial letter written, Dad set off with Picard on what had become a regular and demanding multi-state trek through golf's winter pro tour. After a shot-making clinic and exhibition match at Wichita Falls (TX) Country Club, where my uncle Dick was the golf pro, the Grout-Picard duo returned to Colonial in Forth Worth for a pro-amateur event. Then, a few days later, they drove off for Phoenix to launch their winter season at the Western Open.

Unfortunately, the flu that Dad had been battling for two weeks caused him to withdraw from the Phoenix event after three rounds. I know Dad must have been feeling very sick, because he didn't attend the annual big dinner thrown for all the pros by Bob Goldwater and his brother Barry, the future U.S. senator and Republican presidential candidate. The two brothers were avid golfers and owned Goldwater's Department Store in Phoenix, and each year during the Phoenix tournament there would be a wonderful steak cookout at Barry's house.

Again the next week, in San Antonio, Dad was ill and couldn't play. He was able, though, to send his second letter to his new girlfriend, urging her to write often:

February 5, 1941

Dear Bonnie,

You make me very happy when you write those encouraging letters. So, you must, if possible, write me at least once a week, as I will be looking forward to hearing from you. Please tell me more about yourself and what you are doing in your spare moments.

The tournament in New Orleans starts a week from tomorrow. I like to play there as the course has fine greens and is very long.

I am traveling with Mr. Henry Picard who is the pro at Hershey PA. You, no doubt, have heard his name. Ed and Vera met him in Miami.

There are about ten more tournaments to be played before April 1st; New Orleans, Thomasville, GA, St Petersburg, St Augustine, Pinehurst, Greensboro and Asheville. I am going to leave the tour after Pinehurst for Hershey to have my tonsils taken out. I believe that is what makes me have so many bad colds ...

Bonnie, let me hear from you real soon. Write me at the Jung Hotel in New Orleans, LA.

With best wishes, Jack

A fortnight passed before Dad heard from Bonnie again. She had sent him a letter via New Orleans, where he'd gone for the tour stop but again didn't play because of illness. But it didn't catch up with him until St. Petersburg. Dad wrote, "I guess I have mail all over the United States because of moving around very fast during tournament season." He told her, "Being in this crazy game, with life on the road and all, you have many frustrations." But the delayed letter was a new kind of frustration for him. Never before had he longed to hear from someone as he did Bonnie Fox. Finally receiving and reading her latest letter, though, made him very happy. She told him that she liked the powder box he had sent her as a surprise gift from New Orleans. My father was also beginning to think that he'd struck pay dirt, because Bonnie said she was going to give him a kiss for everything he gave her. He told her, "If that's the case, I had better keep count."

My father's physical condition slowly improved, and his non-playing week in New Orleans was followed by a good performance in the Sixth Thomasville (GA) Open at Glen Arven Country Club. He played well on the quick greens and finished fifth, one stroke behind Ben Hogan and one ahead of Jimmy Demaret and Byron Nelson.

Dad took seventh and won $130 in his next event in St. Petersburg, and as a bonus he was rewarded with one of Bonnie's "sweet letters" that he found sitting on the scorer's table before the tournament's final rounds. The next day, in his room at the Hotel Bennett across the state on the St. Augustine waterfront, he settled in to write again to his sweetheart. He started by congratulating her on her new job at a downtown department store in St Louis called Stix, Baer and Fuller, then slipped in a pretty un-subtle plea for sympathy over his upcoming tonsillectomy:

March 11, 1941,

I play at Pinehurst next, then on to Hershey, Pennsylvania, to have the doctors chop me up. How about writing me everyday, if possible, when I am on the operating table?

... Bonnie, tell me more about yourself, what you are doing - when your vacation is - your hobbies, if any?

I know that I will be in Chicago this summer - I believe in September. So how about taking your vacation then? We could have lots of fun ...

After a second-place finish to Sam Snead and his amateur partner, Wilford Wehrle, at St. Augustine, Dad finished out of the money in chilly, windy Pinehurst and then started the drive back to Pennsylvania for his much-dreaded tonsillectomy. The hospital in Hershey wasn't the place where Dad wanted to spend his thirty-first birthday, but his physician, Dr. Donald B. Stouffer, gently reminded the anxious golf pro that he was in capable hands. Dr. Stouffer also assured Dad that having his tonsils removed would keep him from being sick so much.

The successful surgery soon behind him, Dad wrote again to Bonnie on March 31, this time adding a request for his sweetheart's photo:

> *... I haven't been able to eat since the operation so the result is that I have lost 20 pounds. I look like a bean pole for sure. Doc says I had very bad tonsils and it was a good thing that I had them out when I did.*
>
> *I am leaving here Tuesday morning for my new job at Fox Hill Country Club. It is in Pittston, PA which is only 100 miles north of here ...*
>
> *I came up here with Henry Picard a week ago last Friday from Pinehurst. He has changed jobs this year and will be in Oklahoma City as the golf professional at Twin Hills Country Club for 1941.*
>
> *I learned today that the PGA Championship in Denver will be played in July so I know that I will be through St. Louis then. I will also be in Chicago around September.*
>
> *Say Bonnie, how about it? Have you got a spare picture? I would very much love to have one, so see what you can do for Jack - don't forget now.*

***

The formal announcement was made on March 15, 1941, and all the news services picked up the story: Two-time major-tournament winner Henry Picard no longer would be employed at Hershey Country Club. He would be succeeded by tour player Ben Hogan. Milton Hershey always insisted that his pro represent the company on the PGA Tour full time, and Picard wanted to reduce his tournament schedule; he was a family man who longed for more time with his wife and four children. His new job at Twin Hills in Oklahoma City would offer him an improved lifestyle. His employment there also neatly closed a circle: Picard's connection with Twin Hills actually began during the 1939 New Orleans Open when my father introduced him to the Oklahoma oilmen who owned the Twin Hills club.

Just two weeks after Picard's announcement, my father made the approximately ninety-minute drive from Henry's home in Hershey to

Jack Grout, Dick Metz, Del Webb, Ky Laffoon and Henry Picard posing with the Western Open trophy in 1941 at Phoenix CC. (Grout family photo)

Fox Hill Country Club, where he would begin his work as the head pro. He was excited about diving into his new assignment and had much work to do. After the long winter lull, the pro shop needed to be organized for the new season, new merchandise ordered, and member tournaments scheduled.

My father had held the title of head pro at Edgemere in Oklahoma City when he was just seventeen years old, but in reality, Fox Hill offered him his first real opportunity to prove himself as a club's number-one man. Dad's contract stipulated a salary of $15,000 and ownership of the golf shop. What the typical head-pro contract also stated was specifically how many—or how few—professional tournaments the pro could play in during a given year. In this respect, Dad had a generous agreement with Fox Hill. The membership there wanted him to participate in big tournaments as often as he could.

This arrangement, in which club pros with particularly strong games spent a portion of the year playing on the pro tour, still was common in the 1940s. It allowed professionals such as my father to keep their golf games in competitive shape, continue to build their credibility and thus their careers through tournament success, and also to spread the good word about their home clubs.

In Dad's day, a few of the tour's very best players had club jobs that were jobs in name only. Ben Hogan, Sam Snead and Jimmy Demaret represented big-time clubs or resorts such as Hershey, The

Greenbrier and The Concord at Lake Kiamesha in upstate New York. They weren't required to work regular hours or be at these jobs for any length of time during the year. Rather, such establishments were content to use the player's name as "representing" them and bask in the prestige associated with his wins. This comfortable arrangement gave the big-name players more time to practice and work on their games. It also enabled them to participate in as many as twenty to twenty-five paid exhibitions per year, while their less-prominent tour brethren actually worked their club jobs and, as was the case with my father, hustled an exhibition assignment now and then. Besides being lucrative—often paying as much as $500 for a single day—these exhibitions gave the pros a terrific advantage by keeping their competitive skills sharp.

Dad spent his first few days at Fox Hill simply meeting a number of people and becoming familiar with his surroundings. Cold weather lingered into April, so there weren't many members around. In those days, it was common for golf courses in colder climates to open around the middle of April, but there usually wouldn't be much activity until after Decoration Day—what's now called Memorial Day. So Dad felt comfortable taking time on April 3 to commandeer some club stationery and write another letter to Bonnie:

> *... I forgot to tell you that during my stay at the hospital I had a birthday. Your nice card came on the same day and it made me very happy. I am getting to be an old man now and pretty cards and a picture of you would make me feel most happy. So, you see you must send me one.*
>
> *I am sitting down, where I have marked an arrow on the picture above, and writing you this letter. (The letterhead of Fox Hill Country Club included a picture of the clubhouse). The juke box is really going to town playing boogie-woogie and a couple of my little boy friends are practicing new steps for the coming season...*
>
> *Bonnie, you asked in your letter for me to tell you 'all about myself.' That's something that I have never checked myself over on very much. So, it will have to wait, honey, until I see you this summer ... Anyway we will have something to talk about when we see each other ...*

As time went by, Bonnie would realize that it wasn't her man's nature to talk about himself. He avoided being the center of attention because it made him uncomfortable. Dad was a man of few words, but his words always had impact. He had a high regard for decency and felt that it was one's personal behavior and accomplishments that did the talking.

***

West Pittston is a small town located halfway between Scranton and Wilkes-Barre. In those days there weren't many golf clubs in the area, even though the sport actually was quite popular. When my father got to Fox Hill, it had a nearly full membership and was in good financial condition. To build on that strong base, he actively promoted the club by operating a quality pro shop and golf program and by using the many contacts he'd made as a touring pro to arrange exhibition matches for the enjoyment of his members and their guests. In fact, my father scheduled the first of a number of exhibition matches shortly after he started. To make that happen, he had to drive to New York to pick up his special guest—his good friend Martin Pose of Argentina.

Pose and my father had been close since early 1940, when the South American first came to the United States to play the winter tour. Pose was a striking fellow, slender and swarthy, a bit in the way of Rudolph Valentino, with raven-black hair smacked flat with pomade and parted down the middle. One of several fine Argentine players, he was the first from his country to win a European tournament, the French Open in 1939, and one of the first two to compete in the Masters (with Enrique Bertolino) in 1940. From tee to green, Pose rated among the best in the game, but on the greens he was much less facile.

That weakness was compounded at the start of the 1940-41 winter tour when Pose somehow lost his favorite putter—a blade model— during a pro-am in Hollywood, California. A search of pro shops failed to turn up another one like it, and Pose's short game suffered significantly. At the Masters shortly before his appearance at Fox Hill, Pose took thirty-six and thirty-eight putts in successive rounds on Augusta National's slick greens. He estimated that he should have taken no more than thirty putts a round, and had he done so, he would have been right there at the end with the tournament winner, Craig Wood. He finished twenty-

Jack Grout and his Argentine buddy, Martin Pose, at Fox Hill Country Club in 1941. (Photo courtesy of Fox Hill Country Club)

ninth instead. Citing the lamentable tale of Pose's lost putter, long-hitting Jimmy Thomson—famed for hitting 300-yard drives in an era when very few players could do so—called Pose "the bad-luck golfer of 1941."

April 9, 1941,

Please excuse the long delay in answering your letter. I have been in New York all week and just returned this morning. We are having a golf exhibition today with Martin Pose from Buenos Aires. We are very good friends. He will return home on the 25th of this month by boat.

I feel much better now. But I am not gaining any of the lost weight ... The weather has been very nice and lots of golfers are playing every day ...

I hope you are happy with your new job. Maybe you can get to be a private secretary someday or do you just work to pass away time?

Well Bonnie dear, be a sweet girl and don't forget I am looking forward to your picture which I want very much.

Martin Pose spent about ten days with my father at Fox Hill, and during that time the two bachelors enjoyed themselves on and off the golf course. When the day came to tell each other adios, Dad was sad to see his friend go. While the two men were shaking hands and about to go their separate way, Pose told Dad, "I go home to Buenos Aires now. But I come back. I work and save my money until November 1942. Then, I make the winter tour again with you, Jack." His good intentions notwithstanding, Pose's plans would have to wait. The Japanese laid a bomb on the hopes and dreams of a generation.

April 18, 1941,

Thank you so much for your sweet letter and for promising to send me your picture ...

My friend Martin, from Argentina, left this morning. I was sorry to see him go as I like him very much ... He tried to teach me the rumba but said I had two right feet so the lessons were called off. Maybe I will surprise him on his return next year by learning from someone else. Can you rumba?

... Be sweet, Bonnie, and take good care of yourself and if you please, won't you autograph your picture to me ...

***

My father's job at Fox Hill gave him plenty of opportunities to play golf with the club's members and work on his game, as well as travel to pro tournaments. Dad usually would try to play in four or five "opens," as they were called then, because they were open to not only professional players but also amateurs who could qualify. Dad had to be selective in taking time to play tournaments because he lost lesson fees and shop income when he was away. Plus he had travel expenses of food, lodging and caddie fees and faced the pressure of not making any money if he played poorly.

The life of tour pros in those days was a world away from the pampered existence most enjoy today. There were no fine courtesy cars for the players or lavish spreads of food during the tournaments. Nor were there many free-spending sponsors lined up to pay hefty endorsement fees and provide unlimited golf equipment and clothing for rank-and-file players. Those perks would come during the 1950s and 1960s as more graduates of respected college programs began coming onto the tour full time and there were fewer men on the circuit who spent months of each year as working club pros. To paraphrase actor John Houseman in one of his marvelous television ads for Smith Barney: If a professional golfer of the 1940s had a good life, including financial success, "He did it the old-fashioned way. He earned it!"

Almost all the touring pros with seasonal club jobs faced this conundrum. They had to focus the majority of their time and efforts on the club business at hand, as that was the source of most of their income. Occasionally they might participate in some of the big-money tournaments and, maybe, the majors – if they made it through the qualifier. But financial implications were always a determining factor. To that point, both my father and his brother Dick decided at different times against making a trip to play in a major championship because of the expense. In May 1940, Dick, then pro at Wichita Falls Country Club in Texas, was one of five Texans who qualified to play in that summer's U.S. Open at the Canterbury Golf Club in suburban Cleveland, Ohio. Dick decided, though, that he couldn't afford to play. And in July 1944, my dad got through PGA Championship qualifying at the Tam O'Shanter Country Club in Chicago but decided not to travel to Manito Golf and Country Club in Spokane, Washington, because of the expense. In both cases, the brothers figured to make more money in the end by staying home.

The realistic price of qualifying for the PGA Tournament hadn't yet entered Dad's mind, though, as he settled into life at Fox Hill. With the busy club golf season bearing down, he wrote of his aspirations (as well as reiterating his desire to receive her picture) in a letter to Bonnie on April 29, 1941:

> *You sure are a lucky little girl to be able to travel so much — Florida, New York, and now California. I have been out west five times, always during the rainy season that has made me dislike the state very much ...*
>
> *If I qualify for a certain tournament (PGA Championship) I will fly to Denver in early July. It will be my first trip in an airplane so I have ample time to prepare my fate ...*
>
> *I think your mother has a good idea in the exchange of pictures. I do want yours very much so I would gladly trade. All of the pictures there are of me are taken around the golf course. Do you want one of those? Or do you want a pose-y one ...*
>
> *Well Bonnie, please send yours as soon as possible as I still want one very much.*

***

In the late 1930s and early 1940s, Fox Hill had the biggest golf operation in northeastern Pennsylvania's Wyoming Valley. During a busy summer day, with the course crowded with golfers, it wasn't uncommon for the club to have more than one hundred caddies milling around hoping for work. School-age kids could always count on making a few dollars by caddying or shagging balls, just as Dad did during his youth in Oklahoma City. While welcome as workers, though, the kids also were kept in their place. Fox Hill policy stated that until being summoned by the caddie master, all caddies should remain around the caddie shack, which was located down the hill from the pro shop and out of sight of the "fussy" membership.

A number of the club's more dependable caddies were schoolboys from the nearby town of Exeter, which in those days had a very good high school golf team. The captain of the 1941 team and one of Fox Hill's best caddies was a boy named George Mehallic, the younger brother of Mike Mehallic, Fox Hill's assistant greens keeper. In a conversation in 2006, George (who changed his last name from Mehallic to Mihai) told me that he and the other caddies thought highly of my father's work as Fox Hill's golf professional. He said that Dad actually would take the time to talk with the boys and to be kind to them. Mihai added that Dad "cut a dashing, dapper and charismatic figure around the club—kind of a Cary Grant type."

Apparently my father's favorite young caddie at Fox Hill was Billy Masters, a good player who became his protégé. Among truths my father taught Billy was that around a country club, one of the best ways to receive attention is to play good golf. Masters understood this, worked hard on his game, and won the club's caddie championship two years running, including in a playoff with George Mihai in the summer of 1942. Both of the fine young men went into the armed services in 1943, with George choosing the Navy and Billy the Marine Corps. Sadly, Billy was killed in the Pacific about six months after his enlistment.

I visited Fox Hill Country Club in the summer of 2006, just to poke about a bit, and among those I met was club's starter. He was a tall, elderly gentleman who looked to be in his late seventies; his name was John Yakobutis. Mr. Yakobutis told me he had lived in the area his whole life, and he remembered my father very well. In fact, Mr. Yakobutis said he was "one of Mr. Grout's favorite caddies at Fox Hill." He recalled, though, that in his first stint as caddie for my dad he earned a scolding. It seems that Dad had just played a shot into a green and had taken a pretty good divot, and in young Johnny's haste to replace the divot, he casually dropped my father's golf bag and darted after the chunk of turf. Dad waited for his caddie to return, then calmly yet firmly told him always to lay the bag down gently and never just drop it.

The kindly pro, who had spent many days caddying in his Oklahoma City youth, understood that his caddie was just eager to do a good job. The best part was that the youngster learned from his mistakes and was pretty savvy about taking instruction, proof of that being that my father used him again many times. Johnny would routinely meet Dad in the bunker nearest the pro shop and shag balls as Dad blasted practice shots out of the sand.

Chapter 9
The Inevitable Question

"Competition, whether it be for the U.S. Open or a mere 50-cent Nassau match, is the stimulant that all successful golfers relish. It's the spice that makes all the hours of practice worthwhile." — JACK GROUT

***

The 1941 U.S. Open was played at Colonial Country Club in Fort Worth, a famed layout where Dad and Henry Picard had played a practice round just five months earlier. There were compelling reasons why my father wanted to compete in that Open. The key one, of course, was that he would once again be playing for the national championship. Since the tournament was being held back in Fort Worth, it also would give him a good chance to see old friends and family. And a major bonus was that it might give him a nice opportunity to stop in St. Louis to see the love of his life. My father knew it would be a long and costly trip, though, and admitted to her that when he submitted his tournament application and $5 entry fee, he really hadn't firmly committed himself to playing:

> *May 19, 1941,*
>
> *Thank you for your nice letter and I know when your new pictures are finished they will be swell ... I will attempt to qualify next Monday for the National Open ... The Open will be played in Texas, June 6-7-8; that is a pretty long trip this time of year and I haven't decided to go or not. If I do go I'll stop in St. Louis to see you if you don't mind ...*
>
> *I will play in about four opens this year or maybe five - so if I ever get close to you I will let you know ...*

Toward the end of May, Dad played in the U.S. Open qualifier at the Philadelphia Cricket Club's Flourtown Course. When he arrived, his game from tee to green was sharp, as it usually was, and his short game was in good shape, too. His problem was his ambivalence about actually making the long trip to Texas. That internal conflict robbed him of concentration and led him to absolutely butcher his very first hole in the qualifier. He shot an eight there, and in the end, missed one of the four qualifying spots by one stroke.

Weeks later Dad would manage a better result in his effort to make the field for the twenty-fourth PGA Championship, to be held at the beautiful Cherry Hills Club in Denver. When he teed off in the June 23 sectional qualifier at Lancaster Country Club, he had none of those mixed feelings he'd had during qualification for the U.S. Open. His 36-hole score of 145 won him a ticket into the PGA, and with it, perhaps, an opportunity for a side trip to see the woman he loved.

June 27, 1941

... I am happy that you have a picture for me. I hope you like the snapshot of myself I sent you, taken right here at the club. It was taken just after I had my tonsils taken out.

I, too, am sorry that I couldn't see you early this month. One bad hole (in the U.S. Open qualifier) kept me away. It was a pip!

I am flying either on the 2nd or 3rd of July for Denver. So far I have been unable to make connections through St Louis. It seems that Chicago is the only line from here.

Do you think you will be in Chicago on those dates? If so, let me know, maybe I could stay there for a day or so and we could have some fun ...

In early July Dad flew to Denver, an exciting trip for him as it was his first airplane flight. Unfortunately his hope to make connections through St. Louis so that he could see Bonnie, or to have her meet him in Chicago, didn't work out. Perhaps adding to any disappointment she might have felt about this, she didn't hear from Dad when she celebrated her twentieth birthday on July 1. Apparently he didn't know when her birthday was!

The PGA was held July 7-13, and Dad entered the tournament with high hopes. He had advanced to a very good club-pro job, and knew that the club's members wanted their professional to play well in big tourneys. My father had seen the way his brother Dick was lavishly praised by members at the Okmulgee Country Club in Oklahoma after he won the Oklahoma Open. He wanted to earn the same kind of response from the members at Fox Hill, and he did, in fact, get off to a good start in Denver.

The PGA's first two days consisted of a thirty-six-hole stroke-play qualifier, with survivors advancing into match play. Defending champion Byron Nelson was exempt, and sixty-three others qualified for the starting field, Sam Snead being low qualifier with a 138. A score of 153 or better qualified for match play, and Dad advanced in the middle of the pack with a 75-73-148.

Back then, the PGA Championship was an endurance test. Following the qualifier, most matches were played over thirty-six holes. Though my father was tall, lean and relatively strong, he had limited stamina, so the grueling PGA Championship schedule did not favor him. Dad drew a formidable opponent in the first round of match play – Jimmy Demaret, his traveling buddy in 1935-36. Demaret was perhaps one of the toughest competitors on the tour. It was a shock, then, when my father eliminated him four-and-three (ahead by four holes with only three left to play).

Dad kept things going in the next round when he faced a California pro named Fay Coleman, whose claim to fame was losing to Bobby Jones in the quarterfinals of the National Amateur at Merion as Jones marched toward golf's Grand Slam in 1930. Coleman's match with Dad was a bit more suspenseful than the six-and-five pasting he received that day from Jones. Dad was ahead for most of the match, and beat Coleman one-up.

Next up for Dad was Vic Ghezzi, a big Italian fellow from New Jersey who loved to laugh and carry on. Back then, most of the tour pros were short or of medium height, so my father stood out at six foot two. But Ghezzi was two inches taller, and while he wasn't a long hitter for a big guy, Ghezzi was deadly around the greens. Their third-round match was close the entire way. My father remembered that he struck the ball well and hit more greens in regulation that day than Ghezzi. In the end, however, Ghezzi's mastery of the little shots around the green turned the tide. When my father's approach to the island green on the 550-yard seventeenth hole found the water, Ghezzi had the margin he needed. Both men parred the final hole, and my father lost one-down. Still, he would finish a very respectable ninth, equaling his ninth-place effort in the 1945 PGA as his best-ever finish in a "major."

Just after that tournament, he wrote again to Bonnie.

July 16, 1941

Thanks for your letter in Denver. It was sweet of you to write me and I am sorry that we didn't get to see each other when I flew through ...

I am still planning on going to Chicago in the first week in Sept. probably around the 2nd-8th for the Tam O'Shanter Open. Do you think we can see each other then?

We are having the darndest time making connections...

Dad's good finish in the PGA earned him $200, but maybe more satisfying was the hero's welcome he received from the membership at Fox Hill when he returned to his job there. The members liked and respected Dad, and now their head pro had performed well in a major championship! His nice finish quickly resulted in more members signing up for lessons from him—an extra bonus for his good play in Denver. Club members everywhere thought if you could play well you must know something about the game. Certainly, as much then as today, the better you played in the big tournaments, the better your chances of landing the best club jobs.

The glow of his good performance in the PGA aside, it still was summertime at Fox Hill, the golf season was in full bloom, and things were busy. Dad's responsibilities as the pro were numerous and consumed long hours; at quitting time he often was so exhausted that he could only wonder where the day had gone. Adding to his misery that August, the last letter he'd received from Bonnie was the one she'd written when he was in Denver nearly a month earlier. Was she OK? Were *they* OK? Finally, from his room at the Berkshire Hotel in Reading, where he was playing in the Central Pennsylvania Open, Dad reached out again:

> *August 10, 1941*
>
> *As I haven't heard from you in some time I will write again hoping you are well ...*
>
> *I received a letter from Ed (Bradley) last Friday from New York. He said they will be through to see me Aug. 25th. I might be gone at that time as the Hershey Open is played that week. After that I will play in Chicago at Tam O'Shanter the week following. Ed says he is a member there so maybe we can have a game there.*
>
> *Do you think we can see each other then? If not I will come to St Louis and see you for a day or two ...*
>
> *Please let me hear from you real soon ... Also try and come to Chicago the first week in Sept ...*

Another two weeks went by, and still my father hadn't received a response to his letters. He was puzzled. What was going on? Why hadn't she written him back? All Dad could do was bury himself in his job and try not to obsess about whether there remained a future with his girlfriend. What was going on in Bonnie Fox's world?

Actually, Bonnie's life was typical for a young woman at that time in America. She was happy, single and carefree. Her dreams were about romance, travel and, of course, what the future held in store for her. She had a menial job at a downtown St. Louis department store, made little money, and lived with her parents in a small apartment located over a downstairs storefront. She had girlfriends who liked to talk about their young lives, and all of them went on plenty of dates, mostly with fellows their own age.

One of my favorite photographs: Bonnie Fox and Jack Grout in downtown Chicago, September 1941. (Used with the Rod Munday family's permission)

A month earlier my mother had turned twenty, and the thirty-one-year-old man she had been exchanging letters with hadn't even known it was her birthday. What did they really know about each other? From his letters, it was evident that Jack Grout was a man of few words. Now this guy, who wouldn't talk about himself and whom she had met only briefly eight months earlier, was gung ho about actually seeing her again. Being the youngest of seven children, it had been easy for Bonnie to be evasive and procrastinate when pressed with things. Now, though, she was being pressed to act like a mature adult.

While his sweetheart pondered all of this, Dad traveled to Hershey in late August to join most of the nation's top golfers for the $5,000 Hershey Open. My father knew the beautiful course well from having worked as Henry Picard's assistant pro there for three seasons, and his game was in good shape. His disposition, though, was poor. Even the golf course, one of the prettiest he'd ever seen, did little to inspire him. So Dad wasn't sharp at all; he seemed just to go through the motions. His score on the opening day was an indifferent 77, and it placed him far behind the leaders.

As he listlessly handed in his scorecard, Dad made an about-face and headed straight for the club's locker room. He just wanted to change his shoes and get out of there. When he reached his locker and flung open its green metal door, though, he couldn't believe his eyes: There was the letter he desperately wanted and had waited so long to receive! He felt a wave of happiness and relief. And those emotions swelled as he read the letter.

His young sweetheart told him everything was fine and she'd just needed time to think things over. She said she had missed him a lot, and she wanted to meet him in Chicago as he had asked. Her sweet letter with its warm tone made my father so happy he could hardly stand it.

Inspired by Bonnie's words, my father went out the next morning and shot 66. It was the lowest round of the entire tournament and got him right back into contention. The great round included seven birdies and bested even the fine 67 posted by Ben Hogan, the new professional at Hershey. With his peace of mind restored, my father played consistently the rest of the way, finishing third behind Hogan and Lloyd Mangrum and winning $500.

With the tournament over, Dad wasted no time exchanging telegrams with Ed Bradley in Chicago, telling his future wife's brother-in-law to expect him there by dinnertime the next evening. It was a six hundred-mile drive from Hershey to Chicago, but Dad couldn't wait to get there. At that point, his utmost desire was to see the woman he was courting by mail—in person.

The other golf pros were racing to Chicago also, but for a very different reason: They were anxious to play in a new event put on by businessman George S. May, an extravaganza at the May-owned Tam O'Shanter Country Club in suburban Niles. Called the Tam O'Shanter Open, it carried a healthy total purse of $11,000 and offered a first prize of $2,000. Beginning in 1941 and extending through 1957, May would draw national attention by putting up almost $2,000,000 in prize money and giving the pros their first taste of really big stakes. Another tournament he originated at Tam O'Shanter, the World Championship of Golf, in 1953 became the first nationally televised golf event when May paid ABC (the American Broadcasting Company) a reported $32,000 to show it. First place in the tournament paid an astronomical $25,000, and Lew Worsham won it by holing out from 115 yards—the first winning shot broadcast on national TV. May was also the first to erect grandstands on a tournament course and first to allow club members to ride in golf carts. An unabashed showman and master promoter who has been called the P.T. Barnum of golf, May saw golf as strictly a game, and a golf tournament as merely entertainment—which didn't bother the pros at all as they stuffed their pockets with his cash.

***

Dad arrived in Chicago on Tuesday evening, September 2, checked into his hotel, and immediately telephoned the Bradley residence. "I'm on my way over," he said. There was a heightened sense of urgency to everything Dad did now, because in only about an hour he would again see the girl who had stolen his heart. It had been almost nine months since they first met and he couldn't wait any longer. While he was in Chicago, he wanted to spend as much time as possible with her, but he also needed to get ample rest because he had a big-money golf tournament to play.

As it turned out, Dad's desire to play well in the tournament didn't keep him from having a delightful week with Bonnie. Their time together included listening to the Glenn Miller radio show and going to the hit movie *Sergeant York*, starring Dad's favorite actor, Gary Cooper. They both enjoyed listening to the Jimmy Dorsey Orchestra play "Green Eyes" on the 78-rpm phonograph. And they had dinner together every night and played cards with Ed and Vera.

On the golf course that week, Dad had less fun, driving poorly and finishing out of the money. As far as he was concerned, the tournament could have ended sooner, but not the time he spent with Bonnie. Their week together was everything he'd hoped it would be. He clearly was ready to settle down at this stage in his life. He found himself falling head over heels in love with the girl from St. Louis and proposed marriage to her by the end of the week!

Bonnie must have been expecting his proposal, yet her feelings were mixed. She had come to love and respect Jack Grout and understand that life with him could be comfortable and rewarding. But she still was very young. She greatly enjoyed carefree times with her friends and wondered whether she was ready to settle down. It was a lot to weigh, and she didn't want to make a mistake. Clearly, though, she'd thought carefully about all this and was prepared with a decision that made my father a very happy man: She said "yes," she wanted to marry him and be his partner for life. Though no definite date was set, they agreed the wedding should be sometime the following spring.

With the Chicago tournament finished, Dad had to say good-bye to his future bride and the Bradleys and move on to the next tournament, this time in Atlantic City. This was a routine my father found wrenching, given his natural inclination to be a homebody. Here he had decided, once and for all, that he wanted to spend his life with Bonnie, but then he had to say good-bye and drive away without her. That was the life of a touring golf pro, though, a life he would stick with for several more years before opting for a more stable existence.

Dad arrived in the Atlantic City area the following day and, after a practice round and dinner, headed to bed early. As he walked through the hotel lobby the next morning, a clerk handed him a letter, the one Bonnie had promised would be waiting for him in Atlantic City, and her sweet words only confirmed in his mind that they were going to marry. Dad wrote back to her that evening and said, "I knew I would get one (letter) today as sure as I am a foot tall because you always tell the truth."

Buoyed by the deepening relationship, Dad played good golf that week, tying for fourth and winning $387.50. He enjoyed sharing a hotel room with Horton Smith, whom he had met in 1929 when Smith and Walter Hagen barnstormed across the country playing exhibition matches. The two stars made a stop in Oklahoma City where, as a teenager, Dad got to play eighteen holes with them.

***

Dad's next letter reflected, as well as any of the more than one hundred he penned to Bonnie, the old-fashioned male attitudes of his day—that the husband's place was to make a living, while the wife's place was in the home cooking, sewing, tending to their children, doing housework and generally "taking care of her man." Reflective of the way most American males were programmed a century ago, these expectations showed up in many of Dad's letters to his future wife. I don't feel they portray my father as a chauvinist, as some might judge him when reading his words. Rather, I believe they merely reflect the values of the day, values that today seem woefully out of touch with this country's more enlightened, modern view of the intrinsic value of women.

September 16, 1941

Darling Bonnie,

... I have been on the go ever since leaving Atlantic City and now I have the worst cold I have ever had. I am writing this letter in bed in Mr. and Mrs. Sam Byrd's house here in Ardmore. I had a massage this afternoon and I feel a bit better. Honey, I wish you were here to take care of me. I am such a baby.

I play the 1st round with Ralph Guldahl at 1:50 o'clock Friday. When you're paired with him you're in for a long day because he plays too slow. There will be a large gallery out everyday. I sure hope I can do some good.

I was at Pittston for only six hours, just in time to get your two letters, and I am glad to know you still love me and little Bonnie is learning to cook for her Jack. Won't that be swell ...

(I've) been looking for a place in Pittston for next year that will be our home. But as yet I can't or haven't had time to find a good place. But when I do it will be a cozy nest ...

Be sure and practice cooking and sewing, housework, phone calls, letter writing and taking care of me. Boy, you sure got a big job ...

With Love Forever, Jack

Sam Byrd, with whom Dad stayed in suburban Philadelphia during the Henry Hurst Invitational, was one of those interesting characters Dad encountered so often on the tour. An outfielder for the New York Yankees from 1929 through 1934, he played six seasons with Babe Ruth. (His nickname was "Babe Ruth's Legs" because he frequently pinch-ran for Ruth.) Sammy, as he was known during his playing days, quit baseball in 1937 after two seasons with the Cincinnati Reds and went to work as a golf pro at the Philadelphia Country Club. He won six pro tournaments between 1942 and 1946, lost in the finals of the 1945 PGA Championship to Byron Nelson, and is the only person to have played in both a World Series game and the Masters (finishing third in 1941 and fourth the next year). During the time when Dad stayed with him and his wife in 1941, Byrd was working at the Merion Cricket Club as teaching and playing professional.

Dad was feeling better by the start of the first round of the Hurst Invitational, but neither he nor playing partner Ralph Guldahl scored particularly well that day. Dad shot 75, Guldahl 74. Nor did Dad's golf improve as the tourney progressed. There was a time when a poor performance like that would have had a sobering effect on him. But now things were different because he knew that his sweetheart's feelings for him weren't going to change no matter what he shot on the golf course. In a way, my father had been liberated.

September 23, 1941

... I have been telling Ky and Irene what a good little housewife you are going to make. I also showed them your picture and you passed.

Sweet, I love you. Please write me more often. I always enjoy reading your letters. They are so cute ...

By the time the Philadelphia tournament ended my father had been on the go for about a month. He was tired and needed a break from playing before heading for late-fall tournaments in Florida and Texas, but the irrepressible Ky Laffoon somehow persuaded him to play in the City of Providence Rhode Island Open. Dad finished twentieth in that event, which was notable mostly for the obscurity of the fellow who won it—a twenty-three-year-old pro named Louis Barbaro of Mamaroneck, New York. Barbaro's Rhode Island victory was probably the biggest surprise on the tour in 1941; he shot fifteen under par and won by six strokes over a crack field that included Sammy Byrd, Sam Snead, Gene Sarazen and Lawson Little.

Maybe more important to Dad during that week in Providence was what seemed like an extraordinary event that had nothing to do with golf—his first long-distance telephone conversation with his fiancée. In those days, a long-distance call was considered by many to be a wild extravagance, especially given that a postage stamp cost three cents and air mail was just twice that. In any case, Dad was feeling a bit unsettled because he hadn't gotten a letter in a couple of weeks. He thought it was best to hear Bonnie's voice and corroborate his true feeling for her.

There actually was no telephone in the modest Fox apartment in St. Louis; my father got through to her by calling the phone in the storefront below. Bonnie had given him that number, but she didn't want him using up all his money talking to her. She told him to call there only in an emergency. As soon as my father heard her voice, he knew that things between them were fine. It was a relief to him that their relationship was on solid ground and that she really missed him. The warm and engaging conversation actually went a long way toward reassuring them both. In a much larger sense, though, the whole exercise made my father realize that his "business as usual" way of doing things had to be modified.

First and foremost, it was apparent to him that his usual routine of heading south every November to begin the new year's pro tour would have to be reconsidered. No longer would it be automatic for Dad to play in events such as the Mid-South Open or run here and there to see Ed Bradley or some other fellow. Instead, his new way of scheduling his free time soon would have to include his wife. It was proof that my father was ready to change his lifestyle. Dad loved golf, but he loved home life more. He looked forward with great anticipation to settling into married life.

October 6, 1941

Please don't scold me for not writing more often. I have written you, in the past year, more than any one in my life. So when we are married you will have to do it all as I am going to turn the whole job over to you. Would you like to be my secretary? I will pay you 5 kisses a day...

I have been going to more shows lately for the lack of something to do. All my old running mates have turned me loose now that I am engaged ...

Well Bonnie, please be sweet, remember I love you dearly and don't break my heart ...

Though my father's contract with Fox Hill called for him to close up shop at the end of October, by the middle of that month the weather had turned cold and the golf season had virtually ended. This sudden arrival of winter conditions made it both physically uncomfortable and lonely for Dad, and during the bleak afternoons and evenings of that October's final weeks he saw more picture shows than he usually would see in a year. He also did a lot of thinking about a visit he was planning with his future wife, this time in her home city.

November 8, 1941

I should be in St Louis Thursday or Friday. I had intended leaving Thursday of this week but had to go to New York this week to sign a contract.

The weather is cold as hell and I am very anxious to leave.

I will see you next week ...

***

My father certainly wasn't a wealthy man, and one of the helpful aspects of golf-tour life was establishing relationships with successful people who could lend assistance to the touring pros from time to time. Thus it was that when Dad finally made it to St. Louis in mid-November for a much-anticipated visit with Bonnie and her family, he stayed at the splendid home of Sidney Salomon Jr., a successful businessman and member of a wealthy family. A fine amateur golfer whom Dad had befriended while playing in tournaments around the country, Salomon once had been runner-up to Chester O'Brien in the Missouri Amateur. In 1967-68, when professional hockey expanded by six teams, the Salomon family owned both the St. Louis Arena and the brand new St. Louis Blues. Salomon Jr. quickly became known as a player-friendly owner, pampering his athletes with cars and Florida vacations. His upstart team reacted magnificently to this first-rate treatment and actually made the Stanley Cup finals in their first season, losing a tough series to the Montreal Canadiens.

This visit to St. Louis was an important one for Dad. It represented a long-awaited opportunity not only to deepen his relationship with the woman he loved, but also, finally, to get to meet her extended family, whom he would come to enjoy very much. At dinner one evening, he and the Fox clan all drank champagne, which apparently was a real delight for Bonnie's mother, Annie. My father remembered how Annie's eyes sparkled when she laughed. She was a person that Dad quickly came to love and would forever hold in the highest regard.

One afternoon while young Bonnie and her beau were sitting around the apartment, Bonnie got up and left the room. She returned moments later carrying a pretty cardboard box in which she had stored all of Dad's letters—every one of them. After seeing them, my father told her that he was a bad boy for not saving her letters. He said he wouldn't have wanted anybody else reading what she wrote, so he always burned them.

On November 19—far too soon for my father—he had to say good-bye again so he could drive to Oklahoma City for the Thanksgiving holiday with his parents. Dad arrived in his hometown feeling drained, and only after spending practically three whole days in bed at his parents' house did he begin to feel better. In a letter on November 22, Dad wrote, "I thought I would die when I couldn't get my breath." His next letter, though, noted improvement in his health, perhaps inspired by a couple of Thanksgiving feasts:

> *November 28, 1941*
>
> *Your letter was very sweet and I am glad that you didn't scold me again, as it makes me feel pretty bad when you do.*
>
> *We will probably leave for Florida tomorrow ... I feel better now, getting lots of sleep, practicing every day and playing good. I sure hope to do good in Florida. Ky Laffoon and Pic and myself are going to split on our prize winnings in Florida and Texas opens ...*
>
> *I am not going to send you a picture until you send me one. I like the picture of you sitting on the sand in Florida very much. Your mother showed it to me ...*
>
> *I had two Thanksgiving dinners yesterday, one at home and one at Henry Picard's home. Boy, I am really stuffed, feel like a big owl. Also, went to the zoo yesterday and saw all the monkeys. They reminded me of you as they are never still. Always jabbering and jumping around like a bull frog.*
>
> *We had a long discussion last night on how tough things are going to be in the future. They pointed out how single men are better off. No worries, no responsibilities. But, I love you. I can't live anymore without you, so I will have to suffer with the rest of the world ...*

Dad's reference to pooling winnings referred to a common practice throughout his days on tour—frequent occasions when two or more pros would form a "syndicate" and pool their prize money. Generally this divvying up happened between close friends, as when Dad and Jimmy Demaret pooled winnings for a time during 1936, or during the early part of the schedule when players were unsure how well they were playing and whether they would finish in the money.

As late as the 1950s, there were numerous pairs of pros playing the circuit who agreed to split their combined winnings in tournaments. There also were occasions when two pros involved in a play-off for a tournament would agree privately to split first and second money evenly, then would battle it out on the extra holes to see whose name would be etched on the trophy. These collaborations were eliminated as the tour matured, and for good reason. While often innocent by nature, they tended to cast doubt on the authenticity of the competition, which was not good for the sport's image.

Chapter 10
In the Aftermath of Infamy

"In any of life's activities you can do a better job with today and tomorrow if you understand a little bit about yesterday." — JACK GROUT

✻✻✻

On Friday evening, December 5, 1941, my father checked into Miami's Venetian Hotel with his traveling companions, Henry Picard and Ky Laffoon. It had rained through most of their three-day drive from Oklahoma, so, as happened too often, Dad was feeling poorly upon his arrival. The tropical weather in Miami seemed to revive him, though, as it always did.

Dad spent Sunday, December 7, with Vera and Ed Bradley, and the trio went sightseeing in Bradley's car that morning along bustling Collins Avenue in Miami Beach. As they drove, their casual conversation naturally included the current status of Bonnie and Jack's relationship and engagement. In the beginning, the chitchat was light and fun with laughs all around. As Dad and the Bradleys drove happily beside the Atlantic Ocean, though, events were unfolding 4,861 miles west of there that would bring a far different mood to the country and the world.

The Japanese sneak attack on the headquarters of the U.S. Pacific Fleet at Pearl Harbor on the island of Oahu, Hawaii, began at approximately 7:00 a.m. in the Hawaii-Aleutian Time Zone—midday on the U.S. East Coast. It was a jolt for the nation the next day when President Roosevelt asked Congress to declare war on Japan, even though most citizens had felt that it was just a matter of time before the United States would become involved in the escalating hostilities overseas.

Prior to the Japanese assault on Pearl Harbor, the future of our nation looked so bright. For my father and his colleagues in the golf business, the coming years had held much promise. The United States was taking the game of golf more seriously than at any time since the market crash of 1929, and the consensus was that unless the country was dragged into war, golf could experience a tremendous boom. But war indeed intervened. Suddenly huge amounts of our manpower and raw materials were diverted to the war effort.

Even though golf had been gaining traction, the sport had to be considered just a diversion during these perilous times. Once again, my father and all those from his generation were slapped in the face by devastating worldwide circumstances. A dozen years after the Great Depression crippled the national economy just as many of them were entering the job market, they were faced with a catastrophic world war at the very time they were about to enter their peak years of earning potential.

Beginning the week of the annual Miami Open and for several months to follow, national surveys showed U.S. citizens favoring a policy of allowing normal life to go on, at least as much as possible. Many citizens considered it more important than ever for our sporting events and recreational pursuits to continue, to help boost the nation's morale, but it was obvious to my dad and the rest of the touring pros that, in the short term anyway, things were going to be very different for professional golf.

Thousands of athletes interrupted their careers to serve in the military during the war years. Among the pro golfers in that group, Jack Fleck, who would win the U.S. Open in 1955, participated in the Normandy off-shore bombardment aboard a ship at Utah Beach. Lloyd Mangrum, who won the 1946 U.S. Open and was the tour's leading money winner in 1953, earned four battle stars and two Purple Hearts as a staff sergeant in the U.S. Third Army under General George S. Patton, and Bobby Jones himself reached the rank of Lieutenant Colonel in the U.S. Army Air Forces.

***

After a ninth-place tie in Miami—for which Dad won $212.50 to throw in the pot with the $112.50 won by Ky Laffoon and $50 or so won by Henry Picard—the three friends had a long and tiring drive to Harlingen, Texas, for the next tour stop. "Arrived here late last night," my weary father wrote to his fiancée, "and I feel as if I had been beat up with a club, sore back, legs and throat." Days later, he wrote again:

> *December 20, 1941*
>
> *I spent the day in Matamoros Mexico today. It's a very old city and not much to see. I had a quail dinner and lots of wine. It made me very sleepy so here I am writing my baby ...*
>
> *I guess I will play in Beaumont on Dec. 26-27-28. I will be up (to see you) just as soon as the good lord will let me. I will stay a good week and we will have a swell time, just you and me ...*

Somewhat refreshed by his foray across the Rio Grande into Mexico, Dad played well through the first two rain-soaked rounds in Harlingen, trailing leader Picard by six strokes. He followed with solid rounds of

70-67 but finished eight strokes behind Picard, whose eighteen-under-par total of 266 was the lowest score on the pro-golf tour for 1941.

To close out the year, my father, Picard and Laffoon moved on to the Beaumont Open, an event that drew pros in droves. Beginning the day after Christmas, it had the largest starting field in PGA history—223 players. As happened too often, Dad played poorly in the final round, shooting a 76 for sixteenth place in an event in which a solid finish could have put him in the top ten. The truth is that he just ran out of gas.

Dad's poor finish cost his three-player alliance a little cash. When the Grout-Picard-Laffoon syndicate divided its accumulated three-tournament earnings, each share came to about $750, or $250 a week. My father would have earnings of $4,200 from tournament play during 1941. Including an additional $15,000 under his Fox Hill contract, he managed total average weekly wages of about $370, not including modest earnings from pro-shop sales and private golf lessons at Fox Hill. In today's dollars, and even with the considerable expenses he faced during his cross-country travels on the golf circuit, Dad's 1941 earnings actually look pretty good. His average of $370 weekly would mean about $5,570 weekly today, or almost $290,000 a year. To put that into perspective, the average earnings for PGA Tour players in 2008 were $751,618, or on a fifty-two-week basis, $14,454 per week

My father couldn't have been too disappointed with the way 1941 had treated him on the golf course. He had played the most tournaments of his career and, for the most part, had played quite well. It had been a solid year but unspectacular. Dad was a very good player, with a golf swing admired and even envied by other players. But there was something in him that was more observer than actor, more student on the golf course than dominant figure. This is why, I think, he eventually became one of the greatest-ever golf teachers, as demonstrated through his work with Jack Nicklaus and many other top players. Even on his worst days on the golf course, my dad was learning from his own mistakes, and he was watching and studying the players around him. He was learning, always learning; which meant that when it was time to shift his full focus into teaching golf's intricacies, Dad was prepared in a way that few men ever have been.

***

Although the United States was involved in a world war at the start of 1942, tournament golf had not yet been deeply affected. That would soon change, though. The United States Golf Association discontinued all of its events, including the U.S. Open, for the "duration" — the term used to indicate the uncertain length of the war. The PGA played a reduced schedule, and the U.S. government even halted the manufacture of golf equipment as part of its wartime materials-rationing program.

My father spent the first few days of the New Year with his immediate family and buddies in Oklahoma City, going there because of his commitment to participate in an event at Picard's Twin Hills Country Club. That Oklahoma City All-Sports Jamboree provided an exciting week for Dad, with famous athletes such as baseball stars Carl Hubbell, Lloyd Waner and Pepper Martin showing up to play golf. Dad enjoyed the fellowship, but as soon as the event ended he made tracks for St. Louis. He'd come to Oklahoma City out of loyalty to his good friend, Picard, but he also had been planning a wonderful week with his beloved Bonnie.

Dad enjoyed being around Bonnie's family. He wrote later that "Annie never gets a spoon. Isn't it a hell of a game?" "Spoons" is a fast-paced game that requires a player to get four cards of a kind and then grab a spoon before an opponent does. Dad was a wonderful card player, and during his week in St. Louis he delighted in trying to teach Annie all about "Spoons," apparently with little success.

Leaving St. Louis, my father carried with him Bonnie's heart. About all she could do for the next several days was mope around the apartment and talk about Jack Grout. For Dad, though, there was no time to mope about having to leave Bonnie again. The new year brought with it a new winter golf tour that he would be a part of.

After visits to Oklahoma to see family and friends, then to Fort Worth to visit the infant daughter of his brother Dick, Dad headed back to Oklahoma City. From Picard's office in the Twin Hills pro shop, he wrote to Bonnie about his busy upcoming schedule:

> *Ky (Laffoon) just drove in, so I guess we will leave tomorrow for Phoenix ... Little Irene (Laffoon) will meet us in Florida or N. Carolina. Expenses are too tough now so Ky is going to save for a rainy day.*

Another letter followed as soon as Dad hit Phoenix, and this one made it clear that marriage was very much on his mind:

> *February 2, 1942*
>
> *We arrived here yesterday and we sure are tired. It will take me about three days before I feel good ... I promise to write my love more often now because you are on my mind all the time, darn you. I am counting the days when I will see you next, and they*

sure are long ones. I love you Baby-believe me. Please believe me I do.

The Open starts here Friday and we will leave here Sunday night. I will be in San Antonio Plaza Hotel Monday night. I wish I were going to meet you there as Mrs. Jack Grout. Wouldn't it be swell?

I ... believe that now is the time to announce our wedding in church. Please ask advice from your Mother, she would know ...

Well Lover, don't work too hard as you know you have to take care of me real soon ...

As Dad mailed this latest letter to Bonnie and thought about how much he missed her, he must have recognized that he was falling into the same routine he'd known for many years, and that this routine was keeping them apart. There was a symmetry to life on the tour, with most players running golf shops and giving lessons during the summer, then laboring as playing professionals during the winter and spring in the warmer climes of California, Arizona, Florida and other good-weather southern and western states. It could be a good life, although it was demanding. As the years passed, it was comforting for the touring pros to return to the same cities—Phoenix, Fort Worth, San Antonio, Miami and others. Over time they made friends in each, found the good and affordable hotels, the best places to eat, the best movie houses and, for many of them, the best bars and nightclubs. Then, the tour season completed, the typical pro headed back to a job as golf professional at a good club and settled back into familiar and satisfying routines there.

It was a life that carried considerable pressure: to play well and bring honor to the golf club you represented as head pro; to make money on tour, and to augment that by making as much as possible giving lessons and selling equipment back at the home club; to maintain a normal family life while traveling so much in an era when there were no cell phones or email to facilitate communications with the folks back home. For my dad, there was also his dream of life with Bonnie. Dad wanted desperately to be with her, to marry her, and to raise a family. As he moved into February of 1942, he was anxious for the months to pass so he could get her to the altar.

The familiar venue of the forty-second Western Open—the Phoenix Country Club—offered little relief for Dad as he slogged through two indifferent rounds and missed the thirty-six-hole cut by one stroke. For some reason, my father's golf seemed to falter out West. He was beginning to think it was a jinx.

February 8, 1942

We will leave today for Texas. The weather has been very nice but I played like a diddie bump. I guess I need you more than ever as you are on my mind all the time, believe me.

I received my (draft) classification Saturday and I am in 3A which is ok by me. Some of the boys have already left and some go very shortly.

I have been losing a little weight around my tummy. In about 30 days I'll be just about right as I don't want to be fatty face ...

On our way out here we shot Ky's pistol every 100 miles, must have shot up 5 boxes of shells. We hit every tin can in sight, jack rabbits, and bottles. It sure was fun. I'll bet you are a good shot also.

So, Baby since I have fallen in love with you I have really taken the veil — no drinkie, lots of sleepie and no dates. It has made me feel much better. I should have married you 10 years ago then I would have been world's champion.

Well baby be sweet. Write me at the Plaza Hotel, San Antonio Texas ...

During that weekend in Phoenix, my father's fanciful existence as a professional golfer had come face to face with a grim reality of life in 1942: the first notice of his military classification from the Luzerne County (PA) Draft Board. Being classified 3-A meant he was supporting people who were dependent on his income, namely his parents, to whom he regularly sent money to help with living expenses. And that meant that many others would be called up before he would. It was a comfort simply knowing how he stood with his draft board. It was better knowing instead of wondering when or if he would be drafted, if he would have to fight, or if he might die.

By early 1942, some tour players had been called into service and others would be called up shortly. Dad thus knew he could be called for service and was ready and willing to serve as needed, but he admitted that he wasn't attracted by the military life.

Compounding his distress, the war started badly and got worse. Following the destruction at Pearl Harbor, the battle news coming out of the Pacific was upsetting, the war clearly becoming a horrific slog for all involved. Gas rationing and blackouts began in the United States, and many items that once were readily available were taken off the shelves. Even though professional sports were officially deemed a worthwhile diversion for a worried nation, it was obvious that the pro-golf tour of 1942 and perhaps beyond would labor in the dark shadow cast by world events, still functioning but certainly less important.

***

After Phoenix, the pro tour shifted to San Antonio for the Texas Open, where the tourney's main attraction was the high-energy first-day foursome that included Bob Hope, Bing Crosby, Byron Nelson and Jimmy Demaret. While that pairing thrilled the gallery of eight thousand and raised a pile of cash to support the Red Cross, my father quietly set about having a solid tournament: He shot 68s in the first and fourth rounds and finished fourteenth.

The next day, Dad settled into a room at the St. Charles Hotel in New Orleans, ready for another tour stop and, maybe more important to him at this point, yet another letter to his sweetheart. The back-and-forth letter writings of Jack Grout and Bonnie Fox now were filled with shared hopes, dreams and forebodings. It was becoming clear that the war might spoil their plans, as it already had done for many people they knew. After the first round in New Orleans, for example, Clayton Heafner, who was tied for second with my dad and Henry Picard, went into the clubhouse and received a telegram that somehow had been delayed. The wire ordered him to report to his draft board at Linville, North Carolina, on February 18, already two days past. The big fellow said that he was going to leave as soon as the tournament ended. That sort of thing was happening to a lot of the players.

February 18, 1942

How is my little sweetie? I enjoyed talking with you very much last Wed. your voice was very sweet ... I still want to marry you April 6 or 7 and I am waiting for that day to come ...

Baby thanks for your sweet card , it was very thoughtful of you. Someday I will make you very happy, always believe me ...

Dad was in fourth place after two rounds of the New Orleans tournament, but slipped thereafter. He shot 76-75 on the weekend to tie for ninth and win $162.50.

February 22, 1942

... I still love you dear with all my heart. Irene (Laffoon) speaks of you all the time to all her friends. She is a grand good girl. Old Ky is getting fat. Pic wants to meet you and he and his wife will see us this summer in Pittston ...

It was back on the highway the next day, with Dad and Picard heading for the west coast of Florida. There would be no tourney to play right away, though. In those days, just as in Dad's earliest days on the tour, there wasn't a PGA event each week; sometimes there were as many as two weeks between events. A week off before the St. Petersburg Open gave Dad an opportunity to get caught up on his letter writing with his future wife. There was, after all, a lot for the two of them to arrange for their impending marriage.

February 27, 1942

It has been terrible down here for this time of the year—rain and cold winds. I have been wearing my long underwear everyday. I went out today and saw the Yankees and Cardinals practice baseball then I practiced for 3 hours ...

Sweetheart I think of you lots and I love you much more everyday. I will be up a few days ahead of time to get things arranged with you. Won't it be fun? I'll probably be nervous as hell, but who wouldn't the first time!

... Darling, I hope I can play well in the next five opens as there probably won't be very many (tournaments) next year. But everything will be ok shortly ...

For the previous month or so, Ky Laffoon had been traveling with my father and Henry Picard. Then, when the tour hit St. Petersburg, Laffoon's wife, Irene, checked into the Hotel Seneca and joined the group. Dad liked "little Irene," as he called her, but having her around made him long that much more for the wife he soon would have. Dad was on tenterhooks about his upcoming nuptials yet still managed a ninth-place tie in St. Pete before penning another note to Bonnie:

March 5, 1942

Look what date it is, the Big Affair is coming to the climax and old Jack is really coming up that way soon. I can't believe it's me but I guess it is. Tell me, have you made any plans whatsoever...?

My father and his playing partner, Ben Loving, reached the finals before losing in the Miami Four-Ball to a pair of future majors winners: Herman Keiser, who would upset Ben Hogan by one shot in the 1946 Masters, and Chandler Harper, winner of the PGA Championship in 1950. While the loss was deflating to him, it was clear that Dad's tournament golf had gotten much better. His golfing temperament had improved significantly since he met Bonnie Fox in December 1940. Her support seemed to have helped him develop more confidence and be less anxious, and he was better able to focus. His concentration and ability to perform under duress seemed to have taken a quantum leap now that she was in his life.

March 14, 1942

I arrived here (in St. Augustine) last night with Pic ... Sure has been a rough week. I played pretty good in Miami, with a little luck we might have won. The Pathe News took pictures of the match, you should see them in the movies soon ...

I enjoyed talking to you very much. You are so sweet, I love you when you say "and I am not a baby." Don't kid yourself you're my baby ...

Sweet I'll be here a week then to Pinehurst NC ...

(The Pathe Newsreels to which Dad referred were produced from 1910 until the middle of 1956, when the newsreels in general stopped production. These news clips were shown in movie theaters, silently at first with title cards explaining the action on the screen, and then with voice-over narration that was added in the early 1930s.)

On the evening of March 24, my father sat down in his room at the Park View Hotel in Southern Pines, North Carolina, and prepared to write yet another letter to Bonnie. It was his thirty-second birthday, and as Dad penned the letter it was his fervent hope that this birthday would be his last without her.

I received your letter addressed to Miami today. I'm glad to hear it is getting warmer up there as I know how cold it can get in St. Louis.

I have been losing weight in the past month, have been playing and traveling every day, haven't even had time to rest or think...

Have you had the marriage announced in church? Hope so as now it is too late for such things.

My tires are still ok and the car is running swell, should be ok for 20 thousand more miles ...

The $5,000 North and South Open was held each year on Pinehurst's No. 2 course, and in those days it was one of the more coveted titles on tour and an event that always attracted the top players. It seems, though, that my father was struggling to keep his focus on golf at that point; it was difficult for him to keep one eye on the ball, the other on his wedding date and still play well. Nevertheless, he somehow managed to finish tied for thirteenth.

With $95 in winnings, Dad headed for his home base at Fox Hill to spend a few days catching up on work there instead of playing the tour stops in Greensboro and Asheville. That way he would be well rested before making the trek to St. Louis, where he hoped to marry Bonnie on either Monday, April 6, or Tuesday, April 7.

Chapter 11
Waiting for Twenty-One

"The more you try to forget something that's still present, the more impossible it becomes." — JACK GROUT

❊❊❊

My father hit the road early on the morning of April 2 and arrived in St. Louis two days later, tired from the long drive but energized by thoughts of his long-awaited wedding day. He found the right neighborhood and parked his car on the street in front of the Fox residence at 3039 Minnesota Avenue. As he closed the car door his thoughts were pretty simple: Up a flight of stairs, a couple of knocks on the door, then, buddy boy, there she'll be.

When the front door did open, Dad came face to face with his true love, the woman who seven months earlier had agreed to become his wife. He held her in a warm embrace for several seconds and gave her a kiss on the lips. They had their arms around one another as he entered the apartment. It seemed the perfect moment, the much-anticipated culmination of a sweet and honest courtship. Yet it quickly became apparent to my father that something was amiss. Where was everybody? Bonnie's family and friends usually were right there to greet him when he arrived. Why did she seem so nervous and fidgety? The mood inside the tiny vestibule where they were standing and talking was definitely strange and uncomfortable. When Dad finally asked her what the heck was going on, she broke down and informed him that she wanted to postpone their wedding.

Bonnie Ann Fox had three older brothers and three older sisters. Being just twenty years old and having been somewhat pampered as a younger sister to so many siblings, Bonnie had very little experience in dealing with longterm commitment. Besides, it's not unusual for a young person to be both elusive and evasive, preserving a range of prerogatives. Basically, this one found herself in the classic predicament of wanting to have her cake and eat it, too. She loved my father and was intrigued by the thought of life with him. On the other hand, she wanted to go on dates like her girlfriends. She liked to roller skate, swim and go horseback riding. She wanted to go dancing and have some romance. And while she didn't mention this to Dad, she was taking seriously a $100 bet she made months earlier with her eldest brother, Famous Peter Fox, in which she'd said she would not be married before July 1, her twenty-first birthday!

My father's heart was broken, and he surely was embarrassed over the feeling of being jilted. He even had told some of his closest friends that everything was a "go," and now this. On Sunday, April 5, the *Oklahoman* newspaper carried a story regarding their wedding. Dad's great pal and confidante, Henry Picard, had told a reporter, "Here's a tidbit of information you might find interesting. My friend Jack Grout will be getting married in St. Louis any day now."

Dad spent the following two days with Bonnie and her family, slowly reconciling the shock that there would be no wedding—at least not one involving him anytime soon. By Monday morning, April 6, Dad thought that if he wasn't going to get married, he might as well get back to work. Things definitely hadn't turned out as he'd hoped and planned, but not all was lost. The love of his life told him that she still wanted to marry him; she just needed to delay the big event, at least until the fall. On his drive back to Pennsylvania, he took that bit of consolation with him and, of course, the wonderful jelly and preserves that mother Annie had made for him.

> *April 9, 1942*
>
> *I arrived here (at Fox Hill) Tuesday evening right in the middle of a snow storm that's really a pip. I am just about to freeze to death. I wish I had stayed in St. Louis for another week at least.*
>
> *Sweetheart I miss you terrible. The next time I come to visit you, we will either get married there immediately or we will in Chicago. No more postponing. It's either the next time or never and I mean it!*
>
> *... I do love you more than you know, as you know I am a terrible romance but after awhile you can change me...*

As he returned to Pennsylvania, my father was perplexed by the temporary delay in his wedding plans but still aware that he was, in many ways, a lucky man. He loved what he did for a living, had many good friends to share his life with, and always had goals for tomorrow, next week and next month. He was comforted that those goals included sharing the rest of his life with his sweetheart, even if he had to wait a few more months to finally get married.

Back at Fox Hill, Dad was ready for the golf season to get rolling. He knew that once the club got busy, it would remain so until the first snowfall. It turned out, though, that the 1942 season was slow to gain momentum. The spring and early summer weather that year was unpredictable; one day it was nice, and the next it would turn cold and wet. Dad wrote in one of the letters he sent to St. Louis: "The weather has been terrible here ... rain everyday and colder than billy hell. I have been wearing winter clothes and top coat, don't believe I like the cold weather—Florida for me!" It was so unseasonably cool even by the middle of June that the local swimming pools hadn't opened yet, and it seemed that everyone was still walking around with a cold.

April 15, 1942

I was sorry that you were out when I called last night. I had been thinking about you. I just wanted to hear your voice again...

The weather is very nice again and it makes me feel like playing or practicing once more. I must go to Philadelphia soon as I qualify for the PGA there ...

I have seen lots of (motion) picture shows since coming here-nothing to do, must stop as you know they are tough on my eyes ... Are you having lots of fun? I hope so as you enjoy yourself very much going out ...

Then again, on April 27:

I hope you are enjoying the nice weather. We too are having our share of it.

We have had lots of golfers out and everybody is having a swell time. I play in Philadelphia next Monday qualifying for PGA. I sure hope I can get in as I want to play very badly.

Baby, why don't you send me a picture also your size for some new boots? The man was here and I didn't know the size ...

I have been practicing everyday and I am playing pretty good. I want to see you during the Tam O'Shanter Open (in July), so save your vacation for that week.

You say you have had two dates. I'll bet you had a nice time, didn't you? I know I am a terrible romance. I guess to be a good one-one must need plenty of practice or be a natural ...

I won't be able to play in very many tournaments this summer as we won't be able to buy over 7 gallons of gas each week. That's going to be bad. Sure hope U.S. wins the War quick as things are a mess ...

On April 30, there was the first indication in one of Dad's letters that an actual wedding date was under discussion:

... I ordered your boots yesterday and I know you will like them very much. They will be brown ones and you should receive them in a week at your house.

So you want to get married during the Tam Open. Well maybe so—but I guess it would be better to wait just three more months which would be November. You see darling there are lots of things I would have to change if we got married in July. For instance, my house, trips, and all plans. This crazy country up here is badly in need of apts ... The nearest good ones are 10 miles away. Also after May 15 each car gets about 7 gallons per week. I guess I'll start riding the bus too ...

Sweetie I must ask you again when your birthday is? I have forgotten. Would you send me a picture? You know you promised. Don't be a diddie bump and think I wouldn't like it. I want one - believe me ...

My father missed the cut in the early-May qualifier for the PGA Championship, writing later that he "couldn't do anything at all with my putter and I didn't play any too well either." But his disappointment with not getting to play the major championship was no greater than his concern about what was going on in his courtship of Bonnie, and events in the world around them. Voluntary gas rationing proved ineffective, and by spring 1942 numerous eastern states had instituted some form of mandatory rationing. By December mandatory controls extended across the entire country. On average, motorists who used their cars for "nonessential" purposes were restricted to three gallons per week.

The swimming pool at Fox Hill never opened because of cold and wet weather that extended beyond the Fourth of July, and many of the club's usual summertime festivities had to be cancelled. When my father heard that everyone had to sign up for the gasoline rations by May 15, he told Bonnie that he'd be lucky to get four or five gallons a week. Nevertheless, when he received his gasoline ration card, he wrote and told her the relatively good news: "I got 3-B, which entitles me to 57 gallons for seven weeks, could be worse, I guess."

The war's toll was felt everywhere, and deteriorating conditions had a dramatic effect on professional golf competition. Dad watched all of this with a mixture of emotions, writing at one point, "Hope the war is over soon as business is getting tough. I will stay around (the) club a lot this summer as traveling is too expensive; can make more being here. I will only play in a few, this summer the Tam for sure to see my baby ... "

By the spring of 1942 the military draft was in full swing, and it seemed that all of Dad's friends were going into the Army. By the end of June as many as fifteen members of the Philadelphia Section of the PGA were in the armed forces, and many more were in defense plants and shipyards. With what seemed an indulgence in self-pity, Dad lamented in one of his letters that "I haven't been having any fun since arriving here (at Fox Hill). I don't feel the urge to go out ... I have no gasoline now that the ration is on—so I am a dead old bird."

Given the conditions, my father increasingly missed his Bonnie and ached to be with her. To accommodate his young fiancée, Dad had reluctantly agreed that maybe she ought to go out for some fun at night with her friends. There were times, though, when this accommodation on his part meant that she would have dates with other boys. It was hard for Dad to understand and tolerate this, and one evening, feeling tired and dejected, he wrote: "Seems so foolish to be apart—but maybe it's best, I don't know." Then he added, "But I can't blame the boys for rushing. I guess I would, too."

Dad tried to avoid obsessing over his frustrations by staying as busy as possible. That spring, for instance, he accepted an assignment as judge at a local boxing contest. "Won't that be fun?" he wrote. "I hope my decisions will be ok as the spectators get mad as all hell if you don't. I think I'll get me a bodyguard."

During the spring and summer there would be other welcome distractions. One of Dad's club members gave him a season pass to see the Class-A Scranton Red Sox baseball team, and he reported also that "I went to the circus Sat. night ... I got a big kick out of the clowns, they sure are funny. Tonight I go to the fights, they will be very good ones. Do you like prize fights? Maybe we will go some time."

Throughout this period, my father continued to monitor his draft status. He wrote, "Sweetheart, I am still in Class 3-A! And, I know I will be so for a good time as I am last to be called ... " But, as if to sound optimistic that military life might not be so bad, he added, "My brother Dutch has been in for some time and likes it very much."

While waiting for the draft board's summons, Dad found opportunities to play in golf events that contributed to the war effort. Exhibition matches such as one he played in front of a nice crowd in Harrisburg were both popular and necessary in that they gave spectators a diversion from the war effort and they supported war-bond drives.

In early June 1942, the region surrounding Fox Hill experienced an aspect of the war that brought home dramatically the seriousness of the global situation when a blackout plunged the region into darkness. Blackouts were just another disruption to everyday life in America, brought on by the war. Beginning in the spring of that year, these precautions against enemy air raids became more frequent, especially along the Atlantic coastline. The blackout system was designed so that electronic sirens would scream the warning that enemy bombers could be approaching and that a raid could occur within minutes. Everyone would scramble to black out all lights and lamps. Citizens were instructed that if they were driving an automobile, they were to pull to the side of the road immediately and douse their headlights. Streetlights went out. Patrol cars would drive around to make certain that all lights were extinguished. Every town and city would be enveloped in blackness. My father wrote that "our blackout on June 2 was a success, but we had a big fire just as the whole affair got underway."

During June, my father kept up his steady pace of letter writing, sending a note every five or six days. Besides the iffy weather and the worsening war, those letters mostly focused on the plans the future Mr. and Mrs. Jack Grout had for seeing each other at the Tam O'Shanter National Open and Bonnie's pivotal twenty-first birthday on July 1. Clearly Dad was anxious; his letters had repeated references such as, "I will leave for Chicago on July 19 and will arrive in Chicago on the 20th by train. I hope to see you then, if not I'll be terribly hurt," and "Honey, why don't you tell me what you want for your birthday? Do you want some more boots? Or would a little doggie do. A fellow here has some of the best little dogs I ever saw and they are cute, too."

Dad was delighted when Bonnie's parents finally got their own telephone and he no longer had to coordinate his calls to her with the store downstairs. He wrote, "Some night I'll surprise my baby and call her. Do you want me to call you on your birthday? I'll do it if you want!" Of course, my father did place a telephone call on her big day. And in a letter the next day he wrote, "I sure was happy to hear your voice last night. You sounded so sweet. I guess it was pretty late when I called, but the ball game lasted too long. I thought there was only one game." Then he added, "Just think, you are 21 now, maybe I shouldn't call you baby anymore, eh what."

July 8, 1942

Your letter was swell ... I know we are going to have lots of fun in Chicago. You go ahead and enjoy yourself swimming and horseback riding, you enjoy that better than riding around or walking the old golf course.

It will probably be hot there so bring along some cool dresses ... I want you to meet "Jukebox" Munday. He is a pal of mine, so - when we go out to the club I want my baby to have on the cutest dress in the world ...

July 13, 1942

I hope by now you are enjoying yourself in the big city. Your letter was swell and I am sorry I can't arrive before next Monday ... I hope you can meet me at the station. I want to kiss my baby as soon as possible so please be there ...

We will have some fun, you bet—maybe even have a cocktail or two ...

On Monday, July 20, 1942, my father pulled into Chicago's Central Station aboard a Michigan Central train. As he'd hoped, both Ed Bradley and Bonnie were waiting there to welcome him. On paper, it appeared the purpose of his visit was to take part in a big golf tournament, but there was so much my father felt he needed to accomplish that week. First and foremost, he wanted to spend as much time as possible with his sweetheart. He also hoped to play well and make a good showing in the tournament, but maybe just as important to him was that a few of his closest pals were going to meet his future bride. Dad was anxious to hear what friends such as Rod Munday and Mr. and Mrs. Picard thought about the young woman he planned to marry.

The Tam O'Shanter National Open that July was rightly billed as the biggest golfing extravaganza in history. It was also the most unusual —like a circus with sideshows for practically everyone in the expected large galleries. The tournament was, for example, a golf double-header, promoted as a first in the history of the game. The whole affair began early in the week with the All-American Amateur Tournament and its field of two hundred golfers. Then the Tam's National Open started on Thursday with the sixty-four lowest-scoring amateurs carrying over into the open competition against the pros.

Both the size of the Tam's starting field and the total prize list were advertised as the largest ever. The combined fields in the two tournaments totaled nearly five hundred players, and there was a purse of $15,500 for the pros and $1,300 in war bonds for the winners in the amateur division, making it the richest event in the history of American golf.

While the tournament seemed destined for success, the week had its share of calamity. The event's colorful founder and promoter, George S. May, issued each professional a numbered placard about six-by-four inches and expected it to be pinned to the back of the player's shirt. Always an innovator, May wanted the numbers to help the gallery identify their favorites, as in other sports that had adopted uniform numbers. The pros, however, thought this insulting, and they revolted. At the start of the third round, for example, Joe Kirkwood Sr. angrily declared that he would not be a "circus horse" for anybody and refused to wear a number. "I've been playing golf for twenty-five years," the veteran trick-shot artist said, "and I don't propose to start plastering a number on my back ... "

A group of stars including Byron Nelson and Paul Runyan eventually held a meeting with May to fight it out. May wouldn't back down, though, and several pros, including Tommy Armour, eventually withdrew from the tourney.

My father and Henry Picard were paired during the Tam's first two rounds, and as Bonnie stood near the practice area one day, Picard sauntered her way for a chat. "Look Bon," he said, "you know you got a good man there and he's not going to wait around forever." Henry was doing his best to convince her that she should stop dating other fellows and quit dragging her feet about it!

Despite the controversy over player numbers, the tournament was completed. Dad finished in a tie for thirty-fifth, thirteen strokes behind Byron Nelson's winning score, and had a calm and happy week with the woman he looked forward to taking as his wife.

Soon the letters flowed again:

> *Aug. 11, 1942*
>
> *I talked to Ky today. How about going on a mountain trip after we are married, down near Arkansas? They have boating, fishing, hunting, eating and horses to ride. We will have lots of fun. Ky and Irene might go too, also the Revolta's and Picards—lots of cabins that are clean ... I don't think there will be any golf tournaments, so we'll just lie around and have fun ...*
>
> *Honey, I thought about you all day and even dreamed about you last night. Again, I say I love you and adore you. I miss you terrible ...*

By the fall of 1942 the tour was playing a truncated schedule because of the war, but local and sectional PGA events continued in a limited way and contributed to the war effort. Tournament officials set aside twenty percent of prize monies from all PGA events for defense bonds. A number of exhibitions to raise money for the Red Cross were staged by the golf association, with stars such as Hogan, Snead, Nelson and other players, including my father, Picard and Demaret participating and taking their expenses in bonds. Hollywood stars including Bob Hope and Bing Crosby showed up at various stops on the tour to give a boost to the fund-raising exhibitions.

My father was paired with Crosby at a celebrity exhibition match at the old IBM Country Club in Binghamton, New York, in early September. The crooner had been hopping from city to city on sleeper stops and doing his bit for the war effort. The Grout-Crosby pairing won the match before a crowd estimated at more than three thousand, and then from a platform near the first tee the singer wowed the audience with songs. "Crosby sang eight songs that were dudes," my dad reported.

After each song someone would shout out something like, "I'll give five hundred dollars if Bing will sing 'Sweet Leilani.' " Or "I'd pay one thousand dollars to hear him sing 'Deep in the Heart of Texas.'" Besides the substantial money generated for the war effort by Bing's auction, all attendees paid one dollar to watch the exhibition. To cap the day, Dad got Bing to agree to send Bonnie Fox an autographed picture once he returned to California.

***

Soon after his Chicago foray, my father was abruptly tugged back to earth by two disparate events. At Fox Hill he had to deal with a pay-related strike of the club's caddies at the start of a busy August weekend, an unwelcome occurrence in any club pro's life. He got an even bigger jolt from a story in the next day's newspaper reporting that the draft timetable for men of military age was being moved up. In essence, all those classified 3-A were going to be called to active duty within the next six months. Dad had begun to think that he might not be called up at all, so this latest bit of news led him to think seriously about his options for military service.

As the war dragged on, single men became prime targets for induction, and my father now knew that he could be called up at any time. If the call came, his first choice would have been service in the Navy. He continued to search for options, though, and when he heard that his tour buddy Jimmy Thomson had enlisted in the Coast Guard, he began to consider that branch of service. But then he found out that his eyesight was too poor for the Coast Guard.

As of the third week of September, Dad hadn't heard anything from the Luzerne County Draft Board in quite some time, and he wrote to Bonnie that he was beginning to think maybe they wouldn't be contacting him anytime soon. The very next morning, though, he heard from the draft board: Dad received a questionnaire and was required to hand it in on September 28. While he anxiously awaited the processing of his paperwork, he witnessed five more of his friends depart for duty.

At about this time Dad received a letter from his younger brother, Dutch, who was stationed at Fort Hood, Texas. Dutch had been in the Medical Corps for ten months, and, while he was having no particular problems with military life, he advised Dad against getting involved in any branch of the service. Dutch understood how uncomfortable his quiet, often-shy brother would have been under the rigid discipline of the armed forces.

In late September, Dad heard from his draft board that it was likely they would contact him in December for induction. Wanting to serve his country but also hoping to control his own fate, my father made arrangements to join the Auto Transportation Corps, which carried troops, their equipment, civilian aid materials and Army dependents to distant points. Dad said "even that would be better than being an army buck private!" By this time, Dad knew he was a clear target for the draft, being unmarried and with no children.

Growing more anxious, Dad visited the Navy induction board in early October. He thought that if he could be a Navy petty officer, once he and Bonnie were married, perhaps they could be stationed in nearby Philadelphia. To Dad's disappointment, though, there were no vacancies in the Navy officer program.

Dad had decided by now to travel to St. Louis to see his future wife, but just before departing Pennsylvania he learned of another potential wartime opportunity. Henry Picard wrote a letter encouraging him to consider taking a five-month radio course that was being offered at a civilian flight school in Oklahoma. Picard himself had already been there for about six weeks and was studying to be a pilot. Thus when my father closed the door to his Fox Hill pro shop for the final time that fall, he was seriously considering enrolling in that flight-school program.

***

In the late fall of 1942, with the world at war, with gas rationing and other war-imposed inconveniences affecting every American citizen, and with daily life across the globe marked by fear and uncertainty, two young and earnest products of the midwestern United States of America came together in mutual determination to make their partnership permanent. That is, John Frederick Grout of Oklahoma City, Oklahoma, and Bonnie Ann Fox of St. Louis, Missouri, decided together that it was time for them to become husband and wife.

Though my parents first met nearly two years before they got married, the number of days they actually spent together prior to their wedding was less than twenty. Their long-distance and sometimes difficult relationship was nurtured over that long period by an occasional brief personal visit and a few long-distance telephone calls, but primarily by a steady stream of warm, loving, and at times unintentionally comic letters.

Dad's frustration with the long-distance courtship had boiled over at times, as in June 1942 when he wrote to Bonnie:

> *Darling I have to see you. I can't go on forever just writing you and maybe seeing you for just a short time like we have ... Ours is the darndest romance I have ever heard of. I guess ours will come after we are married.*

Even as he finally was able to feel that Bonnie really would marry him, Dad expressed the anxiety he was feeling about the impact the war was having on day-to-day life:

> *Our honeymoon, the way it looks, might be disappointing ... No gas, no tires and lots of headaches. Isn't it awful?*

Finally, on Saturday, November 7, 1942, some twenty-three months after he and my mother had their first date on a magical moonlit night in Miami Beach, Dad was able to put aside his frustrations and anxieties and celebrate the launch of a new life. On that date, my father took his beautiful Bonnie's hand in marriage in the tiny Ave Maria chapel of the Annunciation Church at 1009 South Sixth Street in St. Louis.

The couples' exchange of wedding vows was witnessed by a small group of friends and family during an evening service with the good Father William A. Hawkins officiating. True to his oft-demonstrated desire for privacy in his personal life, my father had made it clear that he didn't "want a bunch of people there" that he didn't know, and he "would rather be married in the rectory where it would be private." There were, for sure, a few people whom Dad very much wanted to be there, but even in this modest hope he faced another disappointment: His great friends the Laffoons couldn't attend because Ky, Henry Picard and Byron Nelson were in Oklahoma City, preparing for an exhibition match they would play with Bob Hope the next day for the benefit of the Oklahoma City War Chest. Friendship was one thing. Service to country in a time of war was another.

By all accounts, Dad was more than happy to put the life of a single man behind him. He was thirty-two and had been on his own for more than a dozen years. He was ready to settle down. At twenty-one and having lived a somewhat sheltered life, however, his bride was too young to have had vast life experience. Bonnie's older sister Vera, in fact, saw her as not having a very good self-image or much self-confidence. Even though she seemed very much in love with this man she was marrying, she probably was not as prepared to tie the knot as was her eager fiancé.

Perhaps fittingly, the exchange of vows had barely been completed when the young bride got an eye-opening look at the social awkwardness she occasionally would see from her husband through the next forty-six years. After the ceremony the wedding party and guests were gathered in front of the church, exchanging pleasantries, when suddenly the bridegroom jumped into a car with his best man, Ed Bradley, and the bride's father, Pop Fox. The trio headed off to the reception, leaving my mother at the church with the rest of the family! This was one of Bonnie's first lessons in my dad's lack of regard for formality; he knew there would be more than enough time at the reception to talk about things. Besides, it was cold outside and he didn't like cold weather. As the men's car turned a corner and sped away, mom's sister Renie called out, "Look, there goes Jack!"

My father's unfortunate departure from the church was not the only bump the couple would encounter in their first days as man and wife. The next came during their camping honeymoon at the beautiful Grand Lake O' the Cherokees in northeastern Oklahoma. The Laffoons had joined the newlyweds at the lake, and Dad and Ky went fishing one day. When they returned, Dad discovered that Bonnie and some friends, plus some soldiers they had befriended, had gotten into a case of champagne he had brought to share with his bride. Dad was upset about this and told Bonnie so. She told him not to leave her alone if he didn't like what was happening!

Next there was car trouble and Bonnie's first exposure to Dad's considerable temper. As the couple drove to Oklahoma City after the honeymoon, their car had a flat tire. Months earlier, Dad had written to Bonnie that his car was running well and that two tires that were "iffy" should be fine for quite some time. One of the tires blew. When Dad got out to change it, he was angry. In fact, Mom said the temper he displayed scared her; she'd never seen him this way. He hoisted the tire iron up like he was going to whack the car with it!

Taken in the context of the day, my father's occasional frustrations were understandable. Here he finally had taken the hand of the young woman he loved so much, and he desperately wanted to settle into a quiet, warm, loving life with her. Yet he faced possible separation from her for service in a war that was consuming the world. As the newlyweds spent time with Dad's parents in Oklahoma City over the Thanksgiving holidays, then moved on to Fort Worth to see his brother, Dick, Dad had to be feeling more and more pressure.

With time through the holiday season to reflect on his situation, Dad finally decided to follow Henry Picard's advice and enroll in the Spartan School of Aeronautics' Wartime Training Service Program in Tulsa. Beginning in January 1943, Dad worked in what was called a civilian pilot training program, learning the basics of aircraft takeoffs, landings and navigation but shifting eventually to aircraft sheet metal work with his buddy Ky Laffoon. It wasn't military service, but it was preparation for jobs that would allow him to help in the civilian war effort if needed.

Eventually, though, months after his marriage, Dad received an unexpected message that removed permanently the cloud of uncertainty that had darkened his mood. America needed personnel for the war effort, but it didn't want to draft men who had medical issues that might become worse during military service. Even though he made his living as an athlete, playing and teaching golf and even supporting the war effort through his charity golf exhibitions, Dad had a chronic back condition. He was also terribly nearsighted. The war effort may have needed him, but, in truth, it didn't want him. He was married now; he was in his thirties, and he had medical issues. For the U.S. military, he was an unacceptable risk.

The official word came from Dad's draft board in a message both brief and direct: John Frederick Grout had been classified 4-F: physically unable to serve in the armed forces of the United States of America.

Chapter 12
Husband, Father and Club Pro

"If you know what's right, always do what's right" — *JACK GROUT*

✻✻✻

It was, in my view, a huge bonus for a man of Dad's quiet personality that his work in golf threw him together with a wide range of unusual and sometimes downright bizarre characters who brought frequent laughter to his life. Dad and his new bride would get a full dose of one of these characters—maybe, as it turned out, too heavy a dose—when they shared an apartment with Ky and Irene Laffoon in Tulsa through the winter and spring of 1943 while Dad labored in the civilian pilot training program.

The tiny two-bedroom, one-bath apartment gave Mom and Dad a close-up view of the lusty and rough-hewn Laffoon, an Arkansas native first befriended by Dad in the fall of 1927. With his noble nose, sturdy chin and high cheekbones, Laffoon was a striking person and considered himself quite a ladies man. He had raven-black hair slicked back and parted down the middle in a style mimicking Dad's Argentine friend, Martin Pose. When Ky was getting dressed, he'd preen in front of the mirror, pat his hair into place and say, "Boy, you're the best looking man around. I don't know how the women can stand it!"

The two men traveled and played golf together for nearly twenty years, and Dad always enjoyed being with his unpredictable friend, quietly tolerating his often-eccentric behaviors. Ky Laffoon was an intense man, capable of spontaneous fits of temper both on and off the course. He was known to overindulge robustly in all manner of things, including drinking, eating, chewing tobacco and playing cards. Part of his legend involves the range of articles he kept in the trunk of his car, said to include not only his golf clubs but cans of sardines, bottles of scotch, several pistols, a shotgun, boxes of shells and old newspapers.

The Laffoons had been married for about seven years when my parents moved in with them. Ky and Irene were like a number of other couples who were regulars on the pro circuit—the Hogans, Nelsons and Demarets included—who had no children and thus were able to focus all their energies on the business of golf. Their investment with Ky's brother-in-law in a chicken farm in Elgin, about forty miles northwest of Chicago, had provided them with income to fund their travels together on the tour for many years.

For a while, my parents had fun living with the Laffoons, although at times Ky could veer out of control. Occasionally, for example, the two couples would engage in the ancient game of hide-and-seek. Before their game would begin, all lights in the apartment would be turned off. Awkward moments can ensue in such a setting, especially among four healthy young adults. Generally it all was pretty innocent, but Laffoon always had eyes for Mom, and while they hid together in a tiny closet one evening, he put the move on her, to no avail other than to give offense.

Ky apparently decided one day that he would find out for certain whether my mother could resist his self-perceived charms. Laffoon convinced my father, his gullible friend, he ought to drive with Irene so that my mother could ride with Ky as they all went off somewhere. As Dad's car disappeared into the distance, Ky feigned car trouble so that he and Mom had to stop. Once he pulled over, he made a lurch for my mother, but she screamed and jumped out of the car. Ky got out, too, and chased her around the vehicle several times until she convinced him to stop. A short time later Mom told my father about the incident, and she said it really shook him up. Ky had betrayed his friend, and it hurt and angered Dad so much that, Mom said, "At the time, he wanted to kill Laffoon."

Through the months it became clear that golf was the sole interest my father and Ky Laffoon shared. Nor was my mother anything like Irene Laffoon, Valerie Hogan, Louise Nelson or many of the other pros' wives. Mom was at least a decade younger than most of them and had different tastes and interests. Also, Jack Grout had no desire for his wife to traipse around the country, following him from tournament to tournament. My mother did travel to a few events with Dad in 1943 and 1944 and then to others later, but she didn't enjoy the whole tournament scene.

Faced with these differences in personality and style, my parents eventually opted out of their apartment-sharing arrangement with the Laffoons. Unfazed, Ky and Irene quickly paired up with the fine Australian pro Jim Ferrier and his wife, Norma, who followed her husband step for step on the golf course. Laffoon laughed and cavorted his way to a good career, winning ten tournaments, but he is remembered more for his unusual antics. Once, exasperated by his erratic putting, he took a gun out of the trunk of his car and shot the offending club several times while yelling, "Take that, you SOB! That's the last time you three-putt on me!" Another time, Ben Hogan, asleep in the back seat of a car as Laffoon drove, awoke to feel air rushing in. Peeking over the seat, Hogan was startled not to see a driver. Eventually he realized that Laffoon was driving with his head out the open window, his extended hand holding a golf club that he was dragging on the pavement to sharpen the lower edge of the face!

***

With my mother having become his permanent partner and with the knowledge by the spring of 1943 that he would not be drafted into the military, Dad could focus on the career path ahead and on life with his new bride. Clearly, given the quality of his golf swing, Dad could have chosen to intensify his efforts to become mentally tougher on the course and develop more of the competitive fire that Byron Nelson, Sam Snead and other great pros said was the only thing missing from his golf arsenal. Or he could focus on being a first-rate club professional and playing the tour as a sideline when it was convenient or when such play could help elevate his status at his club of the moment.

Making that decision easier for Dad, at least in the short term, was that the PGA slashed its 1943 tournament schedule to only three events because of World War II. Even the four "majors" were cancelled that year, with Bobby Jones suspending the Masters Tournament for the duration of the war and allowing a small herd of cattle to graze the manicured grounds of his Augusta National Golf Club. Dad thus would play in only a couple of tournaments in '43 and three more in '44. He had decided that the bulk of his energies during this period would be devoted to building his résumé as a club pro while simply maintaining his game for the day when the golf business came back full force.

After five months of training at the School of Aeronautics in Tulsa, my father was furloughed along with other trainees, their places taken by pilots returning from the war. Dad and Mom saw this as the opportunity to achieve a graceful end to their apartment-sharing with the Laffoons and announced that they would head for Chicago to spend the summer with Vera and Ed Bradley. There, Dad did some teaching and played in Red Cross benefit matches, and he also interviewed for a few positions at area clubs. Laffoon had recommended several Chicago-area jobs, including the Illinois Golf Club at Northbrook, soon to be renamed Green Acres. The club featured an A.W. Tillinghast layout, and Laffoon had told Dad the operation had "vitality" and that he could make some money there.

Bouncing from club job to club job might be viewed negatively today but was not at all unusual in Dad's time. The midlevel tour pros tried hard to continue advancing up the ladder of better and better clubs, and when they left a job, there always was another pro ready to take their place. In this case, before heading to Oklahoma City that fall to work on a six-month contract with Henry Picard at Twin Hills Country Club, Dad signed on with Green Acres as golf professional for the 1944 season.

***

With the Green Acres contract in his pocket, Dad found welcome respite going back to Oklahoma City that fall of 1943 to work for Picard, then in his second year as Twin Hills' head pro. Even in the welcoming turf of Twin Hills, though, Dad found that the war had had considerable impact. While Picard and his family lived rent-free in a Twin Hills-owned house next door to the club, Picard actually worked at the club only on weekends. He was employed during the week in a war-plant job at Douglas Aircraft Company. It was useful to Picard, then, to have a trusted friend around to run the golf operation in his weekday absence. And it was a good situation for my dad; good club jobs were increasingly hard to come by as the war deepened.

That fall, in a gesture to help the war effort, Twin Hills hosted a servicemen's golf tournament and exhibition that attracted fifty-four soldiers and sailors to the upscale club for a day of golf and recreation. Prior to an exhibition of shot-making for the servicemen and their families, my father and Henry played an eighteen-hole match against two hot-shot Oklahomans named Labron Harris and Jimmie Schatz. While the amateurs won the match, it was my father who provided the day's highlight, scoring a hole in one—his fourth—on the par-three, 168-yard eleventh hole!

Given the success of the day, the club quickly decided to sponsor another exhibition match to support the government's war-bond drive. That late-October event drew players such as Byron Nelson, Johnny Revolta, Jim Ferrier, Leonard Dodson, Toney Penna, Bo Wininger, Labron Harris and Ky Laffoon and attracted about two thousand spectators who paid a buck apiece to see two days of golf.

***

After the truncated tour season of 1943, the pro circuit began returning to normalcy in 1944, offering twenty-three events and more than $250,000 in prize money. Golf clubs across the country rebounded, too, and Henry Picard was among those caught up in the revival after

Douglas Aircraft released him from his full-time job. At the urging of friends, Picard accepted the head professional job at the Harrisburg Country Club, only about twelve miles from his former home club in Hershey. My Uncle Dick succeeded him at Twin Hills, resigning as club pro and manager at Glen Garden in Fort Worth to return to his native Oklahoma.

As they watched this golf version of musical chairs unfold, my mom and dad were planning their new life together in Chicago, where Dad soon would begin his duties at Green Acres. They took a tiny apartment—all they could afford—in Winnetka, about nineteen miles north of downtown. It was a good spot for them, situated just a short drive from mom's oldest sister, Vera, and her husband and children, and less than five miles southeast of Dad's new place of employment.

In his later years, my father would talk freely about the lessons he'd learned along the way, both as a touring pro and as a club professional. And it was clear that he learned some interesting lessons about human nature at Green Acres. For the thirty-four-year-old new head pro, these members were a handful. They seemed to have fierce likes and relentless dislikes. Dad saw their behaviors as coarse and fine, crass and noble—all at the same time. He was impressed by the way his members treated their offspring; nothing was too good for their children. They spared no expense to give them the best education possible. Yet Dad noticed that the club's membership did not always treat one another with the same amount of regard and respect. He explained it as a bit of a caste system, meaning that some families were "in" and some families were "out." It wasn't always a matter of how much money a family had, either. It seemed to be more about how a member made his money, and a family's history.

By season's end, Dad would come to sense that his position as the golf pro was treated with little respect. He felt things had been different at clubs where he'd worked in Oklahoma and Texas; the members were proud of their clubs but somehow less demanding. He knew, though, that his best chance to make serious money in the club-pro business was at the larger clubs of the East and Midwest, and he thus accepted his time at Green Acres as a valuable and necessary learning experience.

My mother's introduction to Ben and Valerie Hogan occurred during Dad's one season at Green Acres. The Hogans had invited my folks to join them for dinner during a Chicago-area tournament. When Mom and Dad entered the dining room, the Hogans were seated and waiting for them. As my parents approached, Valerie nudged her husband and said, "Ben, stand up when a lady comes into view." He looked at his wife and gruffly replied, "Aw goddammit, I'll stand up when it means something."

Both my parents overheard the snub. Dad knew how gruff Hogan could be and whispered to Mom to just let it slide. But my mother didn't forget the insensitive remark and told me about it many years later. In a number of personal accounts, Hogan would state that he "always stood when a woman entered the room." It's true that at times Hogan was gracious and polite, but at others he was rude and one of the world's greatest putdown artists.

***

While Dad opted to play a very limited number of pro tournaments in 1944, he still looked forward to competing when his schedule allowed. Thus when the PGA Championship returned after a one-year war absence, Dad eagerly drove to Chicago's Tam O'Shanter Club for the qualifying rounds. He played well, too, qualifying with a very solid 72-69. It was a sign of the tough economic times, though, that as much as he wanted to play in the major championship that August, Dad decided he couldn't afford to travel all the way to Spokane, Washington. He wasn't the only one who made such a disappointing decision: Dad's friend Ky Laffoon also qualified but decided to stay home on his Illinois chicken farm.

Even if Dad had made the trip to Spokane and had finished well, he likely wouldn't have won enough cash to cover his expenses; the tournament's total purse was just $14,500. Bob Hamilton, a twenty-eight-year-old pro from Evansville, Indiana, was the surprise winner that year. He shocked Byron Nelson in the 36-hole final. This was Nelson's third loss in four PGA finals matches, and the disappointed Texan declared, "Four times in the championship finals and I've won only one; maybe I should just give up the game." Nelson would get over his disappointment, though; he won the PGA the next year, taking his fifth and final major championship.

Dad played only one other significant tournament in 1944 – George May's popular extravaganza at Tam O'Shanter, which by then was called the All-American Open, a combination of his Tam O'Shanter National Open and the All-American Amateur from 1942. This time the entrepreneur and showman was offering a total purse of $30,100, but after opening the tournament with a solid 71, Dad faded in the following rounds and finished out of the money.

By this time my mother and father were settling down nicely in marriage and, in fact, were beginning a family; Mom was five months pregnant with my brother John. Mother was only twenty-three years old but was well on her way to becoming the woman Dad had expressed a yearning for in many of the letters he had sent her during their two-year courtship. She'd done an excellent job of heeding his call for her to "practice cooking and sewing, housework, loving, phone calls, letter writing and taking care of me."

While now his views seem quaint, or worse, my father's belief was that a wife's place was in the home, that it was his function as the husband to take care of his spouse by being a good provider. He worked hard to ensure that Mom wouldn't have to take a job. He wanted her to be contented at home so that she would be there to take care of him when he returned in the evening and always available to tend to their children. His were old-fashioned views, for sure, but the arrangement was satisfying to him, and to my mother and they settled into a happy partnership.

Having children was important to my parents, both having come from large families. But Jack and Bonnie differed a bit on the matter of ideal family size. Dad's experience as a youth seemed to have convinced him that smaller families were more manageable. He recalled clearly the limitations that came with having too many mouths to feed and too much clothing to buy. Before he and Mother were married, Dad even went on record that he'd be content with having just one child, especially a girl who looked just like the lovely Bonnie. My mother, though, had other ideas and let Dad in on the plans a short time after they were married. She told him they were going to have four children and was quite definite that their family would be made up of two boys and two girls. And that's exactly how things worked out!

❊❊❊

The onset of fall's cooler temperatures in the Midwest is a clear first signal that winter is on the way, and those cooler days and the changing colors tend to stimulate a surge in play at most golf clubs. At Green Acres, though, by early October most of the members had stored their golf clubs for the winter. With cold weather advancing, Dad's ability to make money from lessons had just about dried up, so he and mom decided to give up their rented apartment and spend the next several months near her family in St. Louis. Mother's baby was due, and she knew she could count on getting personal care from her relatives.

Before he and Mom left Chicago, Dad shifted career gears again: He accepted the head professional position at Butterfield Country Club on Chicago's west side for the 1945 golf season. Another year, another job change. As was typical for club pros in his day, Dad was building a varied résumé and also a strong tolerance for new challenges. Each club provided new teaching situations, new lessons about the golf business, different types of people, new preparation for long-term success. Dad was building toward the day when his jobs would be in more prominent clubs and of longer duration. He was learning to be a true professional in the business of golf.

***

The first of Jack and Bonnie Grout's four children, my big brother, John Frederick Grout Jr., was born on December 18, 1944, in St. Louis. Dad and Mom, though, barely had time to celebrate John's arrival. Just a month later, Dad's mother died unexpectedly of a heart attack at age sixty-eight, shortly after returning home from the installation service for Catholic Bishop Eugene J. McGuinness at the Cathedral of Our Lady of Perpetual Help in Oklahoma City. Dad had left Oklahoma when he was only nineteen, and his relationship with his parents was loving but not especially close. Still, he was deeply saddened as he traveled back to Oklahoma to grieve Nellie Grout's passing with his father and the rest of the family.

My father wasn't stoic, but he tended to accept quietly most of what life threw at him. This included his mother's death and, later, the passing of his father and four of his seven brothers and sisters. Dad tended to move steadily through the bad times and the good with even approaches, always anticipating that things would work out well in the end. And usually they did.

Dad's new job at Butterfield Country Club didn't require him to be there until early spring, so he was able to play some of the tournaments on the 1944-1945 winter pro tour. The tour rebounded from its wartime slowdown in a big way in 1945, with thirty-eight events scheduled and total prize money of $435,380. For a winter-tour veteran like Dad, it must have seemed enticing, if only for a little while. Dad enjoyed the camaraderie of the tour, and there was some comfort in knowing that he would be on the road and away from his family for only six weeks. With no income from golf lessons or pro-shop sales during the winter, the idea of winning a few bucks on the winter circuit was appealing. So off he went, through New Orleans and on to Gulfport, Pensacola, Jacksonville, Miami and Charlotte. Playing very well at times, poorly at others, Dad managed only about $500 in winnings through the six tournaments. His smooth swing aside, it was becoming clear that Jack Grout was not going to get rich playing golf!

My father had spent many of the previous fifteen winters on the tournament circuit. During that time he'd grown accustomed to the too-often-mediocre food, middling hotels and low remuneration he found on the road. He began to feel more and more that it was time for him to say "enough already." His total transformation from tour pro to club pro didn't happen overnight, but the process began to accelerate as the winter of 1945 gave way to spring.

When Dad arrived at Butterfield CC in March 1945, America was ready to transition from wartime to peacetime. American cities would explode in celebration when Germany surrendered to the Allies on May 8, and again on August 14 when word of Japan's capitulation marked the end of the dreadful conflict. The U.S. economy began a period of exceptionally strong growth due to pent-up consumer demand. The automobile industry converted back to producing cars, and new industries such as aviation and electronics grew rapidly. A housing boom, stimulated in part by affordable mortgages for returning members of the military, added to the expansion.

The economic rebound renewed Butterfield CC. The club, founded in the early 1920s, had seen its membership sink to 263 in February 1942, but in the postwar period the number again approached three hundred. Revenues spiked, also, as guest fees nearly doubled from their prewar days. Importantly to my father, club members seemed anxious to learn all they could about the game from the first "name pro" in the club's history. They made him feel welcomed and appreciated, and the cash he made from a busy lesson schedule helped him and his family.

Finally, at thirty-five years old, it seemed that my father was achieving his dream of being his own man. Officials at Butterfield had great respect for Dad and gave him the opportunity to do things his own way. Moreover, his two decades of playing, teaching and handling golf-shop responsibilities had prepared him to perform at a high level. He was at a high point in his personal life, as well. With a wife and infant son at home, my father was a happy man who was achieving something critically important to him that many of his contemporaries in professional golf never attained the life of a family man.

When Dad began work at Butterfield, he moved his family to a small apartment at 153 North Lavergne Avenue in the community of Oak Park, west of downtown Chicago and about a twenty-minute drive from his work. Oak Park was an interesting place that became known as the hometown of famous persons including Ray Kroc, founder of McDonald's; Edgar Rice Burroughs, creator of the "Tarzan" character, and chemist Percy Lulian, whose research led to the development of cortisone. The Grout apartment often was a bustling place. Ed and Vera Bradley would come over to visit their nephew, little John Grout, and would bring their children, Joan and Barbie, with them. Dad would look back with pleasure at the memory of the group taking walks together and catching fireflies in the backyard.

His new duties at Butterfield and his new baby conspired to keep my father busy as the spring and summer golf season of 1945 hit full swing. Still, always feeling pressure to maintain his profile as a tour golfer, Dad also found time to enter a series of events and continue building his bank of golfing memories. At George May's All-American Open at Tam O'Shanter, he played alongside, among others, a promising young pro named Claude Harmon, who three years later would win the Masters and who eventually saw his four sons all become noted golf instructors. In the $10,000 Chicago Victory National Open, a five-day pro-am held for the benefit of soldiers and sailors wounded in the war, Dad finished twelfth as Byron Nelson took his historic eleventh tournament title in a row on the way to an unbelievable eighteen-win season.

Dad soon had an opportunity to endear himself even more to the Butterfield membership and to elevate his national profile and prestige, and he took full advantage: He posted scores of 70-70-140 to qualify for the National PGA Championship, to be held in July at the Moraine Country Club in Kettering, Ohio, near Dayton. At the Ohio championship, Dad shot 147 for thirty-six holes of stroke play to qualify as one of thirty-two who would advance to the tournament's match-play rounds.

This was a big deal for my father. He recognized at this point in his life that he was not going to dominate the pro tour. Rather, Dad understood that his best long-term career opportunities would be as a club professional and teacher and mentor for other players. He also knew, though, that the only way he could get a top-notch club-pro job was to continue building a name for himself as an excellent player on the tour, particularly in major championships.

Given his thirst for success in Kettering, my father must have groaned when he learned his opponent in his opening match: defending PGA champion Bob Hamilton! An Indiana native who won five pro tournaments and played on the Ryder Cup team in 1949, Hamilton was one in a long line of interesting characters my father encountered in golf. Writer Al Barkow reported that as a young man, Hamilton shilled for Titanic Thompson, who was both a very good golfer and a renowned gambler. Their scam began with Thompson sending Hamilton ahead to caddie at a small-town golf course and find some likely suckers. Then the personable Titanic would meander in, approach the unsuspecting locals about playing in a money game, then graciously offer to handicap himself by taking as his own playing partner—that "caddie over there." The caddie, of course, was Hamilton, and he and Thompson would mop up their surprised opponents.

There was to be no scam in the Hamilton-Grout match at Moraine Country Club, though. After Hamilton birdied three of the first five holes to go two-up, Dad rallied for a one-up lead after the first eighteen holes. Then he played tenaciously on the day's second eighteen, winning the match five-and-four with a par against Hamilton's three-putt bogey on the thirty-second hole. My father, who had longed to show his true mettle in this major event, had whipped the defending champion!

Dad played solidly again in the second round, the opponent his longtime buddy, Ky Laffoon. Their match was a great one. It was tied after the regulation thirty-six holes, but Laffoon stunned Dad by holing a thirty-foot chip for a par on the third extra hole. When Dad missed his par putt, Laffoon had the match.

My father finished tied for ninth in that PGA, matching his best-ever performance in one of golf's "majors" and taking home $350 for his efforts. His pal Laffoon finished tied for fifth, and Byron Nelson was the winner, beating the former major league baseball player Sam Byrd four-and-three in the final match.

Typically, Dad wasn't discouraged by his tough loss to Laffoon and proved it later in July at the Illinois PGA Section Championship. Playing the par-five eighteenth in the final round at Skokie Country Club's hilly Donald Ross layout, Dad went for the green in two, landing just over the back edge. Then, showing none of the jittery nerves he'd occasionally displayed under competitive pressure, Dad calmly chipped in for an eagle and a one-stroke victory over Welsh-born pro Errie Ball.

PART THREE: THE FIRST LITTLE BOY ON THE TEE

Jack Grout's junior golf class at Scioto in 1950. Ten-year-old Jackie Nicklaus is third from the right.(Bill Foley photo, used with permission)

Chapter 13
Coming of Age

"As human beings, we persist in wanting to make the golf swing complex, but it isn't. Instead, it is quite simply a swinging motion of the arms, assisted by other parts of the body in a sequence of motion, toward a target."
—JACK GROUT

***

I once heard it said that "if you don't take care of yourself, then you won't get taken care of." Whether it's during the severe recession of 2007-2009 or the war-marred 1940s of my father's era, the fact is you do have to take care of yourself. So despite his relative happiness at Butterfield Country Club, and despite the respect and appreciation of the members there, by the end of 1945 Dad was preparing to move on after just one season at the club. Again, his good friend Henry Picard was involved in Dad's decision to move.

The prestigious Canterbury Country Club in Cleveland, Ohio, reached out to Picard in the fall of 1945, offering the two-time major tournament winner its head-professional position. It was a bit of a no-brainer for Picard; Canterbury was to host the U.S. Open the next year, and Picard believed that deep familiarity with the course there could give him an edge in the big tournament. When Picard told his employers at the Harrisburg Country Club that he was headed for Cleveland, the club quickly set its sights on my father. Dad, after all, had served as an assistant to Picard at the nearby Hershey Country Club and had distinguished himself with solid work there.

Ordinarily my father wouldn't have had any qualms about leaving a club for a better opportunity, but this time was different. The membership at Butterfield had been extremely supportive of him. Also, Dad and Mom were expecting their second child within months, and that made it an awkward time to move. Yet the new job at Harrisburg would be a step up professionally, so Dad decided to make the move. As things turned out, though, the name "Grout" would not disappear from the Butterfield club: Uncle Dick, with recommendations from Henry Picard and from my dad, landed the head-pro job there. And unlike Dad, he stayed—serving as head professional at Butterfield from 1946 through 1957, a period that for club pros in that era must have seemed an eternity.

As the new year approached and winter chilled the Chicago air, Dad ventured off to Harrisburg for a while. He needed to tend to planning at the golf club but also found time to rent a small home for his family in the borough of Lemoyne, across the Susquehanna River from Harrisburg. He was back in Chicago for the December 13 birth of my sister, Veronica Ann, whom my parents called Ronnie. But then Dad was off for another trip, this time heading south with Picard for some warm-weather golf. To her dismay, Mother was stuck in the Chicago apartment for several weeks, left alone to handle the infant Ronnie and her older brother, John, himself just a year old. Mother would say later that Dad had left her with little money, and that, for the most part, she subsisted on crackers and carrots. This led to a serious discussion upon my clueless father's return, my mother informing him that this was *never* to happen again!

❄❄❄

To a large degree, the Harrisburg years were a turning point in my father's career. They marked his coming of age as a club professional and, for the most part, signaled the end of his days as a tour player. He would qualify for the U.S. Open at Henry Picard's Canterbury Golf Club that summer of 1946, but he failed to make the two-round cut (while Picard finished the tournament in what was for him a disappointing tie for twelfth.) But Dad's intention at this point was to settle down as a home pro and make that the bedrock of his future years in golf. Even as he watched Byron Nelson win six more tournaments during 1946 before retiring from full-time competition at the age of thirty-four, and as his friend Ben Hogan became the world's dominant golfer that year with thirteen wins, Dad held firm: He'd had enough of the tour life.

Before Harrisburg, most of my father's club-pro jobs had been for short stints. Belt-tightening during the Great Depression and then the onset of World War II forced him to move around in order to survive. That nomadic way of life was especially tough for a man who enjoyed being at home and sleeping in his own bed at night as Dad did. Furthermore, it tended to hinder his development as a golf teacher. Although Dad gave many hundreds of golf lessons at various clubs in the '30s and '40s, he'd seldom been able to stick around long enough to monitor the results of those lessons. Prior to 1946 Dad couldn't be sure that his teaching approach was truly effective.

Fortunately, that set of issues now was behind him. With the postwar economy showing strength, my father finally was able to put down roots in Harrisburg. Dad spent the next four years at the busy upscale club, and during that time he gave an extraordinary number of lessons. Besides being a primary source of income for his growing family, this intense focus on instruction also provided him feedback on his impact as a teacher. Through his continuing work with the same group of students over a period of years, he now could learn which parts of his swing philosophy translated into improved student performance, and which didn't. He was getting his graduate education, not just in the golf swing but also in how to teach it.

My father's approach to golf instruction derived from his personality plus his substantial playing and teaching background. It was natural for him to regard the golf swing in basic and fundamental terms because he was a minimalist at heart. He liked structure and things that were clearly and explicitly stated. When a subject interested him, his mind could absorb a great number of facts about it, and he had a wonderful memory for details.

While all of the great players with whom he traveled the pro circuit influenced my father's playing technique and helped shape his teaching philosophy, Henry Picard had perhaps the greatest impact on Dad's golf education. Musing about his frequent colleague and mentor on the tour and their work as club pros, Dad would say, "If it hadn't been for Pic, I'd still be plugging along in the same old rut, getting nowhere."

Of course, it was Picard who got my father out of Texas to begin with by offering him a job as his assistant in Pennsylvania in 1937. During that first spring in Hershey, Dad began a close working relationship with his buddy, one that included taking golf lessons from him. And in those lessons, Picard was passing along not only his own swing theories but also those of Alex Morrison, the most advanced and controversial swing theorist of the 1920s and 1930s. Through the late 1930s my father would have a number of chances to do additional research of his own with the swing professor, and Morrison actually used pictures of Dad, Picard and other leading pros to demonstrate technique in his 1940 book, *Better Golf Without Practice*.

For a full decade before landing in Harrisburg, my father had been teaching pretty much the Morrison/Picard system. Now, as his own swing philosophy became fully defined, he was having second thoughts, or better yet, his *own* thoughts, regarding certain aspects of his golf mentors' teaching approaches. Actually, Dad was becoming skeptical about how golf, in general, was being taught. It confounded him that, in his view, so many golfers didn't seem to improve significantly even after extensive lessons and practice. He became convinced that the game too often was being presented in a complicated and confusing manner. This growing conviction, nurtured by countless hours of practice, study and teaching, would over the next few years propel him into the ranks of the game's elite teachers. He was becoming a man who truly could help *you* make your *own* game better.

***

My father was aware of the tendency of many people to make things unnecessarily difficult for themselves. His perception was that human beings tend to regard something complicated as having greater meaning or greater value than something simple. But Dad wasn't buying that philosophy as he shaped his teaching technique. His experience and background told him the simple approach to golf was not only the best approach, but really the only approach. In this and other respects, it turned out that Dad, in his own quiet way, was well ahead of his time.

It was through his work in Harrisburg that my father developed true confidence in his teaching philosophy and skills. He became known in the area as a man of calm demeanor who could put any student at ease. During a typical lesson, he'd spend the first five to ten minutes not saying much at all about the student's golf game. Once the student felt comfortable, Dad would succinctly explain an idea or demonstrate a fundamental to perform. Then, as the student began to master a concept, Dad would enthusiastically show his approval. Nothing pleased him more than seeing one of his students hit a good golf shot.

Dad was a great believer that improvement in golf came primarily through rigorous practice and lessons. "Practice as much as you can," he once wrote. "Most people I have taught don't want to pay their sweat equity." Often enough while growing up, I experienced Dad's high regard for "putting in your time." One afternoon on the practice tee during his late-career tenure as a seasonal teaching professional at Muirfield Village Golf Club, I walked over to him and complained about how sore my hands were from hitting balls. He scanned my puffy red paws, then looked me straight in the eye and said, "That's good, now go back and hit some more."

There were times, for sure, when Dad could be a tough bird. He was unyielding in his view that good golf required both dedicated work and precise physical technique. On the subject of taking lessons, he wrote that "even tour players need the analytical eye of a professional teacher to keep their games well honed." Practicing what he preached, my father took more than eleven hundred golf lessons during his lifetime. Dad always held the acquisition of knowledge in high esteem and sought from an early age to ensure that he had a

Gene Sarazen and Ben Hogan with Jack Grout at Harrisburg Country Club in 1946. (Photo courtesy of the Country Club of Harrisburg)

broad and deep understanding of his chosen sport. That thirst for learning would last to his dying day.

With his first season at Harrisburg Country Club completed, my father remained at home during the winter months of 1946-1947, hiding from the cold weather with Bonnie and their two children in their little house in Lemoyne. It marked the first time in more than a decade that he skipped all of the winter tour, even the Florida tournaments, and this was tough on him for a couple of reasons. One, he detested cold weather and thus thoroughly enjoyed his winter forays to Florida. And two, he missed the energizing experience of being on tour and seeing his golfing buddies. Nevertheless, Dad felt that his time was better spent by being around the house where he could help my mother and be a good father.

By the spring of 1947, my father was more than ready for his second golfing season in Harrisburg. He was nicely compensated in the head-pro job there; Harrisburg Country Club wouldn't make him a rich man, but his salary and other earnings would pay the bills and then some. It helped that Dad owned the pro shop and kept several hundred of the members' golf bags in storage. For an annual fee of $20, members could have their bags and clubs cleaned, cared for and tucked safely away in the bag room. Also, Dad's lesson book was as full as he wanted it to be, and there were the usual local and several national tournaments that occupied a special place on his calendar. Those tournaments kept his game sharp, offered a welcome break from his club duties, and also gave him a shot at extra earnings. The whole package worked well for him.

Through the next year and into the fall of 1948, with its explosion of colors across the rolling northeastern Pennsylvania countryside, Jack and Bonnie Grout were a happy, if very busy, couple. They had moved to a slightly larger and more comfortable rental home in the little village of Heckton, just north of Harrisburg. Dad was well established in his job, and Mom was fully involved in the work of maintaining a happy and stable home life for my father and their children.

That fall, however, the normally healthy and perky Bonnie Ann Grout began feeling very poorly. She eventually went for medical tests, and the news that came back was a shock to her and her family: Mom had contracted tuberculosis. She became seriously ill and, given that TB is an infectious disease, had to remain quarantined for an extended period in a hospital room in the mountains of northeastern Pennsylvania. Fortunately her condition was treatable and her caregivers dealt with it quickly and aggressively. She was back home in about seven months.

This proved to be an extremely difficult period for Mom and her family. My sister and brother were about three and four years old, respectively, and all they knew was that their mother was sick. They didn't get to see her for months. It helped that Bonnie's mother came to live with and care for the family until Mom could return home. Grandma Annie's presence allowed Dad to focus on his work as needed and to visit his wife in the hospital as often as possible. How fortunate, in hindsight, that Dad had made up his mind after the 1947 season to cut his playing schedule. With all that was going on with Mom, and with two young children at home, it would have been impossible for him to be away.

***

As late as the 1940s, it was common for a club's head pro to own the golf shop. For some of the pros, this part of the job was a mixed blessing. Many would get overextended with inventory, buying clubs and apparel they almost couldn't give away. My father, however, had become good at evaluating new equipment and golf's fashion trends. I believe his humble background helped in this regard. It taught him to be shrewd and to squeeze everything you could out of a dollar. Dad quickly assessed those items that had merit and stayed away from those that were gimmicks with no lasting value. His pro shop always showed a tidy return, thanks to strong support from club members, who genuinely liked him and always could count on him stocking the latest and best golf equipment. As on the teaching side, Dad's easy way with people had a lot to do with his success on the business side.

In the world of country clubs, word about this kind of competence gets around—word about a club pro's business skills, about his or her playing abilities, about that head pro who is a great teacher of the game. So it was not surprising that by the end of the 1940s, word had gotten out about my dad. He had proved himself as an attentive and effective manager of a series of pro shops. But he had become best known as a man who loved to teach, who often spent all day on the lesson tee with players of all ability levels and who never found it too much trouble to give just "one more lesson."

Accomplished PGA Tour players such as Dow Finsterwald often came to Harrisburg to have Dad take a look at their swings and offer suggestions. At a time when the golf swing was not understood in anywhere near the depth it is today, my father's reputation for having a non-irritating manner, an uncanny eye for spotting flaws, and a knack for transmitting simple solutions to what seemed like complicated problems had spread well beyond the Susquehanna Valley and the Blue Mountains of Pennsylvania.

Dad wasn't looking to begin the 1950s in a new job or in a new city. The four years in Harrisburg, with the exception of the one my mom was ill, had been good for him and his family. But in the fall of 1949, a head-professional position opened in a city that my father had driven through a number of times during his various travels and he had liked a lot. Things happened pretty fast after that. Henry Picard, still the head pro at the Canterbury Golf Club in Cleveland, teamed with Ohio businessman John W. Roberts in contacting him about the position. Then the two men backed Dad's eventual efforts to secure the new job.

The *Associated Press* reported the news on December 9, 1949: Thirty-nine-year-old Jack Grout, head professional at Harrisburg Country Club in Pennsylvania for the past four years, had been named head professional of Scioto Country Club in Columbus, Ohio. The story noted that, as the new head pro, Grout would be the host for the 1950 PGA Championship, scheduled at Scioto on June 21-29, 1950.

The prospect of hosting a major tournament excited my dad. But I know he would have been infinitely more excited had he been able to look into the future and see that within a few months, his orbit would collide with that of a Columbus ten-year-old who would become, under Jack Grout's tutelage, the most successful golfer the world had ever seen. As prepared for that opportunity as a man could be, my father was about to apply the full power of his knowledge about the techniques and theories of the golf swing to the instruction of an athletic and eager boy who, until he met Jack Grout, had never played the game of golf.

It was a pairing made in golf heaven, and it was to last thirty-nine years, ending with my father on his deathbed, giving a final lesson to the great Jack William Nicklaus, the man by then long known to the world as golf's magnificent Golden Bear.

Chapter 14
"The Kids Came out of the Rafters"

"Once a child learns the basics of the swing (or any skill, for that matter), he'll never forget them." —JACK GROUT

***

On January 8, 1950, a picture of my father appeared in the *Patriot-News* of Harrisburg, Pennsylvania, with a caption reading, "At Harrisburg Country Club, we found Jack Grout readying for a switch to Scioto C.C. in Columbus ... so we posed the handsome Texan for a 'last look' glamour picture." Oops! Actually an Oklahoman by birth, Dad's sole Texas background was the time he spent as his brother's assistant at Glen Garden Country Club in Fort Worth. He could laugh off the mistake but not the importance of his four years in Harrisburg. He considered them a significant step up professionally and financially.

In retrospect, though, my father came to view his Scioto assignment as the high point in his long career in golf. The new position at a prominent and successful golf operation in Ohio's capital city didn't make the Grouts financially secure overnight, but it did offer my parents a brighter long-term outlook. His appointment also helped restore a bit of lost swagger to a club that had a long and proud tradition.

Dad's attitude from the start at Scioto spoke of real pride in his appointment there and a conviction that the club was an even better and more important one than its members realized. He brandished that attitude in a club committee meeting shortly after his arrival, when James L. Long, the club's president, mentioned that if Scioto were to do this or do that, they could be just like Columbus Country Club. My father was having none of that kind of thinking. Scioto, he insisted, should start doing things its own way. Then, he said, other clubs would begin patterning themselves after Scioto. Indeed, as time went on, that's exactly what happened. My father was proud of that and also smiled years later in noting that he and Jimmie Long became lasting friends despite Dad's early outspokenness.

***

Dad's ascension to the Scioto job brought him any number of special satisfactions, but few more important to him than ownership, for the first time, of his own home. He and my mother had lived in a series of rented apartments and houses during their seven years together. Now they were able to buy a modest house at 2205 Fairfax Road in the Upper Arlington suburb of Columbus, in a fine neighborhood not far from the club. My mother established a comfortable nest there for my five-year-old brother, John, and four-year-old sister, Ronnie, and Dad quickly dove into his new job.

It was a good break for Dad that he began at Scioto in the middle of the cold Ohio winter. That allowed him to concentrate on building his golf staff, assessing the state of the overall golf operation, and getting up to speed with the club's preparations for hosting the upcoming summer's PGA Championship without being concerned with heavy member traffic through the golf shop or running the club's various leagues and tournaments. With Dad bringing in a new team of assistants—Charles Barnes from Harrisburg, Edgar "Larry" Glosser from Oklahoma and Jay Jack Weitzel from Reading, Pennsylvania, and a new caddie master, Harold Heiser from San Jose, California—an air of anticipation about the new golf season quickly took hold.

Dad had been on the job only about a week when a reporter asked for his thoughts on Scioto's Donald Ross-designed golf course. "It's one of the toughest layouts I have ever played," Dad replied. In that interview, Dad also revealed that he'd decided to compete in the PGA Championship that June at Scioto, and he made it clear that he hoped to make an impressive showing. Receiving less note in the interview was an initiative that Dad had in mind, one that eventually would bring Scioto a great deal of attention—an instructional series for junior golfers. "We're going to have a fine program for the girls and boys once school is out," Dad announced, "and they'll get group and individual instruction along with a tournament."

Attacking his new job with enthusiasm, Dad met as many members as possible and got to know the club's non-golf staff, and he also found time to get to know his new city of residence. In one of his early forays out into that new world, he had an unplanned encounter with a Scioto member, one that would become famous in the history of American golf. "I needed some medicine, and since I was new to Columbus, I stopped at the first drugstore that I happened to see, on the way to the club," Dad recalled. "I didn't know much about Upper Arlington yet, and I saw this Nicklaus Drug Store ... " My father parked his car and went inside, where a smiling, heavyset man walked up and offered his assistance. The man's name was Louis Charles Nicklaus—"Charlie" to his friends and family—and he was the pharmacist.

"Mr. Charlie Nicklaus introduced himself to me and said he'd heard I was starting a junior golf class," Dad said, continuing with this oft-told story. "He said he was a member at Scioto and had a ten-year-old son who was interested in learning golf, and could he get him in my junior class?" Charlie Nicklaus related that his son loved sports and, despite his youth, already had shown real athletic ability. My father, as always, was gracious in his response: "Sure, I'd be glad to have him." He told Mr. Nicklaus when the first session would be held and to "send him over!"

Informed by his father about the upcoming summer lessons, young Jackie Nicklaus was enthusiastic. In fact, my father said in later years, "The first little boy to come in the pro shop and register was Jackie Nicklaus, and the day we started, the first little boy on the tee was Jackie Nicklaus." On that summer day in 1950, said Dad, "little Jackie showed up for the initial class along with about seventy-five other boys and girls. It was the first time anyone had ever taught a junior class in Columbus, so the kids came out of the rafters. But, the earliest to arrive was young Jack Nicklaus. And in the days and years that followed, he almost always was the first to arrive, so that he could be the first in line to be taught."

Dad's new junior program featured a weekly two-hour class that met on Friday mornings. The group would meet at one end of the club's unusually large practice range, which measured about 150 yards wide and four hundred yards in length. Dad would line the kids up in a long row across the teaching area. He would discuss some point he wanted them to absorb, demonstrate it himself or use one of the juniors to do so, then let them all go at it while he moved up and down the line working briefly with each individual.

In those beginning classes so long ago, just as in his later instruction of famous professional golfers, my father taught the basics. He always stressed the fundamentals, which he kept simple and to a minimum. His instructions were clear and easily comprehensible, and the kids could sense from his great conviction and enthusiasm that if they could just master these several simple concepts, they could have great fun at a game that, at first, might not have seemed like fun at all.

As my father saw it, the first fundamental concerned the head. He wanted every member of his class to be aware of the absolute necessity of keeping it steady during the swing. It wasn't good enough to "keep your eye on the ball," because you could do that and still move your head. Dad knew that the violent force of a golf swing must revolve around something that's kept relatively centered.

In this respect, my father felt the need to resort to a rather rough teaching device when the promising young Jackie Nicklaus was about twelve years old. Dad called for one of his assistants, Larry Glosser, to report to the practice tee. Once there, Glosser was instructed to stand in front of Jackie, stick his arm out, and clutch the boy's hair with his hand, the height difference between adult and child making this setup possible. Dad then said, "OK, Jackie boy, now just you go ahead and hit that ball for me." When the youngster moved his head the least bit while hitting a shot, he paid a price! Though my father was a gentle man, he felt these tactics were needed to teach little Jackie to keep his head steady every time and on every shot. Contradictory accounts notwithstanding, Dad did employ this tactic during Jackie's early instruction, as confirmed in Nicklaus' golf memoir, *My Story*. But some side-to-side head movement is necessary to maximize distance, and later, in the interest of the "long ball," Dad allowed Nicklaus to have slight movement—as long as his head remained on a vertical plane between his feet.

The second fundamental was that good footwork means good balance, a concept that Dad first considered back in 1937 through his studies of Alex Morrison's theories on the golf swing. Later Dad had watched as his friend Henry Picard learned superb foot action by hitting balls seven hours a day. Picard's technique, which Dad adopted as his own and taught to Jackie Nicklaus and many others, was not terribly complex, yet it was not a "natural move" and thus could be difficult to master. The move involved rolling the left ankle inward while bracing against the inside of the right ankle on the backswing, then pushing off the right foot by rolling the right ankle inward, shifting all the weight onto the left foot during the downswing, and raising the right foot up onto its toe as the swing was finished.

When Nicklaus protested that the move was hard to accomplish, Dad simply said, "Well, then, Jackie buck, let's see you hit those three buckets of balls without letting your heels come off the ground even a little bit." It was some time before my father permitted his young pupil to raise his heels at all during the swing. Dad said that Ben Hogan used to practice that way, sliding his right foot into the shot as he hit it.

Dad's third fundamental was the importance of developing as full a swing arc as possible. When the club head is traveling through a big, wide arc, he always maintained, it gathers a great deal of speed, which equates to distance. Dad taught that the best way to accomplish this was with a full shoulder turn. His thinking was that by extending, extending, extending, a young golfer stretched his muscles, something that would not occur later when the muscles had become so much less flexible.

From the start, Dad also encouraged the kids to hit the ball as hard and far as they could, an instruction at odds with the traditional method of teaching young golfers to strive for accuracy first. Although Jack Nicklaus would embrace my dad's affinity for the "long ball" and make it famous, this tendency to try to crush the ball was one my father encouraged in most of his students. Under the tutelage of Jack Grout, the moment you first picked up a golf club you were encouraged to hit the ball hard. Dad's reasoning was that the person who can hit the ball farthest has an advantage and that, accordingly, a player should develop a power swing when he or she is young and the muscles are limber. Accuracy, he taught, could come later.

My father was an aficionado of the long drive. It didn't matter whether you were pro or amateur, man or woman, large or small. When you were swinging your driver, Jack Grout wanted you to whack the daylights out of that ball. Even a hint of laziness in this regard would bring his stern disapproval. Dad even had his own lexicon when promoting this long-ball philosophy. "Let's see you peel that onion," he'd implore. Or "Come on; put some smoke on that potato. Hey, quit hittin' it like a girl. Go ahead, wheel and deal this next one. This time, put a little Smoky Joe from Idaho on it!"

When my father watched me practice, we'd typically begin with a few short irons, then some middle-iron shots and maybe another half-dozen or so with my 3-iron or a fairway wood. Then he'd say, "OK, let's see you get out your smoke pole," and I'd spend an hour or so walloping drivers.

During one of these slugfests at La Gorce in Florida, a famous member of the club walked past. "Jack," the man said, "you're gonna kill that kid!" It was the great Eddie Arcaro, the only jockey in history to ride two Triple Crown champions, Whirlaway in 1941 and Citation in 1948. Arcaro had witnessed my workout and apparently was concerned for my well-being!

One morning before one of our sessions, Dad offered me a new challenge. He asked if I thought I could keep the ball up in the air for a longer period of time than he could whistle. Another ploy, I thought, to coerce me into creaming that ball! Our arrangement was this: He would take a deep breath during my backswing. Then, at the moment my club contacted the ball, he would exhale and begin to whistle.

I was about sixteen years old when we began that whistle contest, and through the next two or three years Dad always could out-whistle my best drives. It didn't matter how far I launched one. Even though I was developing into an extremely long hitter, I could never win.

Then, during one of my breaks from college, he and I were on the practice tee once again, going through our routine. I was really cranking them out there, and Dad was whistling away. After one blast that actually cracked the persimmon face of my driver, Dad pursed his lips and blew. I knew it was now or never for me in our little contest. As his eyes were riveted on my rocket that continued going up, up and away, I posed at swing's end and peeked back at him. The ball took so long to come down that Dad had to sneak in a quick breath to keep whistling. But this time I saw him. I cried out, "Ah-ha. I caught you! I caught you breathing!" Knowing the jig was up, Dad nonchalantly replied, "Dickie, I've been breathing for a long time."

His swing-for-the-fences approach to golf came as sweet music to any kid who heard Dad's exhortations for more reckless abandon, and particularly so to the athletic young Jackie Nicklaus. "I didn't have to remind Jackie at all, he wanted it that way," Dad said. "He was a little kid who just wanted to fire that sucker. He had the instinct."

***

While my father eventually would describe Jack Nicklaus as "the greatest golfer who ever swung a club in the entire history of the game," he admitted he hadn't immediately spotted the youngster's special potential. "He was just another little boy out there swinging away, like little boys do," Dad remembered. "He was just one of the kids, a redhead with a crew haircut." Through the summer and fall of 1950, though, Nicklaus began to display signs of having real talent for the game. "That little rascal learned quickly," Dad said. "Some kids forget, but you'd tell Jackie one time and he would remember."

Although young Nicklaus' golfing promise wasn't immediately recognized by my father, his passion for the game certainly was. "Jackie would beat me in (in) the morning!" Dad said. "I'd get to the club about eight o'clock and he was already out there putting." Years later, my father would remind me about Nicklaus' devotion to practice whenever I wasn't working hard enough on my own golf game. "During the summertime," he'd tell me, "Jack would arrive at Scioto early in the morning, hit balls for an hour or two, play eighteen holes carrying his own clubs, have lunch, hit more balls, go out and play eighteen more, come back and hit more balls or chip and putt until dark."

Jackie Nicklaus had ambition and was totally dedicated to working hard on his golf game, and my father appreciated these aspects of the youngster's character. Not only appreciated, he encouraged and rewarded them. Nicklaus later wrote that "Jack Grout got excited about my golf game and he stayed that way until the day he died. He saw in me a future, a young kid who wanted to do something, and he wanted me to have two things I needed at that time: to hit balls and to get help from him."

Nicklaus also recalled, "I'd walk in from playing a round and Grout would say, 'How'd you do, Jackie boy?' and I'd say, 'I hit 'em really good, Mr. Grout, but I hit a couple of bad shots,' and he'd say, 'Let's go out to the practice tee.' We'd go to the practice tee and hit balls. After a while, he'd say, 'Well, how you doin' now, Jackie boy?' I'd grin and say, 'Doing fine, Mr. Grout,' and he'd say, 'Get back out there.' I'd run out and play another eighteen. When I'd come in, he'd say, 'How'd you do?' and I'd say, 'Great' and he'd say, 'Good, see you tomorrow.' "

"I've never seen a youngster practice golf like Jack Nicklaus did," my father said. "He'd come out to Scioto in the worst possible weather you could imagine." Despite such commitment, though, there actually were a few times when Dad felt his young pupil was neglecting his golf. "On these occasions," Dad said, "I'd merely mention this to his father, Charlie, and sure enough, Jackie would show up the next day ready to go." Once Dad mentioned to Columbus journalist and personal friend Bill Foley that, "Jackie's 15,000 to 20,000 balls behind in his practice." Dad said he didn't think any more about what he'd said until the next morning. "Then I saw my comment printed in the paper. That afternoon Jackie was on the practice tee firing away, and he was still there quite awhile after it grew too dark to see the balls finish."

Two decades later, looking back on those early days with Jackie Nicklaus, my father told *Sports Illustrated's* John Underwood of the incredible discipline that set Nicklaus apart. "High winds. Mud. Rain. We'd be out there," Dad said. "'You're going to play in it, you better practice in it,' I told him."

***

The impending PGA Championship was a wonderful bonus for my dad as he worked through his first months at Scioto. The approach of the tournament provided a special impetus for improvements at the beautiful golf course, and Dad looked forward to the chance to showcase his golf operations and, perhaps, his own skill as a player.

Six days before the field descended on Scioto, Columbus sportswriter Paul Hornung wrote: "Jack Grout, tall, bronzed Oklahoman, via Texas and Pennsylvania, is convinced that the competitive record for his Scioto Country Club course will go by the boards before the final shot is fired in the hectic $40,000 PGA next week. The new Scioto pro isn't saying that Snead, Demaret, Mangrum, Ferrier, Oliver and their less glamorized playmates will tear the course apart. But Jack does think 'the boys will score real well.' "

Dad told Hornung the course was " ... in perfect shape. It just couldn't be much better. The fairways are wonderful. The ball sits up nice for your woods and you can get enough bite on your irons. Our greens are just as good. I'll bet that most of the boys agree this is the best course the PGA Tournament has ever played."

Days later, Russ Needham wrote in *The Columbus Dispatch* that my dad could be a factor in the PGA. "When this sportswriter spoke with tour veteran Toney Penna," Needham said, "one thing the diminutive pro mentioned was, 'If that guy (Grout) could see, he'd be right there with the best of them. He has one of the finest swings in the game and everything to go with it but eyesight.' " Penna was correct, of course; Dad's nearsightedness always had been a limiting factor in his play on the pro circuit.

An array of the day's best golfers showed up on June 21-22 to test Scioto's 7,032-yard par-72 layout in a two-round stroke-play qualifier, with the sixty-four survivors advancing to match play. The field of 128 players included Sam Snead, Gene Sarazen, Jimmy Demaret, Lloyd Mangrum, Henry Picard, Bob Toski, Jim Ferrier, Dad's good friend Rod Munday and many other well-known players.

Even though as defending champion he didn't have to qualify, Sam Snead was the low scorer in the play-in rounds with a total of 140. A score of 152 qualified for match play, with seven players who tied at 153 having a playoff for three spots. Unfortunately, Dad could manage only a 154 total. Actually, this might not have been such a great disappointment for him. The host professional in a major championship had numerous duties and responsibilities during the tournament. As much as he said he wanted to advance into match play, it's doubtful that he could have handled all that and also maintained the sharp focus needed for elite-level competition.

Henry Picard, in the tournament through special invitation from Dad and truly a long-shot in the event, had a different fate. Now forty-three years old and pretty much a stay-at-home head pro at Cleveland's Canterbury Country Club, "Pic" overcame severe arthritis in his hands to make it through the stroke-play qualifying rounds, then eked out victories in his first three matches. In the quarterfinals, Picard blew away Johnny Palmer by a ten-and-eight margin. Shockingly, the old pro had advanced to the semifinals, where Henry Williams Jr. awaited. Again, Picard started fast, standing three-up on Williams after their morning round.

During the afternoon, Picard seemed to be headed for an easy victory—six holes up with just eight to play. But a combination of things happened at that point to produce one of the greatest comebacks in the history of the PGA. The multiday grind in the heat plus the demands of the long Scioto course began taking their toll on Picard. Also, Williams, a Purple Heart soldier in World War II, summoned tremendous energy and went on a tear. When Picard bogeyed the thirty-fifth hole, the match, amazingly, was square. Both players made birdies at the thirty-sixth hole to send the match into overtime. Williams, who would lose the finals four-and-three to Virginian Chandler Harper, clinched the semifinal win over Picard with a par on their thirty-eighth hole. Henry was deflated but philosophical. "Well, I stayed in a lot longer than I thought I would," said Dad's longtime friend. "Now, no one can argue me into getting back on this damned tournament trail. I'm going home and be a family man. After all, I'm an old man, and my legs just gave out."

Young Jackie Nicklaus was having happy feelings about that major-tournament week even as Picard dragged home. "Jack Grout introduced me to Skip Alexander, who was one of the better-known players in the Championship," Nicklaus recalled. "Skip took me into the locker room and introduced me to all the pros. I remember Jimmy Demaret, Sam Snead, Bob Hamilton, Lloyd Mangrum, Chandler Harper ... I got autographs of a lot of the players. That was something special Mr. Grout did for me, to have one of his buddies take a young kid back into the locker room. That was my first introduction to pro golf, at the age of ten."

Chapter 15
The Golf Pro's Golf Pro

"After about seven years, they get tired of looking at you and you get tired of looking at them." —JACK GROUT

***

Scioto Country Club's lovingly manicured golf course is one that figuratively knocks a player flat and won't let him up. Artfully designed, aesthetically pleasing, and challenging but fair to play, it has been ranked consistently among the nation's great golf layouts. The club, located northwest of downtown Columbus, was opened in 1916 and gained early fame when Bobby Jones won the U.S. Open there in 1926. Jones made history that hot July day, coming from four strokes down in the final nine holes to overtake noted professional Joe Turnesa by one stroke and become the first player ever to win the U.S. Open and British Open in the same year. Scioto also was the venue for the 1931 Ryder Cup and, after the PGA Championship in Dad's first year at the club, hosted the 1968 U.S. Amateur Championship and the 1986 U.S. Senior Open.

The club's membership included many among the elite of Columbus business, government and society. The atmosphere at the club was somewhat refined and formal, but Dad's arrival at Scioto came at a time when golfers were adopting more relaxed attire on the course. Men were giving up shirts and ties for collared golf shirts, and women traded their below-the-knee skirts for Bermuda shorts and pedal pushers. Dad happily promoted the more relaxed attire for his members, even though he lagged in adopting the latest fashions for his personal golf wardrobe; longtime golf shop manager Dom LePore recalled that during the early part of his Scioto tenure my father wore a white shirt and tie to give lessons, even during the sweltering summertime.

On December 16, 1951, as Columbus coped with zero temperatures and a six-inch snowfall, my dad was enjoying the warmth of Scioto's Men's Grill with club members Allen Rankin, Preach Hoag, Frank Gates and Charlie Cox. It was early afternoon, and they were just finishing lunch when, suddenly, a cloud of smoke wafted past the grill room's big picture window. Hoag dashed outside into the snow, saw the roof of the clubhouse ablaze and called to those inside. Gates immediately summoned the Upper Arlington Fire Department.

"The fire started in the attic," my father said, "and I was up there on the second floor with the manager holding one of those squirt guns (hand-held fire extinguishers), but the smoke got so dense I couldn't see. I knew the club was gone and I had to get out of there. I ran down to the pro shop where I had a fellow working for me named Charlie Barnes. I said, 'Charlie, start moving the merchandise out of here, because we're going to get burned out.' Some of the members helped us—Preach Hoag, Allen Rankin, a couple of other fellows. They were grabbing sets of clubs and boxes of balls and all that stuff and carrying them outside."

The club storage room was in the back of the pro shop, and Dad needed to get as many bags of golf clubs out of there as he could. He initially directed that all members' clubs be hustled to the caddie house, but as the fire spread and expedience became the watchword, everything was simply dumped into the snow at a reasonable distance from the clubhouse. Dad was fortunate that a number of club members were present when the fire started; they helped rescue all of his merchandise and all members' clubs before the flames or water could damage them.

Upper Arlington Fire Chief Samuel Foster and his department were summoned at 1:15 p.m. and arrived within minutes, but they immediately discovered that the intense cold had frozen all of the hydrants shut. Those frozen hydrants severely hampered the firemen in a three-hour struggle to control a blaze that burned out the interior of the clubhouse. The firefighters' efforts saved the men's locker room, and the pro shop sustained only slight smoke and water damage, meaning that Dad's part of the operation had been largely spared. Firemen theorized that sparks from an overheated fireplace started the blaze. The building was insured, and work began right away to repair the estimated $340,000 in fire-related damages.

My brother John remembers Dad entering our front door that night wearing his overcoat and fedora and throwing off the overpowering smell of smoke. "Ronnie and I were asking so many questions (about the fire) that he and Mom told us to go take inventory of our canned goods," John says. "We promptly went to the basement, where we had shelves stacked with the canned goods. We counted each of them and filed our report. Mom and Dad looked at the report and told us that we were fine and would easily make it through the winter!"

***

Jay Weitzel, one of the three assistants Dad brought in when he began his Scioto tenure, remembered my father's friendly but businesslike approach. Dad had just signed on with Scioto in late 1949 when Weitzel, then just out of high school but already a very skilled golfer, interviewed with him for a job. "He was a tall, handsome man, and impeccably dressed," Weitzel said. "He was friendly, but at the same time you knew he was very serious about golf and the golf business." Weitzel was so comfortable with Dad that he accepted my father's offer of a job without even asking about the salary. "I trusted that he would do right by me. This was the beginning of a relationship that would shape the rest of my life."

Weitzel, who worked with Dad at Scioto from 1950 until 1956 and then served for thirty-eight years as head professional at Hershey Country Club, spoke fondly of the "family feeling" of Jack Grout's golf operation. Weitzel often went to dinner at the Grout home with his original Columbus roommate, Scioto pro-shop manager Charlie Barnes. And he said, "Anyone who spent any time with the Grouts knew they loved and were very devoted to each other ... and were a very close family."

In retirement, Weitzel recalled that my father " ... probably had a better grasp of the entire scope of what it meant to be a golf professional than anyone I have ever been associated with ... he was a golf professional's golf professional. Jack's ability to work with everyone was his greatest strength."

The amount of time my dad spent giving lessons to golfers of all skill levels remains a key memory for his former assistant. "He loved to teach and often spent all day on the lesson tee," Weitzel said, chuckling over the memory of what he considered "probably Jack's greatest teaching challenge"—Scioto member Richard Borel. "Jack worked with Mr. Borel for what seemed like close to three years to cure a chronic shank," Weitzel recalled. "I don't remember if he was ever completely successful in correcting the problem, but it demonstrates Jack's patience and love of teaching."

Weitzel also spoke of the stream of excellent golfers who sought Jack Grout's help. "It was not unusual for accomplished players to come to Scioto to have Jack take a look at their swings and offer suggestions," he said. "Often these sessions were 'tune-ups' rather than complete makeovers. As an assistant, I remember watching Jack work with notables such as Dow Finsterwald ... I gained valuable insights into teaching (by) watching Jack work with good players."

When not on the lesson tee or in the pro shop, my father devoted himself to smoothing the way for new members of the club. Businessman John Bishop talked of being one of those on the receiving end of Dad's welcoming approach. Bishop's invitation to join Scioto came with the backing of Charlie Nicklaus, and, on his first visit to the club as a new member, Bishop found my father waiting to greet him. "He was such a lovely person," said Bishop, "and he said, 'I've got a game for you today—I'm going to play with you.' That just about knocked me down, but then he said, 'I've also got Allen Rankin and John Roberts.' These were the two greatest players at Scioto before Nicklaus came along. I just got so nervous."

A talented amateur player in Ohio circles, Bishop quickly found his nervousness assuaged by the friendly demeanor of his host and later viewed that day as the launching pad for "many, many happy years of golf there." My father, Bishop remembered, "was well liked by the membership. He'd have lunch with us, and he'd always want to order pie at the end. He never ate the crust; he only wanted the filling, and we used to kid about that. He had a lot of influence ... he was a true gentleman."

***

The spring and summer of 1953 found my father dealing with a series of significant events, including both a personal loss and positive developments within the Grout family in Columbus and on the golf course. On May 10, Dad was saddened to learn of his father's death in Oklahoma City. Herbert Duane Grout had succumbed to cancer at the age of seventy-eight, and Dad traveled alone back to Oklahoma to join his seven brothers and sisters in mourning. On May 24, almost as if by some grand design to distract Dad from his grief, Dad wowed the Scioto membership by shooting a seven-under-par 65 to establish the course record on the club's tough layout. The next day, he shot 72-72-144 at the Columbus Country Club to qualify for the national PGA Championship, scheduled in July at the Birmingham Country Club in Michigan. And to top all this off, on June 19 I came along, the second son and third child of Jack and Bonnie Grout. The *Columbus Citizen Journal* noted my arrival with a headline that read, "Scioto pro Jack Grout now has his very own threesome."

It was an exhausting period for my father, yet as he prepared that summer for the PGA Championship, he could look with great satisfaction on the life he'd built. With the Scioto clubhouse restored after the devastating fire of 1951, with Dad established as a wonderful teacher and mentor for golfers in the club, with young Jackie Nicklaus beginning to blossom as a player of real talent under Dad's guidance, and with his family secure in an established home and having just added its third child, my father had developed the well-rounded life he'd aspired to for so long.

The upcoming PGA in Michigan was one of only two professional events Dad would play in 1953, the other being one of his favorite tourneys, the Greenbrier Pro-Am Invitational at the luxurious Greenbrier Resort in West Virginia. At this point in his career, Dad played just a few significant tournaments each year—to keep his game sharp and to remind Scioto's membership that their head pro was a strong-enough golfer to play with the "big boys."

***

My father was a serious and responsible man, a hard worker. But just as he relished the challenges of his days at Scioto, he also cherished quiet evenings at home with his family. Jack and Bonnie Grout and their children lived a happy and relatively uncomplicated life together, with the focus on home, school and friends.

When Dad came home after work, he and the children often would gather in the kitchen to watch mother prepare our evening meal. After dinner, Dad typically would retire to the living room to smoke his Camels, read the newspaper, work crossword puzzles, or watch the "Gillette Friday Night Fights," the "Lucky Strike Hit Parade," or the "Ed Sullivan Show" on our first television, a prized round-screen Zenith. We never really knew much about what Dad was thinking. It was not unusual for him to work seven days a week, and he usually was tired when he came home and just wanted to relax. He would open up more to the family in later years, although he never talked about country club politics with us, or with mom. He was also mum on the subject of his personal religious faith, leaving it to Mom to be the regular church-goer and overseer of our Catholic upbringing.

Sometimes in the evenings, card or board games would be played. One day when he was sixteen, John came upon a backgammon set in a closet, and Dad began teaching him the game. John recalled that Dad was "merciless, and would win most of the time." Dad taught John the opening moves of the game, but then, John recalled, "I was on my own. If he got behind in the game he would love the 'backgame.' When he had achieved the ultimate goal, he would announce, 'That's called a Backgammon!'" John eventually read a book about the game and said that "I surprised (Dad) one night by not hitting an exposed blot—an unprotected checker—which would have enabled him to set up his backgame. He asked me if I was not going to hit the blot, and I just smiled at him. He smiled back. He had suddenly realized that his days of backgammon domination were over."

On an occasional evening, my parents would venture out on the Columbus social circuit. The two never drank much, sometimes sharing a beer while Mom was cooking or a cocktail at home before one of the club's dinner dances. Mother was a beautiful and lively lady, and Dad was very proud of her and enjoyed taking her dancing, relaxed in the knowledge that the children were safely in the care of the babysitter, Mrs. Mamie Nolan. Mom would mention on occasion that someone had flirted with her during one of their evenings out, but Dad didn't mind. He just smiled.

I've long believed that Dad's devotion to family had a deep impact on young Jackie Nicklaus. I suspect that while diligently practicing the golf techniques my father was teaching him, Nicklaus also might have been quietly studying Dad's way of going about his day-to-day life. As Nicklaus proceeded through his spectacular career, he would, as my father did, make sure that his family got as much attention from him as did his work in golf. Nicklaus adopted a personal rule that he never would be away from his family for more than two weeks at a time—and he stuck with it. He devoted himself to finding adequate time to be involved in the lives of his children, rather than being a slave to his golfing career. These were personal values he shared with not only his own father, but also my dad.

***

The 1953 PGA Championship was played July 1- 7 on the compact 6,465-yard, par-71 Birmingham Country Club course in suburban Detroit. As usual at that time, thirty-six holes of stroke play determined the sixty-four qualifiers for match play, and Dad shot 74-72-146 to make the cut by two strokes. Meanwhile, excellent players such as Henry Picard, Horton Smith, Lawson Little and Toney Penna failed to qualify. Johnny Palmer was low qualifier with a 134.

On the first day of match play, defending champion Jim Turnesa, heavily favored Sam Snead and tournament co-favorite Cary Middlecoff headed a list of golf's brightest names—including Gene Sarazen, Vic Ghezzi, Jim Ferrier, Chandler Harper, Chick Harbert, Lew Worsham and Porky Oliver—who were buried in an avalanche of upsets. Dad pulled off one of those stunning surprises, defeating medalist Palmer. The newspapers called that first day "a carnage of name players," and termed it the darkest "black Friday" in PGA Championship history.

Though my father was a forty-three-year-old club pro who hadn't been a touring player for six years, he played steady golf that week. Against Palmer, he won two of the first three holes and led three-up at the turn. He jumped the margin to four-up with a birdie at the twelfth, then saw Palmer make a match of it by winning two of the next four holes before Dad held on for a two-and-one win. It was a significant and satisfying victory for my father. Johnny Palmer was a seven-time tour winner, after all, who proved his golf mettle by winning the Western Open at the Salt Lake City Country Club in 1947, when that tourney was considered one of the leading events in American golf. A veteran of the U.S. Army Air Corps who was a B29 gunner on thirty-two missions over Japan in WWII, Palmer was an accomplished golf pro who was nicknamed "Old Stone" because of his calmness and lack of expression when playing.

Dad had reason for elation over his morning match-play victory, but the afternoon round pulled him back to earth. He lost that match four-and-two to Claude Harmon, who that morning had defeated Ted Kroll by the same margin. Harmon was eight under par for his two matches on "black Friday" and played well the entire week, making it to the semifinals before losing one-down to the eventual champion, Walter Burkemo.

Heading back to Columbus with a seventeenth-place tie in a major championship, my father had proved again that he could compete with golf's elite. But while that gave him renewed credibility (and perhaps more income) on the lesson tee, he really didn't need the ego boost it provided. My father was fully focused by this time on being a great club pro and teacher, and especially on being a mentor to the teenage golf phenom, Jackie Nicklaus.

The rest of Dad's life would be built on sharing his knowledge with the many accomplished professional and amateur golfers who sought him out, and sharing his love with his family. It was a life he could only have dreamed of in those long-ago days when he crisscrossed the country in drafty automobiles with Ben Hogan, Byron Nelson and Henry Picard, sharing the hardships of travel and the delights and demons of his sport with the other dreamers and achievers of professional golf.

Dad's final major tournament was the 1956 U.S. Open at Oak Hill Country Club in Rochester, New York. He shot two not-very-good rounds there and missed the cut.

Chapter 16
Wisdom from a Legend

"High winds. Mud. Rain. You're going to play in it, you better practice in it." —*JACK GROUT*

***

By the summer of 1952, group golf lessons with my father had become passé for the impatient perfectionist Jackie Nicklaus. The youngster talked his father into letting him supplement his weekly group lesson with some private lessons from the pro. A month after these one-on-one sessions started, the Scioto charge slips began arriving at the Nicklaus home. When the elder Nicklaus went over his club statement, he'd rub his forehead in amazement and mutter, "Good gracious Jack what's this, another lesson from Mr. Grout, and a dozen buckets of balls in one day?" But Jackie's father was just teasing him. Mr. Nicklaus actually received great enjoyment from the time and effort his son was putting into golf.

Nicklaus was a slave to practice. My brother John has vivid memories of watching the youngster stroll to the range, full of purpose. "It was always a treat when Jack Nicklaus would come out to hit balls," John says. As Nicklaus advanced into his late teens, John remembers, "Jack had a shag bag loaded with slightly used Titleist 5's, and we always waited anxiously for him to pull out the driver."

This steady practicing and extra tutoring from Dad led to real progress, with young Jackie breaking 80 for the first time while still twelve. He had shot eight straight 80s, and just when the little bomber began to wonder if breaking that barrier was an unreachable goal, he shot a 74. My father actually remembered the day it happened, because one of the kid's tee shots almost clobbered him. By chance, Dad was playing just ahead of Jackie. In a subsequent interview he related the moment this way:

"I smoked a good one off the tee at number sixteen, over the hill in the fairway. I hit onto the green with a seven-iron. Just after I started walking toward the green, a ball came whizzing by me. I looked around and I couldn't see anyone. Pretty soon, here comes little Jack ... playing all by himself. That was his drive. I knew right then this kid was something. When you're only twelve and hit the ball that far—it must have been 275 yards—wow!"

*Scioto junior golfers in 1953 include: (second row) my sister Ronnie, third from the left, and brother John, tenth from the left; (back row) 13-year-old Jackie Nicklaus, fifth from the left. (*Columbus Dispatch *photo by Jack Hutton)*

A near-identical incident happened a year later, when the by-then thirteen-year-old clobbered a tee shot down the sixteenth fairway and right through the legs of long-hitting Scioto golfer Bob Hoag. "I said, 'Who the hell is that?' " Hoag said later, "and the guy I was playing with said, 'That's this little thirteen-year-old kid. Jackie Nicklaus is his name.'" (Hoag would soon forgive the near miss. In fact, he became one of Nicklaus' best friends and for many years was his playing partner in the Bing Crosby Pro-Am Tournament.)

My father delighted in his young student's proclivity for smashing the ball. Nicklaus heard my father say repeatedly, in different phrases but all with the same meaning, "Go on, Jackie boy, let this one have it. Don't worry about where it goes. We can fix that later. Now whack the daylights out of this next one." Dad was preaching the same sermon a dozen years later, when it was my turn to get serious about golf. "Dickie, this time I want you to really smoke it," he would say.

Inspired by my dad's encouragement and spurred by his own huge competitiveness, the young Nicklaus continued to make fast progress. In the summer of 1953, at age thirteen, he reached a key goal he had set for himself, breaking 70 for the first time. Par at Scioto was 36-36-72, and Jackie fired 34-35-69 while playing with his father.

The youngster had temporarily gained entry into golf's "promised land." Yet all golfers know that the game has a fickle nature; one minute you're on top of the world, and the next minute you're ready to quit. Later that summer, the hard-charging phenom was sorely tested. Since Jackie had begun to gain some recognition, he was invited to play in a celebrity outing at Scioto, staged by Columbus Mayor James A. Rhodes for the benefit of the National Caddie Tournament. Dad was charged with running the tournament and decided to pair Jackie in a foursome that included Patty Berg, the greatest woman golfer of her time. Before the whole affair started, Dad delighted in the opportunity to build up his young protégé by telling Berg all about his wonderful talent.

Occasionally my father would reminisce about that day, and when he did, he'd really throw his head back and laugh. "Jack shanked all over the course," he said. "I think he shanked every iron shot he hit." Nicklaus wound up with an embarrassing 53 for nine holes—a score that was easily ten strokes higher than he had been shooting on his poorest days. It was, to say the least, a humbling experience for the youngster. The truth was, though, that young Jackie had not been feeling well. His back was sore. He had a slight temperature and a persistent dull headache that caused him some dizziness. Eventually it was discovered that he had a mild, non-paralytic type of polio. His sister, Marilyn, had a more severe case that affected her walking for quite some time.

***

In 1955, Emerson L. Davis, veteran golf writer of the *Ohio State Journal*, later the *Columbus Citizen-Journal*, wrote a piece in which he detailed the rise of Jackie Nicklaus within the golfing firmament. Davis wrote:

"Five years ago, Jackie was just another 10-year-old carrot top in a junior class at Scioto, getting his first peek at golf under the supervision of professional Jack Grout. But now Jackie, thanks to some fine teaching by Grout and his own determination to conquer the game, has blossomed into a good golfer. A number of people, followers of the game, and others have asked us on occasion these questions: How good is Nicklaus? Will he become a great golfer? Where will he go to college?

"We had a talk with Jack Grout. He told us that the youngster, right now, is a better golfer than a lot of much older leading amateurs, and his shooting in the 60s on tough courses was remarkable. Grout added, 'Jackie cannot do much better scoring, but he keeps learning a

Wintertime in the quonset hut at Scioto,1960: Jack Nicklaus (with friend Bob Obetz) under Dad's watchful eye. (Bill Foley photo, used with permission)

little more about the finesse of the game each time out. He's eager to absorb everything he can on golf and practices for hours trying to improve on the different phases of the game. Once in a while, like most everyone, he tries powdering or slugging his drives, but that's only a natural instinct, and as long as he's straight it doesn't make any difference.'

"Grout, one of the finest pro shooters in the state, was on tour with the nation's top pros a few years back and is sure that if Jackie continues to improve and not lose sight of the fact that he still has a lot to learn, he could become one of the greatest golfers in history ... He's an amazing youngster. Golf is easy for him and don't forget that he's a natural athlete, adept at basketball, swimming and any other sport he tries."

According to Davis, my dad figured that Nicklaus would "reach his peak when he's around 20 years of age, because by that time ... the youngster will have mastered all the shots, will have the know how, and nothing is likely to ruffle him."

Years later, in his first book, *Let Me Teach You As I Taught Jack Nicklaus*, my father—the very player Byron Nelson said was "too nice a guy, not a tough enough competitor"—wrote that "competition, whether it be for the U.S. Open or a mere fifty-cent Nassau match, is the stimulant that all successful golfers relish. It's the spice that makes all the hours of practice worthwhile." Given that philosophy, it was natural for Jackie Nicklaus' teacher to urge the precocious teen to enter every junior tournament he could. The Nicklaus family made every sacrifice, financially and otherwise, to see that Jackie had the opportunity to compete often. Making all this easier was the young player's tremendous natural desire to challenge himself against other good players.

The record shows, obviously, that all of this competition, plus frequent lessons and obsessive practice, resulted in quick improvement in Jackie's game. As my father put it, "Although he wasn't a standout from the very start, after about six years he was." What happened then was the golfing highlight of Nicklaus' high school days. At sixteen years old, competing against a field that included solid professional players, Nicklaus emerged with a flourish from the golfing shadows by winning the Ohio State Open at Marietta Country Club. His four rounds of 76-70-64-72 represented the young man's coming-out party as a substantive golfer.

***

Through his middle and late teens, Jackie Nicklaus remained as close as ever to my father. During this period, Dad worked especially hard with him on two phases of shot making that were to become outstanding characteristics of Nicklaus' style of play: hitting the ball in a high arch, and hitting it so that it flew on a left-to-right trajectory, known to golfers as a "fade." Seeing Jackie's vast potential, my father was looking ahead, as he had been from the start, to the years when his protégé might be competing against the finest players in the world. He thought it important that the budding star learn to hit the ball high, because this would be to his advantage when he was faced with playing long irons to firm, fast greens on which the pins were placed in spots that offered little margin for error. The value of fading the ball is that a fade generally is thought to offer more control than a "draw," or right-to-left flight, the latter flight pattern too often resulting in sharp hooks of the type that plagued Ben Hogan during his early golfing years. The very best players are able to play the ball either way, depending on the shot that is called for by the design of the hole and the way the wind is blowing at a given moment. However, over the long haul, as Dad emphasized to Jackie Nicklaus, the player who fades the ball is likely to have better control than the player who draws it.

Nicklaus practiced these lessons with a vengeance, even through the bitter cold of Columbus winters. "In those days," Nicklaus wrote later, "following the weather-enforced winter layoff from sustained practice, I would usually begin working intensively on my game with Jack Grout at Scioto in early February. If it were not too cold or windy, we would hit balls outdoors, if necessary clearing a patch of snow or packing it down and hitting off the top. In really bitter cold conditions," Nicklaus wrote, making fun of himself, "we'd become sissies and work from the open-ended Quonset hut."

My father and his staff had devised a setup that facilitated practice on harshly cold or snowy days—a wood-framed, plastic-covered half Quonset hut that sat on the Scioto practice range. Equipped with mats and a small heater, the homey little shelter allowed Dad to give lessons during the off-season without freezing himself or his pupils. "Well," Nicklaus would say later, "Jack didn't give many lessons (to other players) once I started using the hut, because there weren't any golf balls left for anyone else to work with. I'd hit my own practice balls, then Jack's teaching balls. We'd hit everybody's practice balls." Nicklaus recalled that "it was a lot of fun when the snow melted, trying to sort them all out."

Even in bitterly cold weather, Nicklaus could be found on the Scioto range. "I'm sure some of the older members thought I was mentally impaired, even downright crazy," Nicklaus said later. "They probably thought the same about Jack Grout, too, for standing out there in the cold with me." About those days in the hut, Dad said, "Jack will practice in weather a brave man wouldn't venture out in."

As Nicklaus attended Ohio State University in the late 1950s, my father's habit would be to take a look at the young man's game for a few minutes periodically, maybe offer a thought or two always keyed to golfing fundamentals, and then tell him to go play. Scioto member John Bishop remembered watching these sessions and marveling at the quiet communication between student and teacher. "Jack's hitting those terrific shots out there, and Jack Grout is saying nothing," Bishop said. "But every once in a while he'd just go up to (Nicklaus), and he'd tell him to stop at the backswing and he'd just move his hands a little bit, not so I'd even notice it. Then he'd just say, 'Try that.' And Jack would try that. I didn't see any difference in it, but they both agreed it was better."

Veteran Columbus sportswriter Kaye Kessler, recipient of a PGA Lifetime Achievement Award in Journalism in 2001, watched such practice-range work with a journalist's analytical approach and respected what he saw. "Jack Grout was an economist with words, a picture of sartorial splendor with dress," Kessler said. "Clad virtually always in shirt, tie, sport jacket or sweater, he was remarkably perceptive but sparing with his always soft-spoken directions or responses."

Kessler, who covered more than one hundred golf majors and followed Nicklaus from his start at age ten, noted that through the years the Nicklaus-Grout team "became so stunningly in sync that if Nicklaus had a problem, a question, a funk or whatever, he could call his main man for answers. Concise, simple, Grout would quietly ask Nicklaus the positioning of his feet, path of takeaway, follow-through, head movement, ball flight. A quick and calming solution would follow."

Kessler recalled Nicklaus saying repeatedly that, "Mr. Grout was amazing, knew me backwards and forwards, didn't need to be with me, though he usually was, and he could ask me one simple question and have the answer."

The quiet, carefully targeted and specific instruction my father provided to Nicklaus made an impression on many who watched their work together. Keith Schneider, a Muirfield Village assistant pro who later would be general manager and director of golf at the popular Castle Pines Golf Club in Colorado, told Kessler, "What struck me most about Mr. Grout was how simplistic his approach was to his instructions. I remember one year when Jack (Nicklaus) came to Muirfield as he prepared for the Canadian Open. I sat on his golf bag for three hours listening and watching while Mr. Grout worked with Jack, and I was so impressed with the simplicity of his approach. I never learned so much in my life as I did while Mr. Grout quietly went through the grip, posture, ball position, head."

Because Dad remained focused on the fundamentals of the game, Nicklaus did, too, and this without a doubt was a key to Jack's ability to remain competitive on the tour through several decades. Typically my father would deflect credit for his pupil's deep knowledge of the golf swing. "The credit for mastering those fundamentals and for sticking to them through thick and thin must go entirely to Jack," he said.

Once Nicklaus had pretty much mastered the game's basics, Dad's main objective was to build him up with encouragement and help him to believe in himself. My father's supportive nature and his career as a tour professional himself had helped him understand the massive peaks and valleys that the game of golf imposes upon the human psyche. Jack Grout, it turned out, was just the right teacher for someone as naturally golf-smart as Jack Nicklaus. Dad impressed and inspired

Nicklaus. The simplicity of his approach and the respectful manner in which he did things were major reasons why Nicklaus stayed with Dad for nearly forty years.

In my view, the most impressive single thing my father did as Jack Nicklaus' career-long coach was to resist any temptation to dictate specific techniques to him. There are legions of books and countless magazine articles detailing the exploits of golf teachers who teach a certain "system," and who push hard to get their pupils to buy into that way of doing things. My father was not that kind of teacher. He felt great confidence in his knowledge of the game, as he should have, given his years of competition with and against elite golfers such as Hogan, Snead, Nelson, Demaret and many others, plus his work with great golf thinkers and instructors such as Jack Burke Sr., Alex Morrison and Henry Picard. But from Dad's days on tour, he knew that a player must understand his own game well enough to be able to address its flaws not only on the practice tee, but also on the course during competition. He maintained that any golfer, including his own star pupil, would flounder in hit-or-miss fashion unless he thoroughly understood his own swing and could diagnose his own mistakes.

This ability to self-correct is, of course, essential if a player aspires to become a great champion. This is what my father meant when he said that "I taught Jack the fundamentals of the game, but there came a time when he had to figure out his own problems and their cures." In his work with the young Nicklaus, Dad always served not only the usual main course of fundamentals, but also a side order of "how one thing affects another—what causes what." Dad regarded those lessons on independent thinking as some of the most important and valuable he ever gave to Jack Nicklaus.

Nicklaus appreciated the subtlety of my father's teaching approach. "I'd ask questions," Nicklaus said, and "Jack Grout would tell me that I should change directions slowly at the top of my backswing. I'd say, 'Why do I have to change directions slowly?' Then he would explain that if I didn't, my legs wouldn't have time to work in my downswing; my shoulders would take over instead. There are a million things Jack told me to do, but he also always told me why to do them."

Nicklaus' ultimate conversion to self-reliance occurred when he obtained what may have been the single most important piece of golfing advice he ever received. It came from amateur golfing legend Bobby Jones, albeit indirectly through Jack's father, Charlie. As the elder Nicklaus visited with Jones at Augusta National during the 1961 Masters, Jones shared his convictions about the role of a teacher in a golfer's career. "I think I was a fairly good young golfer," Jones told

Jack Grout and Jimmy Thomson with tournament host Bob Jones at Augusta National in 1959. (Photo courtesy of Scioto Country Club)

Charlie, "but I never became what I would call a really good player until I'd been competing for quite a number of seasons. You see, when I started to play in the big tournaments, whenever anything went wrong I'd run home to Stewart Maiden, our pro at East Lake (in Atlanta), who taught me the game. Finally I matured to the point where I understood my game well enough to make my own corrections during the course of a tournament, and that's when I'd say I became a good golfer."

When Charlie Nicklaus passed on those remarks to his twenty-one-year-old son, they hit home. Jack began to realize that, from the age of ten, every time he had missed a couple of shots he would head back to Jack Grout. From the day Jack's father reported his conversation with Jones, Nicklaus continued to work regularly with my dad on refining and honing his game, but he also made a conscious and ever-increasing effort to figure things out for himself. In subsequent sessions with my father, Jack would ask more questions about the "whys" of the various elements of the swing and fewer about the "hows" of executing them.

Like Jones, Jack Nicklaus recognized the need for the ability to, in effect, teach himself. He recognized that he would have to have sufficient mental grasp of proper technique to be able to make his own corrections, not just on the practice tee, but, so far as is possible, also while actually competing. In short, he recognized that he had been playing for too long with crutches. And he understood that the only way to discard those crutches was to gain the independence that comes from internalizing the game's cause-and-effect relationships and developing an ability to deal with them on the fly, without outside help.

It's obvious that this belief in self-analysis on the course isn't universally accepted today, as numerous professional golfers surround themselves with full-swing instructors, short-game instructors, psychologists and other specialists who form their ever-present entourages. Dr. Rich Orlando, a Columbus resident who took golf lessons from my father and later observed the practice routines of hundreds of touring pros as the on-site ophthalmologist for Nicklaus' Memorial Tournament, talked skeptically of this phenomenon. "So many of the current players bring (David) Leadbetter, Rick Smith, Butch Harmon, etc., out on the range at every damn tournament. These guys can't ever take the club back without having their 'guru' with them."

It seems now that Nicklaus was wise beyond his years in moving toward greater self-sufficiency early in his career. Even though he still was barely into his twenties, Nicklaus by the early 1960s was becoming a major figure on the world golf scene. He increasingly was finding himself playing high-level competition far from his golf home at Scioto and without my dad on hand to coach him on short notice. Through the 1950s, encouraged by his father and by my dad, Nicklaus had played an increasingly heavy schedule of local, regional and national tournaments. He won youth championships at Scioto in 1950 and 1951, was a member of the Scioto CC youth championship team in 1952, won the Ohio State Junior Championship in 1954 and 1955, and made that first major splash in 1956 by winning the Ohio State Open at age sixteen. Then, in 1959, Nicklaus won the first of his two U.S. Amateur titles and was chosen to play for what has been called the greatest U.S. team ever assembled in the Walker Cup Matches—the amateur equivalent of the Ryder Cup for pros—in Muirfield, Scotland. Among his teammates: Deane Beman, Harvie Ward, Charlie Coe and Tommy Aaron.

When Nicklaus finished second by two strokes to Arnold Palmer in the 1960 U.S. Open at Cherry Hills in Denver, it was clear that the chunky young phenom from Columbus, Ohio, had matured into a tremendously capable player. His identity as the "Golden Bear" would develop not long after, as well. In his book, *My Story,* Nicklaus wrote that on the day he turned pro in 1961, he got a call from an apparel company. The firm wanted him to endorse a line of its sweaters and sports shirts. Casting about for an emblem or logo that could be used on the sportswear, Nicklaus eventually recalled an interview that an Australian writer named Don Lawrence had done with Mark McCormack, Jack's future agent. In the article based on that interview, Lawrence referred to Nicklaus as the Golden Bear. (Coincidentally, Jack had played high school basketball for the Upper Arlington Golden Bears.) "Jack, that's it," his wife, Barbara, said when he proposed a bear logo. By 1963, wrote Nicklaus, he was "routinely known by the new moniker." I never heard my dad refer to him by that nickname, but I know he thought it was perfect. "Like the bear," Dad quipped, "big Jack was not inclined to leave behind many scraps for others to feast on." He got a big laugh out of saying that.

The Golden Bear began traveling more once he turned pro in 1961 and had fewer easy opportunities to see his golf mentor at Scioto. Not that it was really necessary for him to spend as much time with my father on the lesson tee. They'd spent a full decade of frequent and often-intense work together, and the physical golf fundamentals and strategic considerations my father taught had been well learned. Given his natural athletic ability and his understanding of the game's mental side, it was time for Jack Nicklaus to take command of his own ship and rely on Dad primarily for periodic refresher sessions, with less-frequent in-depth reviews to root out accumulated swing flaws.

Also, something else was happening over which even the mighty young Nicklaus had no control. By the late summer of 1961 my father had been at Scioto Country Club for nearly twelve years and perhaps felt he'd accomplished all he could there. His longtime clubhouse assistant, Dom LePore, suggested that Dad was also feeling the need to make more money to support his wife and four children—the arrival of my little sister Debbie in 1954 having rounded out the Grout sibling foursome. Or maybe after more than a decade in one place—by far my father's longest stay at one club since his first head-professional job way back in 1927—Dad just felt the itch to move on. On Friday, September 1, 1961, a headline in *The Columbus Dispatch* reported: "Jack Grout Will Take Florida Job." The article said that my father had informed Scioto's board of directors the previous night that he would resign his position at the club effective October 31.

Dad had accepted a job as head professional at La Gorce Country Club in Miami Beach, Florida, starting November 1. This was a major decision for him, and he was excited at the prospect of living and working not only in another top-notch club, but also in a warm-weather city. What the *Dispatch* article didn't reveal, though, was that a small "rebellion" within the Grout family had left the La Gorce move in question for a time. After going to Miami for interviews and then accepting the new job, Dad returned to Columbus and awaited a letter from the Florida club that would make his hiring official. And he waited ... and waited. What he didn't know was that his fifteen-year-old daughter, Ronnie, then very happily ensconced at Upper Arlington High School, was appalled at the thought of leaving Columbus and had devised a secret plan to derail the move.

As Ronnie told it, "Our mailman usually arrived at our home around noon, which was about the time I returned (during the summer) from hanging out with my girlfriends ... I decided to sabotage the move by hiding all of the mail postmarked from Florida. Every day I ran home from my friends' houses or the pool to pick up the mail before anyone else got to it. I'd rifle through it, grabbing the important letters and quickly running them up to my room."

A few days passed, and Dad wondered why he wasn't hearing from La Gorce. "One evening during dinner," Ronnie said, "I noticed that Dad seemed restless and sad. I never thought it was because of my secret." But then Ronnie learned from Mom that Dad was concerned because he hadn't heard from La Gorce. "Your father has resigned from Scioto, and he was told that he was hired in Florida," Mom said.

Ronnie began to cry, convinced that she had ruined her father's career. Overcome with guilt, she retrieved the letters from her sock drawer and went downstairs to find Dad sitting in the den, reading his newspaper. "I handed him my secret bundle," Ronnie said, "and admitted what I had done." Fortunately, it hadn't been so long that Dad's new employer had begun to question his interest or dependability; in the stack of mail was just one letter from the club. "I thought he was going to kill me, but he was just relieved," Ronnie said. "I'll never forget how sweet and understanding he was about my scheme. No spanking, no punishment, just a good talking to and the promise to never hide the mail again. I was lucky, I suppose. But we still moved to Florida."

On the surface, my father leaving Scioto and moving fifteen hundred miles south to Miami Beach might not seem so unusual. He always had detested wet and cold weather, and now he was putting frigid winters in the past. In my view, though, Dad's decision said a great deal about him and his personal values. Most other club pros, situated as Dad was at Scioto in 1961 with an excellent golf operation and a golf prodigy under his sole tutelage, would have stayed. Is it possible to imagine any teacher today moving away from such a superstar just when the player is about to hit the big time?

An article in the *Columbus Dispatch* quoted my father as expressing some regret at leaving Scioto, where he'd spent so many happy and successful years. But in it, he also talked with quiet enthusiasm about his new assignment. "La Gorce is the oldest club on the Beach," he explained. "It's a good opportunity for me, and it will give me a chance to do different things. I get July and August off, so I can take trips with my wife and kids."

***

At the Columbus Airport, 1959: Teacher sending protégé off to Scotland for the Walker Cup Matches. (Bill Foley photo, used with permission)

On Thursday evening, October 26, 1961, Scioto Country Club hosted a farewell appreciation dinner for Jack Grout. More than 150 Scioto members and other Columbus friends were there, and the keynote speaker was James Rhodes, the sitting state auditor and eventual governor. In his toast to my father, Rhodes said many kind words:

"Somewhere in our community today are men and women who are successful leaders in their own fields ... men and women who were the children of yesterday, who under the guidance of a professional golfer, counselor and friend have made good in life's endeavors.

"The affection planted in Jackie Nicklaus and other youngsters by wise guidance, sense of right values, and the virtues of integrity, initiative and fair play were fostered in their minds by their dear friend and teacher ... Jack Grout.

"It is by the honesty, proven merit and wise leadership of men like Jack Grout that our boys and girls of Scioto have taken their places at the helm of the ship of life ... and they can carry on as wisely as those who have taught them ... for they have been imbued with the simple and abiding principles of fair play.

"It is with this purpose and in this faith that the teachings of Jack Grout will carry on forever with his students.

"Jack Grout has faith in God—in the Golden Rule—the Brotherhood of Man. And he has been blessed with a wonderful family.

"His faith in youth—The hope of tomorrow—A hope which can never fail ... To have a good friend and a good teacher is one of the greatest attributes of life ... and to be a good friend and teacher is one of the noblest and most difficult of undertakings. Jack Grout has been such a friend and teacher ... His friendship and council is abiding.

"We are sadly parting with our old friend and teacher ... but he will be away from us only in distance. He will always be in our hearts and our minds. Jack Grout is only saying 'good-night' and not 'good-bye.'

"Our humble prayer is 'God make us worthy of such a friend.' "

Unfortunately, Dad's family had to miss the farewell dinner. By then, mom had packed her four children in the new, air-conditioned 1961 Buick LeSabre convertible that Dad had given her for her fortieth birthday and driven us to Florida for enrollment in our new schools. I remember that on the day we left Columbus, I turned around in the backseat of the robin's egg blue Buick to take one last look at our house. Mom then proceeded to push that Buick hard as we motored south toward a new place and a new life. My brother John was sixteen, my sister Ronnie fifteen, and my little sister Debbie seven at the time. I was eight.

That December, while our family was settling into the warmth of South Florida, Jack Nicklaus was toiling in the makeshift little Quonset hut at Scioto. He wrote in his book *The Greatest Game Of All* that it "wasn't quite the same that year. Jack Grout wasn't around."

As 1961 drew to a close, my family was adjusting happily to a new life in the sunny south of Florida. Dad was feeling right at home at an excellent golf club populated by high-profile and fun-loving athletes, movie stars, political figures and business leaders. My siblings and I were in new schools and developing new friends. And Jack Nicklaus was making his own big plans back in Columbus. "That year, for the first time," Nicklaus wrote later, "I said good-bye to the other wintertime practicers just before New Year's Day and headed for the West Coast and a whole new life as a PGA Tour professional."

For my father, for our family and for Jack Nicklaus, it was a time of change, of new adventures and rewarding discoveries. None of us suspected at that time how often Jack Grout and Jack Nicklaus would cross paths in the coming decades, how strong their personal bond would grow, and how effectively they would team to make a deep and enduring impact on the world of golf.

Chapter 17
Where the "Action" Never Stops

"Hitting a ball over the green will land you in the Poor House."
—JACK GROUT

❋❋❋

The golf club where my father became head pro in 1961 was as different from his previous place of employment as the earth is from the moon. Scioto Country Club, tucked into a suburb of sleepy Columbus, Ohio, was a successful, well-regarded operation with a wonderful golf course, solid membership and, throughout the operation, conservative Midwestern values. La Gorce Country Club, by contrast, sat smack dab in the middle of one of the hottest entertainment and tourism centers of the 1960s – Miami Beach. The club was awash in visiting celebrities and numerous millionaire members and was proud of its showy, fun-loving approach to the game of golf. Opened in the 1920s and hit hard by both the Great Depression and World War II, La Gorce had made, by the time of Dad's arrival, a full-bore recovery. In short, the place was rockin'.

La Gorce's clubhouse was a sizable two-story, white-frame structure with a green roof. Typical of first-rate golf clubhouses, the La Gorce facility had a large and inviting living room-type area inside the front entrance. Comfortable couches and chairs were arranged around a fireplace, above which loomed a large portrait of club founder John Oliver La Gorce. To the left of the living room area was an impressively wide, open staircase that led to the more formal dining room upstairs.

Visitors entered the golf shop through glass double doors to the left of the main entrance. Dad's office was near the reception desk there, and players heading out the back door toward the first tee passed a one-chair barber shop, complete with manicurist.

All in all, it was a handsome and functional facility, but at La Gorce merely "functional" wasn't enough. That, at least, was the conviction of a largish, bulbous-nosed fellow named Harry Daumit, who was La Gorce's president during several years of Dad's stint there and who championed a project to greatly enliven the club's interior décor. Daumit, founder with his first wife of Lustre Crème Shampoo products in the 1950s, was given to boldness, and the emotions of La Gorce's members were decidedly mixed when the results of his redecoration effort were unveiled. Some said it looked lush and rich, aptly opulent given the club's wealthy clientele. Others, though, said the place resembled a Gay-Nineties house of ill repute. No question, the red carpets and ornate gold trimmings made the interior spaces stand out.

The gaudy decorating notwithstanding, it was in the grill room, the locker rooms and on the golf course itself that the dazzling personality of the La Gorce Country Club of the 1960s shone through. The place was a magnet for an assortment of interesting characters—the guy, for instance, who one day dashed off into the bushes during a golf round, donned a karate suit, then dashed back to the tee and screamed "kyeee, kyeee" as he hit his drive, or the men who would sneak onto the course before a round and reposition the tee markers to spots more favorable to the types of shots they could hit.

Balancing the zaniness was the dash and style provided by the rich and famous who frequented the club in great numbers. The locker rooms, dining areas and fairways of La Gorce were favored destinations of entertainers such as Bob Hope, Chuck Connors, James Garner and Will Rogers; athletes from Mickey Mantle to Patty Berg, Babe Zaharias, Jack Dempsey and Gene Tunney; high-profile sports franchise owners John Y. Brown, Bob Irsay and Joe Robbie; and politicians including Vice President Spiro Agnew (and his Secret Service entourage). And, as these big-name club members and guests imbibed in and contributed to the intoxicating glamour of the place, they also regularly rubbed elbows with a class of men who saw golf not as a sport but as merely a game of chance in which real money could be made in a hurry, given the right opponent. These were serious, big-time gamblers, tough and unwavering high rollers who could draw large and appreciative galleries of La Gorce members and guests to their high-stakes games on the club's pristine fairways.

***

My father's departure from quiet, conservative Columbus to the rowdiness and glitz of Miami Beach came at a time when the nation was entering a period of serious change and turmoil. The Silent Generation of President Eisenhower's 1950s was giving way to a new generation tortured by America's involvement in the Vietnam War. There were street protests and new kinds of music, dress and morals—all adding up to a cultural revolution that changed our nation and the world. The country would be uplifted by Alan Shepard's fifteen-minute flight on the Freedom 7 in 1961, making him the first American in space. But events as disparate as the civil rights movement in the

American South, the assassination of President Kennedy, the appearance of the mop-haired Beatles—"these youngsters from Liverpool," as television icon Ed Sullivan referred to them—and even the searing focus on female sexuality by the new editor of *Cosmopolitan*, Helen Gurley Brown, all rocked the American psyche.

Amid this decade of societal upheaval, Miami Beach, like its sister entertainment center Las Vegas, provided for those who could afford at least a temporary respite from what seemed like unsolvable problems in our cultural and political life. The beautiful hotels, beaches and nightclubs that lined the famed Collins Avenue were a pleasure-seeker's paradise, though absent Sin City's legalized gambling. And La Gorce Country Club was right in the middle of the action.

Given all that, it seems incongruous that my father—a quiet, unassuming man who definitely was not a party guy—should choose La Gorce as the place for his capstone job as a full-time club professional. The fact was, though, that Dad never felt it was his primary role to keep the club's celebrity members and guests happy or to get involved in the high-stakes wagering that was so common there during his tenure. Rather, he saw his role largely as the architect of a calm, tranquil, professional atmosphere in which he could promote the game of golf to men, women and children through individual and group instruction.

Actually, whether Dad was able to foster a golf operation that was calm and tranquil is debatable. He never talked much about it, but he gave hints from time to time that he was amused, even charmed, by how common it was to see the uncommon at the club. Dad's employees had similar responses, particularly concerning the regularity and ease with which they found themselves in the company of major celebrities. John Scheffler, an assistant pro for Dad for ten years before taking a head-professional position in Massachusetts, marveled in recalling memories of the La Gorce CC of the '60s and early '70s. He told, for instance, of club member and Baltimore Colts owner Bob Irsay popping into the pro shop and saying, "John, what are you doing for dinner tonight? How'd you like to have dinner with the Chicago Bears?" The Bears were having a team dinner at the club, and Scheffler attended, relishing the chance to mingle with stars such as the brilliant linebacker Dick Butkus.

Numerous other pro football stars roamed the halls and the golf course at La Gorce—the Packers' Jerry Kramer and Max Magee, 49ers' (and later Saints and Redskins) quarterback Billy Kilmer, Miami's Bob Griese and many more. "Broadway Joe" Namath, while as famous for his good-natured cockiness as his formidable football skills, was regarded as one of the more polite and personable athletes who frequented the club. "It was really an exciting place for someone like me to work," John Scheffler said. "And Mr. Grout, he just handled it."

Thanks partly to the La Gorce membership of New York Yankees owner Dan Topping, a stream of baseball stars passed through the club's pro shop. My sister Ronnie once played the La Gorce course with Dodgers lefthander Sandy Koufax, and local legend says that Mickey Mantle left his mark by once hitting a drive of about 420 yards on one of the club's par fives!

Entertainers who played the hotels and clubs along Collins Avenue also were regular visitors at La Gorce, and even the fashion designer Oleg Cassini was a frequent visitor. I once played La Gorce with Cassini and still can see him approaching the "halfway house" after the ninth hole to place an order. "I would love a Gatorade," Cassini said. At first, nobody could understand him; he pronounced it something like, "Ghat-tur-ah-dee." After a few puzzled moments, though, we figured it out.

La Gorce was a hospitable haven for all manner of high-profile people who, while at the club, were treated with respect but about whom no "fuss" was made. Still, the club's welcoming posture toward its famous visitors did have limits. One mammoth pro football player, for instance, irritated senior club members when he spent his days as a guest strolling around, constantly flexing his impressive muscles. A former La Gorce member (who asked not to be named in this story) tells of the club's old-timers getting tired of this guy and conspiring to cut him down to size. Inspired by an image from the movie *Paper Lion*, they brought in a mongoose, showed the rat-like creature to the macho fellow, and then set it loose. "The guy jumped up on a locker and was screaming and yelling ... 'Get it away, get it away,'" the former member recalled. Everybody in the locker room was laughing. The guy was a little bit more unassuming after that."

***

The famous coterie that routinely made La Gorce its "second home" provided an atmosphere of excitement to the club, but another part of the club's culture unquestionably gave it much of its allure for the well-to-do. The place was, simply put, a thriving center for high-stakes wagering. Perhaps it was just the times, or maybe it had to do with the famous clientele, but whatever the reason, the authorities looked the other way. The presence of serious gambling at La Gorce wasn't troubling to my father, though. After all, he had worked at the

Father and son at La Gorce Country Club in 1970 during a Golf Digest *photo shoot. (Doug Kennedy photo, used with permission)*

Arlington Downs thoroughbred track in Texas early in his career and had bet on the ponies and enjoyed competitive card games of all types.

A certain amount of gambling wasn't uncommon for a golf club, then or now, of course. Wagering always has been a key thread in the sport's fabric, whether on the professional tours or on the thousands of municipal tracts that dot the American landscape. Author Tom LeCompte put it well in an article titled "The 18-Hole Hustle" that appeared in a 2005 issue of *American Heritage* magazine: "In the days before television and corporate sponsors; in the days before the players became superstars, surrounded by personal entourages and traveling by private jet; in the days before golf became staid and safe, there was a time when the game had a more ragged edge."

That ragged edge, LeCompte continued, has lived through the years in stories about wild and crazy goings-on in golf clubs both famous and obscure. "Traded in clubhouses, across card tables or over post-match beers, the sums (wagered) grow a little larger, the propositions a little more outrageous with each retelling. Over time the stories have taken on the weight of myth." As long as there has been golf, LeCompte concluded, "there has been gambling. And where there is gambling, there is bound to be hustling. Call it human nature."

If LeCompte is correct, then the La Gorce that Dad joined as head golf professional in 1961 was brimming with human nature. The hustlers were plentiful, the action ongoing and expensive. I experienced this firsthand as I moved through my teens and sought to emulate my father by becoming a professional golfer. There was, for instance, the day I was approached on the La Gorce range by a fellow named Al Dobbin, a man not unfamiliar with gambling action. I was a very good player by this time, and Dobbin invited me to be his partner in an upcoming money match. "It'll be big money, kid," Dobbin declared. "But you can't lose. If we win, you get half. If we lose, I'll pay. What do you think?"

Seemed like a sure deal to me, so I agreed. A week or so later Dobbin informed me of the date of our match and, importantly, outlined a few "particulars" that I needed to understand. First, he told me that it wasn't always best to win every hole. Sometimes, he said, it's prudent to deliberately lose a hole—to purposely mishit a shot or two and, without being obvious, miss a crucial putt. Though his advice challenged my strong sense of competitiveness (and sportsmanship), I had to admit it did make some sense. What Dobbin was saying was that we had to make our opponents believe they could beat us. We had to string them along so they would make additional side bets called "presses" during the match, thus increasing the overall betting pot and allowing us to squeeze the most money out of them.

To make sure things went as planned, Dobbin instructed me about certain signs he would give me during the match. He would, for example, lift his arms over his head as if to stretch when he wanted me to hit a poor drive or miss the green with an approach shot. On the greens, when he rubbed his face or scratched his head, that meant "don't make the putt," no matter the length.

On the day of our match, I was hitting the ball quite well. When asked, I told Al I was ready. Well, I was ready, all right: I began the round birdie, birdie, par, birdie, birdie, then hit a booming drive on the next hole. Al came racing up to me on the sixth fairway, declaring in undisguised disgust that "kid, we lost them, you played too good! What the hell's wrong with you? You missed every sign I gave you!" Al was shaking his head as he walked away, and I felt very stupid. Our "pigeons," tipped off by my strong play, didn't make another bet the rest of the round.

At another time, when I'd played my way into a tie for the lead entering the final round of the La Gorce club championship, Dobbin flagged me down in the locker room. I think he was trying to get a rise out of me. "Kid, there's an incredible amount of action being bet on the outcome (of the tourney)," he said. "And I can tell you, kid, the majority of it ain't on you." During the final round on Sunday we had a fairly large gallery, which told me there was, in fact, a lot of "interest" in the final result. The betting action notwithstanding, I won that day, finishing birdie, birdie to break the tournament scoring record set twenty years earlier by a man who would go on to make a big name on the PGA Tour, Doug Sanders. Like Al Dobbin said, most of the dough was on the other guy that day—so most of the bettors lost money. How much I never knew.

With characters like Al Dobbin so much a part of La Gorce, it often was impossible to separate the game of golf from the games of chance there. The distinctive lingos of golf and of gambling seemed to blend into one. My brother, John, talked of hearing this hybrid language around the gin rummy and backgammon tables in the Men's Grill, where Puerto Rican waiters wore white Eisenhower jackets and hustled around doing their duties: "Have you got a game?" "What's our starting time?" "Who's our fourth?" The excitement and the hustling grew more intense on the first tee as bets were made and personal constitutions tested. "You could stand back on the shaded porch by the pro shop and hear them bickering over how many strokes to give or get," John said. "Posted handicaps were never a true and honest

Bonnie Grout dancing with Arnold Palmer at La Gorce Country Club in 1964. (Raymond W. Muniz photo, used with permission)

way to determine the match's final agreement. On occasion, the starter would have to prompt them on the PA to begin playing."

Sometimes the betting action went beyond the normal rough and tumble and into the extraordinary, with substantial galleries following the action on the course. Leaving as little as possible to chance, the golf hustlers would take along their favorite caddies, professional bag toters who would station themselves well ahead of the tee boxes during a round and were adept at using a discrete "foot wedge" to ensure that their players had good lies in the rough. The caddie pen at La Gorce featured an array of interesting characters, men with nicknames such as Oakie, Alabam, Hoss, Rhode Island Red, Little Ricky and another red-head named Shithouse Red, who had the extra job of keeping the caddie shack clean. Most of these men would go north for the summer, scattering around the Northeast. Some would drive members' cars north in the spring, then back to Miami for the season. They rented rooms and had their favorite watering holes up in the North Shores area of Miami Beach, halfway between La Gorce and the well-regarded Indian Creek Golf and Country Club.

A veteran caddie named Albert clued me in one day to an amazing match that perhaps typified the high-level action at La Gorce. I was picking up balls on the range when I noticed a foursome including one of the club's major gamblers playing holes one, two and three, then trudging across the practice ground and playing the same holes again. Then they made the loop a third time, to complete nine holes. Albert told me later that the group had "a stranglehold" on a hapless guest, a relative of a chef who was known worldwide. The group had been carrying out a hustle called "three friends and a stranger" or "man in the middle" with this fellow for $30,000 dollars a hole! In this particular hustle, the group had already played eighteen holes, and their "pigeon" and his "partner" were on the hook. Playing the extra holes afforded the losing twosome a chance to win their way back to even. But the man's "partner" invariably would go in the tank at just the right time, so their unpleasant "situation" only got worse and worse. What had seemed to the guest to be an even match easily could pay all three members' golf expenses for quite some time.

As stunning as that sounds, the legendary tennis and golf hustler Bobby Riggs said it was anything but unusual at La Gorce. In his book, *The Last Sure Thing: The Life & Times of Bobby Riggs*, author Tom LeCompte quotes Riggs as saying that "La Gorce was a den of thieves ... All the ringers, hustlers and smart guys were there." Whether accurate or not, Riggs' colorful characterization of the club seemed not to have been appreciated there. One day when receptionist Molly Lee wasn't in the pro shop, I opened one of her desk drawers and discovered inside a list of names that was headed "Persona Non-Grata." When I asked my father what that meant, he said, "Oh, Dickie, that's a list of people who can't come out here anymore." The name "Bobby Riggs" was on that list.

My father had grown up with golf gambling and with assorted amusing characters from the early days of the PGA Tour, so he would just smile and shrug his shoulders at the shady side of La Gorce. If anything, the sheer fun that seemed to wash constantly over the place —not just the high-stakes wagering, but the loony stories Dad heard on a daily basis—inspired his conviction that he'd found a great new home. There was, for instance, the Southern gentleman named Jim who had a regular game with a La Gorce member. Losing to this member on the eighteenth hole one day, Jim requested to "press," or double, their bet. "Jim, you can't get that; sorry, but I don't have to give you that," the member said. But Jim insisted, "My wife told me not to play with ya'," he declared. "My friends told me not to play with ya'. You are a dastardly bastard. You have to do this!" "No, I'm sorry," replied the member, holding fast. Now Jim showed real outrage. "I hate ya', I hate ya', I'll never talk to ya' again!!" he ranted. Finally the member relented. "OK, Jim," he sighed. "You've got it." Suddenly calm, Jim said, quietly "You are a gentleman and I like you very much."

Another member, an Italian who had worked his way through several marriages to wealthy women, loved my father and, when I was in my midteens, wanted to help Dad by taking me back to Italy for a time in order to make me "a man." He even asked my mother if that would be OK but got a bluntly negative response: "You've got to be out of your mind." Years later, when I was in my early twenties, the Italian fellow somehow cajoled me into taking "gigolo training sessions" from him, including proper dining etiquette, the art of persuasive conversation and other skills designed to impress females, particularly wealthy, older ones. I soon got tired of the charades, though, and withdrew from the "training."

My father would roar with laughter over such episodes, each one seeming to heighten his appreciation for the cast of unusual characters surrounding him at the club. Then, at the end of the day, he would shift comfortably into his other world. That was the one he shared with his family in their new residence, a two-story white stucco home located on a dot of land in Biscayne Bay called Sunset Island, reachable via a small bridge from mainland Miami Beach.

While our family enjoyed many things about their new surroundings, it would be a stretch to say that the Grout children passed uneventfully through their early years in South Florida. During the first year, for instance, I suffered an asthma attack while at school, and big sister Ronnie, alerted to my condition by the nuns, called Mom and told her to "come quickly. Dickie is suffering from amnesia!" Both John and Ronnie faced more significant difficulties in adjusting to Miami Beach, and both wound up changing schools. John went back to Upper Arlington High School in Columbus for his senior year, and Ronnie finished high school at Rosarian Academy in West Palm Beach, the two returning home for holidays and the summertime break.

For the most part, Dad's earlier life pattern was maintained in the new Florida environment. He still worked long days and still enjoyed his quiet time at home, reading the newspaper or his latest favorite book about the Civil War or watching "Gunsmoke," "Bonanza," "The Jackie Gleason Show" or assorted war movies and westerns on TV. Dad's all-time favorite show was "All in the Family," which first appeared in 1971. I suspect that Dad could relate well to the Archie Bunker character; neither Archie nor Dad was comfortable with the political, social and cultural changes that besieged the country in the 1960s and '70s.

Debbie and I delighted in tormenting Dad from time to time, maybe just to get his attention. As he was reading one night, Debbie sneaked up to him with a heavy book balanced on her head. The book fell and smacked the tile floor, the loud bang scaring him badly. He swooped out of his chair, grabbed Debbie, and gave her a good whack on the rear end, all in one motion, before she fled the room. Another night, when our family was in Columbus for vacation, Dad was taking a nap when Debbie and I again sneaked up on him. I thought it would be neat to have "cold pop," so we started putting ice cubes on his neck. When Dad awoke and realized what was going on, he lurched from the bed in time to see me dashing out the door. So he again grabbed Debbie and gave her another good whack on the behind. I thought it was really neat that Debbie would take the grief for my bad idea!

Dad got his revenge, of course. He always took Debbie and me to school in the morning, and as we were driving across a causeway one April Fools Day he told us that a huge amusement park was being built over Biscayne Bay, right there by Mount Sinai Medical Center. Debbie and I were so excited by this that we told all our friends about it. We were still yacking about the exciting news when Dad got home from the club that evening, but he finally said, "April Fools Day!" Boy, were we crushed.

Dad's not remembered by most folks as being particularly lighthearted, but he really did have a good sense of humor. During our Miami Beach days, someone gave him a three-foot-tall toy parrot, and Dad discovered that when the thing was plugged in, its eyes lit up, its wings flapped, and its head turned to look around the room. One Halloween, Dad sat in the dark in our den with that parrot over his head and Mom ushered the little trick-or-treaters into the room. Dad stood up, moved his arms and lurched forward. Mom said the little ones bolted for the door, sincerely frightened by the strange parrot-man in the den.

On another occasion, when we went to Howard Johnson's for breakfast after Sunday services, a waitress asked Dad, "Has anyone ever told you that you look like President Johnson?" "No," Dad replied, "but I am his brother, Howard." Silence. It went right over her head.

While there were many things to do in Miami Beach, golf tended to be at the core of many of Dad's interactions with his children. John, for instance, became a talented golfer under Dad's tutelage, his handicap sinking as low as a two before he headed off for college, then into a career as a first officer for National Airlines, then a pilot on big jets for Pan Am and Delta. Adding spice to John's life was his part-time career as a model in Miami, doing both print work and TV commercials. His regular girlfriend, an airline stewardess named Judy Preston, beat out a former Miss USA for the coveted job of being Miss Coppertone, and her face became a fixture on billboards across the country and in a national TV commercial in which John also appeared.

Little sister, Debbie, had her own special golf experiences. She tells, for instance, of having a golf lesson from Dad at age eight or nine, under one of the big trees by La Gorce's first tee. Dad called Debbie "Dobsie," and he said that day, "Dobsie, let's see you whack a few…" On one of her shots, Debbie swung through and clobbered the inside of her left foot! "I immediately looked up at Dad," Debbie says, "and he said with a quite stunned expression, 'Dobsie, I've never seen anybody do *that* before.' Then we both started laughing."

For my part, devotion to Dad and to the sport he'd made his life's work came naturally. I decided early that the beauty of the golf course and the challenge of the game would be the core of my professional life, and Dad generously encouraged my interest. And, of course, having my personal hero encourage me just increased my desire to master the game. In the evenings, just before time to go home, Dad sometimes would say to me, "Dickie, let's go down (hole) one and up nine." Dad would hail one of the caddies to carry his bag, and I'd sling mine across my right shoulder, and off we'd go.

Occasionally during those two-hole rounds, we'd be joined by a fine golfer named Tim Holland, a close buddy of Dad's who was gaining fame as a champion backgammon player. These were pleasant forays, these two-hole rounds, but I also remember that during one of them Dad got so upset at missing a green that he whacked himself on the head with an eight-iron. "Wow," I thought, "this is serious stuff!"

Dad truly loved the game of golf, and my siblings and I all can remember many times when he encouraged us, and even our mom, to enjoy the special beauties of the game. Thus indulged, we proceeded to delve into the game's mysteries with varying levels of intensity, but always with enjoyment. For Dad, this provided not only the satisfaction that comes from sharing one's personal calling with family members; it also provided him with occasional comic relief. I, for one, certainly was not immune from providing such moments for my father. It's not that I lacked seriousness about golf. In fact, once I found out what Dad did for a living and how he spent his time, golf began to appeal to me more and more. Still, my golf education did have its bumpy and humorous moments.

Dad's philosophy was that junior golfers could best learn the game by playing it a lot. So, wanting me to learn the basics of the game before playing the tough La Gorce layout, he directed me to a local par-three course where I spent practically the entire summer of 1963. On that nine-hole layout, located next to Miami Beach High School and with its longest hole measuring 180 yards, I played as many as sixty-three holes in a single day.

Apparently impressed by my ardor, if not yet by my golfing skills, Dad decided at summer's end to send me out for my first round on the La Gorce course. Providing final pointers as we walked toward the first tee together, Dad noted, among other things, that two obligations of every golfer were to play with reasonable speed, and to be sure I'd picked up my divots. So, fully instructed and wanting to impress my father, I smacked a good drive down the first fairway. Dad just tapped the face of his watch a couple of times and said he'd await me on the ninth green in two hours. So I headed out, thinking that I had to get to the ninth green in time and I was not to make a mess of the pretty course.

Sure enough, as I walked up the ninth fairway two hours later, Dad was waiting. Happy that I'd enjoyed the front nine, he asked if I wanted to play the back, and he cautioned that there were some long holes there and also mentioned the heat. Yes, I assured him, I want to keep playing. So off I went. By the thirteenth hole, though, I began to feel weary, hot and hungry, and by the time I trudged onto the eighteenth green, I was exhausted. The strap on my golf bag seemed to be digging into my shoulder and I felt that the bag weighed a ton. Plus Dad looked upset. He tapped his watch and said I was more than twenty minutes late. Where the heck had I been, and how come I looked such a mess?

I told him I was sorry for being late, but it was very hot and I got really tired out there with having to carry my heavy bag for eighteen holes. "Heavy bag? Well is it any heavier now than it was this morning, and why are you so filthy and dirty?" Dad demanded. I told him that the bag was, in fact, a whole lot heavier than it had been before I began that morning. In fact, I told him, with all those grass divots I'd picked up and stuffed into the bag, it now weighed more than I could handle, and I had gotten dirty from collecting all my divots!

When my father realized what I'd done—picked up all the divots I'd made along the entire eighteen holes so as to keep from littering the course with dried grass—he began to laugh. He picked up the bag to see for himself how heavy it had gotten and then laughed some more. He'd been around the game of golf for a very long time, but this was something he'd never seen before! When he could stop laughing, Dad explained that I'd taken him too literally, that he'd just wanted me to put my divots back in the ground where they came from, not to bring them home. Later that day we went back onto the course to replace as many of the chunks of grass and dirt as possible. And, as is easy to imagine, for quite some time Dad got a big kick out of retelling that story.

That day, and the many subsequent days I shared with my father on the golf course or, more often, on the lesson tee or in the pro shop, defined our relationship. That is, our bonding occurred in places where, in my view then and now, my father was a giant of unquestionable stature. It's the sort of situation that might tend to drive some fathers and sons apart, with the son perhaps disdaining pursuit of a profession in which a parent excels, feeling, perhaps, that he could never match the parent's success. But it had quite the opposite effect on me. I always tried my best to be as much like my father as I could. And I still do.

***

It seems, in retrospect, an ideal life that the Grout family was leading. Dad had achieved elite status in his profession after decades of work and was sharing his life with the only woman he ever loved. And my siblings and I were doing well. There were bumps and detours along the way, of course, but it was a generally healthy and happy life for the whole group.

A special bonus for Mom and Dad was that the relationships Dad built at La Gorce led to a series of exciting overseas getaways. Dad went on a ten-day golf outing to Scotland in 1965, for example, with a group of men including his good friend Bud Wilkinson, the legendary former Oklahoma football coach, and Miami businessman Frank Smathers. The group braved the unpredictable Scottish weather to play British Open courses including Turnberry, The Old Course at St. Andrews, Royal Troon, Carnoustie, Gleneagles and Muirfield. Later, Mom and Dad traveled to Italy at the behest of the Italian Golf Federation. They stayed at Villa D' Este on Lake Como, and Mom reveled in the Italian scenery while Dad worked during the days with the best male and female Italian golfers. Coincidentally, one of the players Dad taught was Stefano Betti, who beat me one-up with a monster putt on the eighteenth hole in the 1976 British Amateur at St. Andrews.

A favorite family photograph: Mother and Dad dancing at La Gorce CC in 1972 and very much in love. (Raymond W. Muniz photo, used with permission)

PART FOUR: TWO JACKS MAKE A WINNING HAND

On the practice tee at La Gorce Country Club in 1964: Teacher and prodigy watching each other. (Nicklaus family collection)

Chapter 18
Home on the Range

"Learning to play golf is like learning to play the piano; you've got to practice a lot of scales before mastering a symphony." —JACK GROUT

***

As Dad was getting things organized in the La Gorce golf operation and spending numerous hours helping the club's members on the lesson tee, his star pupil from Scioto was moving ahead briskly with his own career. Jack Nicklaus had won his second U.S. Amateur title in 1961, during Dad's final year at Scioto Country Club, and finished seventh in the Masters and fourth in the U.S. Open. Then in 1962, Nicklaus' first year on the pro tour, he established himself as golf's most important new presence by defeating Arnold Palmer in a dramatic eighteen-hole playoff for the U.S. Open title at Oakmont. After just eighteen tournaments as a professional, Nicklaus already was threatening the hyperpopular Palmer's reign as king of the fairways.

His Open victory, followed the next year by wins in the Masters and the PGA Championship, vaulted Nicklaus into the top ranks of touring pros. It also brought new acclaim to my father, the great young Nicklaus' lone golf teacher. The phone in my father's office started ringing as the wealthy businessmen who made up the bulk of the La Gorce membership lined up for lessons from Nicklaus' personal instructor. Numerous celebrities also came calling, hoping that a bit of Dad's teaching magic could be sprinkled onto their golf games. Even some of Nicklaus' fellow pros began coming around, seeking Dad's wisdom on the lesson tee.

The emergence of Jack Nicklaus as a great golfer would bring his relationship with my father full circle. They had begun with Dad as the lead partner, the wise and always-encouraging golf teacher to the crew cut, stocky young athlete. Then Nicklaus left Columbus and went out on his own, and a case could be made that he became the dominant partner in the Nicklaus-Grout relationship with his sensational play as a twenty-something golf professional. Soon, though, the relationship between the two men would take on a more balanced feel, with both the awesome professional golfer and the talented golf instructor being successful independently of the other yet relishing their working and personal relationship more and more as the years and decades went by.

Unfortunately my father did not keep a log or diary of his working sessions with Jack Nicklaus. In the contemporary cable TV age, for sure, their work together would be the subject of a reality show or continuing reports on ESPN or the Golf Channel. But my father spent no time thinking about his golf legacy; he just went to work every day and did his job as best he could. What he left behind, for those of us who stood quietly in the background and watched him work with Nicklaus on the practice range, was a rich collection of memories of two exceptional men pursuing their dreams together as a team and always striving for excellence.

As he settled into his professional career, Nicklaus established a pattern of regular consultations with my father—not the frequent sessions so many current golf professionals have with their coaches, psychologists, exercise therapists and others, but just an hour here, a day there to tune up Nicklaus' swing and help him refocus mentally. Nicklaus came to La Gorce every winter for a session with Dad, timing those visits to fall just before his mid-January departure for the West Coast to play in his first tourney of the year, usually the Bing Crosby National Pro-Am. During those early-year sessions, Nicklaus would say to Dad, in effect, "J. Grout, I am a brand new golfer, teach me to play golf." The two would begin with the basics—posture, grip, body alignment and so forth—and go from there. The visit in January would be the first of five to six in a given year, almost always including those periods when Nicklaus was preparing intensely for a major tournament.

During Dad's early La Gorce years, Nicklaus sometimes would fly to Miami for practice sessions, and Dad would summon one of his employees or a club member to deliver Jack to the club. Later, when Nicklaus moved to Florida, he would drive or fly down from his North Palm Beach residence. In the sweltering days of the Miami summer, Dad and Nicklaus would work in the shade of the royal palm tree that loomed beside La Gorce's pitching/chipping green. In fact, this is the very first place I remember watching the great man hit a golf ball. That was in 1962, and I sat on the ground next to the pile of balls Nicklaus was hitting. I felt the ground shake when he took a divot. During this session, I'd look up at Dad with my mouth wide open. He'd look at me and just smile.

Because the tall royal palm where the two men worked was off to the side of the range, the net effect was that big Jack would be hitting his shots across the width of the practice area. His shots would fly into the third fairway on short and middle irons, and his tee shots would soar into the fourth hole's rough, among some tall Austrian Pines, or into the fairway. Always there'd be a caddie shagging those balls. Because of the time of year, there were very few golfers on the course, so Nicklaus really wasn't inconveniencing anyone.

When Nicklaus visited Dad during the wintertime, the routine was different. During those sessions, he and Dad would venture to the far end of the lesson tee, next to the third green. In that location, no one was behind them or could get very close while Nicklaus practiced. By the late '60s and early '70s, the La Gorce members had pretty much gotten accustomed to seeing Nicklaus, and the precedent had been established to give Dad and his famous student plenty of room.

There were exceptions to the rule, of course. Joe Turnesa—one of the seven famed "Golfing Turnesa Brothers," great-uncle of current PGA Tour player Marc Turnesa and himself the winner of fifteen PGA Tour events—did some teaching at La Gorce and was watching with a group of people one day as Dad worked with Nicklaus. A La Gorce member who saw the exchange recalls that, all of a sudden, Nicklaus said to Turnesa, "Joe, what do you think? What do you see here? What do you think about my swing?" And Joe said to him, "Jack, you ought to make your swing a lot flatter than it is." Nicklaus looked at Turnesa and smiled thinly. Dad couldn't bring himself to say anything, and others watching the scene held their breath. Then Joe Turnesa meekly put his head down, and Nicklaus went on hitting balls.

Assistant pro John Scheffler remembered my father always finding time for Nicklaus, even if he had to cancel other appointments. Often, Scheffler said, "They were lengthy sessions, one time until after dinner time. They would work on everything, not just full shots. They would hit chip shots, but not too many bunker shots." Scheffler remembered that in 1965, the year when Nicklaus shot 271—then the all-time low score in the Masters—the pre-tournament practice session "was about ball position. Mr. Grout had him change his ball position ... and whatever that change was, it worked."

Scheffler talked of my father being a refined teacher of the game—an artist rather than a taskmaster. "I remember Jackie Burke saying that teaching is kind of what a wood carver does," Scheffler said. "He takes a piece of wood and keeps chiseling away at it until it looks like a duck." That, Scheffler believed, was very much the way my father thought about teaching the golf swing. There wasn't a lot of chatter, just business. Scheffler remembered the exchanges between Dad and Nicklaus generally being very brief: "What did that look like?" "How did that feel?" "Try this." "It wasn't like the dramatic change that Tiger (Woods) went through with Butch (Harmon)," Scheffler said, recalling that Nicklaus and my dad worked repeatedly on the same

*Practice round at Scioto in 1962 included Bruce Devlin, Jack Grout, Jack Nicklaus and Jazz Pianist Billy Maxted. (*Columbus Dispatch *photo)*

few things: "They wanted the ball to go high. They didn't want it to go left."

Nicklaus sometimes wore golf attire for these working sessions, sometimes not. "One of the first times," Scheffler said with a chuckle, "he came in a tennis outfit. I thought, my God, he has the biggest thighs I've ever seen in my life!" My father's outfits for teaching sessions were more formal, reflecting his traditional and conservative tastes. Scheffler was impressed that Dad "would wear beautiful slacks and a short sleeve cut-and-sewn shirt. He was kind of a character; if it got cold, he'd take a jacket off the rack, and a hat, and he'd go down and teach, come back, put the hat back on the shelf and the jacket back on the rack."

Like his good friend Scheffler, I remember Dad's sessions with Nicklaus sometimes turning into marathons. They would work through the morning and often eat lunch together. At La Gorce, they would sit at a table, ordinarily by themselves unless Dad spotted one or two of

At the 1964 PGA Championship at Columbus Country Club, Dad said, "Dickie, watch Jack." As usual, I followed his directions.(Bill Foley photo, used with permission)

his buddies whom he knew could handle sitting with Jack and with whom Jack wouldn't mind sitting. Then it was back to the range.

Nicklaus seemed, in every sense, a golfing machine. His practice routine was systematic, disciplined; his sessions with Dad always purposeful. He'd begin with the sand wedge and work his way methodically through the entire bag. In his earliest sessions at La Gorce, when there'd be a caddie shagging his practice balls, the caddie would need to move only backward or forward; Jack didn't make the guy run to the left or right. His divots were like bacon strips, and he'd leave a neat patch of torn-up turf when he was finished, just the way you're supposed to.

Sometimes Nicklaus would be trying out new drivers that had been made for him, and during those sessions Dad and Nicklaus would examine every shot carefully and weigh the pros and cons of each club. It was fascinating to see and hear the level of detail and scrutiny they went through just to determine the best driver for Big Jack. It's clear, too, that that kind of dedication to detail was precisely what made Jack Nicklaus the extraordinary player he was. And, of course, it was what made my father one of the best-ever teachers of the game.

Being Jack Grout's son, I was privileged to see quite a number of wonderful players who came to work with my father. When I was a teenager, I not only observed and practiced with them, I also frequently joined them on the course after their sessions with Dad, and I could hold my own with them. In the summer of 1963 Nicklaus visited Dad for a tune-up before traveling to Dallas for the PGA Championship, which he won. It was on that occasion that I first got to play in the same foursome with him—even though I was the age Nicklaus had been when he took his first group lessons from Dad back at Scioto! It was quite a thrill for a kid just ten years old! Nobody hit the golf ball like Nicklaus. His ball seemed to occupy the same place in the air shot after shot. Other tour players who worked with Dad hit the occasional poor shot. Even the great champion Ray Floyd hit some stinkers. Not Nicklaus. His shots seemed always to be good.

My father's La Gorce sessions with Nicklaus sometimes resulted in special benefits for me. Nicklaus would give me permission to go into certain pockets of his big green-and-white golf bag and pilfer any used gloves he had in there. Through the mid '60s, we had hands about the same size. Most elite athletes' hands are large, but Jack's were small with thick fingers; even in my early teens, my hands were almost as big as his. He seldom used a glove for more than one day, so I would find in his bag an ample supply of those nearly new white beauties. I felt honored to get to wear them.

My good fortune aside, what was going on in the background as I rifled through the great champion's bag was the work of serious and talented men laboring together to achieve lofty goals. That, I suppose, was why there was not a lot of kidding around when Dad and Nicklaus occupied the practice tee—with the curious often watching from a distance or perhaps even creeping close enough to hear a bit of what the two men were saying. It's not that these were unpleasant sessions in any way; there was, in fact, some storytelling and laughter and talk about the world outside of golf. But what I remember most about my dad's days with Nicklaus was the purposefulness of it all: The respected teaching professional and his world-champion protégé. A few words. A question. A suggestion. Then a series of rockets through the air, the mighty young student leaving his serious and accomplished coach in silent awe with the beauty and power of his golf swing, the majesty of his shots, his mystifying ability to duplicate those perfect strikes again and again and again.

As Jack Nicklaus tortured golf balls under Dad's attentive and admiring gaze, the relationship between pupil and teacher continued a natural and healthy evolution. As a boy, Nicklaus practically idolized Jack Grout and did whatever the pro told him to do. Even as Nicklaus got older, he watched my dad's every move on and off the golf course, and in the process got reinforcement of what his father had taught him about being a gentleman, a sportsman. For his part, my father initially had been attracted to the drive and work ethic of the young Nicklaus. Then as time passed, that initial attraction turned to fascination for the sheer intensity and steely will of his maturing pupil.

When Dad's special feelings for his young friend and their combined hard work culminated in such brilliant success, my father could only marvel at Jack Nicklaus and his accomplishments. Their union may literally have been the very best in a father-and-son-type relationship. Maybe because both men knew that neither would be going home with the other once their sessions ended, it worked out that their get-togethers contained all the love and respect but few of the hard feelings or other problems that naturally develop within actual families.

Jack Grout and Jack Nicklaus, it seems, were the perfect golf pairing.

***

My father's allure as a golf teacher continued to skyrocket as Jack Nicklaus moved through his first decade as a playing professional. Dad's most famous pupil won seven tournaments in the United States and abroad in 1963, including the PGA. He won six more times in 1964; took five titles including his first Masters championship in 1965; won the Masters, his first British Open and three other titles in 1966; then won six events in 1967, including his second U.S. Open. The British Open victory in 1966, at Scotland's venerable Muirfield propelled Nicklaus into the company of Gene Sarazen, Ben Hogan and Gary Player as the only men to have won all four of the major golf tournaments.

Nicklaus' amazing performance added yet more luster to my dad's reputation as a teacher of the game of golf, bringing to his lesson tee successful players such as Marty Fleckman, Grier Jones, DeWitt Weaver, Steve Melnyk, Jerry Heard, Jim Colbert, J.C. Snead, Gibby Gilbert and Raymond Floyd. Roger Maltbie, Tom Purtzer, Lanny Wadkins and Olin Browne would come along later. Adding additional glitter to Dad's life was the steady stream of famous athletes and celebrities who sought his help. Joe DiMaggio, Andy Williams, Vic Damone, Eddie Arcaro and champion American swimmer Eleanor Holm were among those making the trek to La Gorce.

Alvin Dark, who enjoyed an illustrious career in major league baseball, was among those seeking Dad's help. Dark was the 1948 major league rookie of the year (before each league named a top rookie), a three-time major league all-star, and he played in three World Series—winning with the New York Giants in 1954. He later managed a pennant-winner in each league (Giants in 1962 and Oakland in 1974) and won the World Series with the Athletics—one of only eleven men since 1950 to win a World Series as both a player and later as a manager. Although he'd never had a golf lesson, Dark decided to concentrate on golf after he was fired as Cleveland Indians manager in 1971. Until then, he'd just practiced and played, practiced and played—a routine that had carried him to four titles in the National

Baseball Players Golf Tournament. But now he hoped to play in the U.S. Amateur and some bigger events.

On the La Gorce range, Dad quickly sized up Dark's game. As a right-handed batter, Alvin was a pull hitter; it was natural for him to use his right hand as the dominant one and allow the left hand to just hang on. In golf, however, that tendency results in too many low hooks. Dark was confounded by the narrow fairways and grabby Bermuda rough on Florida courses. He had to learn how to hit the ball straighter and higher.

Years after their first session together, Dark would prepare an audio tape in which he spoke to my father, detailing what had occurred that day in 1971:

"So I went over there with my wife one day and got some balls and went to the driving range. And you said, 'Go on and hit some balls.' So I teed it up and I was hittin' the ball. And I hit about ten or twelve, and I kept thinking every time I swung, 'What is Jack going to do? He's just watching me.' And in a minute ... you said, 'Let me tell you what you do. You see that cloud up there in the air?' And the cloud was not straight up, of course, and it was not right on the horizon. But it was about a 45-degree angle, the cloud that you were pointing to. And then you said, 'Let's see you hit a ball at that cloud.' And so I said to myself, 'Oh, now he's messin' with my mind and I'm not sure I can handle this kind of thing, but I'll do it.'

"So the first couple balls I hit, I kind of fell back in trying to get the ball up in the air. I'd always been a hooker so therefore I wasn't worried about height, I was worried about rolling the ball. And the first thing you know, after I hit about ten or twelve balls—and you didn't say another word to me until after I hit about ten or twelve—but then you said, 'OK, now you remember that swing.' And after about ten or twelve more balls, I hit about six or seven of them on a much, much higher flight than I'd ever gotten on the golf ball. And lo and behold, all the ball did was just draw a little bit. I could always slice a ball if I wanted to, but I never worked on a slice; I just wanted to hook it all the time. So I started hitting a high draw, just a little bit. Then the next thing you taught me was how to hit the ball straight by just being sure that I stayed 'inside' the ball and to make sure that I didn't get out over the ball. So Jack, those new moves changed my swing completely.

"The next two tournaments I had at Miami Country Club; one of them was a match-play and one of them was a medal-play, and it was all those young kids that I was playing against. Well, I won both of them ... and I never will forget you, Jack, because had it not been for you there's no way I could've won. Even to this day, I'm eighty-two years old now—I still win a few tournaments. I win a senior tournament every once in a while. But the thing about it is, there isn't any golf course I can't play because any time I start hooking the ball, I just think about that cloud up there in the sky and just to be sure that I stay inside and behind the ball ...

" ... the guys will ask me, when I'm playing golf, how can I hit the ball so straight. And I always tell them the story about you teaching me to look at that cloud up in the sky and try to hit the ball up at that cloud ... I'll always consider that day as when this old baseball player learned the lesson of a lifetime."

***

Maybe the most amusing of Dad's celebrity students was colorful baseballer Ken "Hawk" Harrelson. After playing for four major league teams, Harrelson suffered a broken leg in 1970, retired from baseball, and set out to build a career in professional golf. He played and practiced a lot at La Gorce in the early '70s and wore great-looking, funky caps. Whenever Ken hit a terrific shot or made a long birdie putt, he would do his famous, or perhaps infamous, "Hawk Walk." He'd have on one of his "pimp-type" caps, stick out his beak of a nose, then shuffle around in that cool way of his, looking just like a hawk.

Besides loving to be around my dad, the Hawk loved the long ball, and he flat-out idolized Jack Nicklaus. He kept pestering Dad to arrange for him to visit with Nicklaus just up the road at Lost Tree Village golf course, across the street from Nicklaus' North Palm Beach residence. So, one morning the Hawk and I drove up to North Palm in his big black Cadillac with a shiny hawk as a hood ornament. Nicklaus couldn't have been more gracious, spending much of the day with Harrelson and me on the practice range, showing us everything he could about every conceivable shot. The Hawk was very impressed. Whether it was because of my father's teaching or inspiration from Nicklaus, Harrelson improved a good bit as a golfer, actually qualifying for the British Open in 1972 and winning some minor tournaments before settling in for a long tenure as a broadcaster for the Chicago White Sox.

Not all of Dad's pupils provided as much fun as Hawk Harrelson, and certainly not Raymond Loran Floyd, the hard-edged but very accomplished tour pro who approached my father in 1972 and pleaded for help with his ailing game. Floyd, noted for his intense on-course gaze that came to be known simply as "The Stare," turned pro in 1963, his victory in a tournament that year making him, at age twenty, the fourth-youngest winner of a PGA Tour event. He and my father met on the practice tee at the 1965 U.S. Open Championship at Bellerive Country Club in St. Louis, but only long enough for Floyd to ask Dad to take a quick look at his swing. In the ensuing few moments of discussion, my father displayed an approach to teaching that made an indelible impression on the young golfer and would draw him back to Jack Grout nearly a decade later for serious work on a golf game gone awry.

That day on the practice tee at Bellerive, my father was struck by Floyd's habit of regripping the club in the moment before he began his backswing. Dad had a suggestion to make, but typically, he prefaced his advice with a bit of praise and encouragement. "I'll never forget it," Floyd said in a 2009 interview. "He said, 'Boy, you are really swinging well. Let me see you try something. Just hold that club. Don't let that hand regrip right before you start. Sometimes that throws your rhythm off.' " That, said Floyd, was typical of my father's approach to instruction. Praise, then teach. Encourage, then inform. "No matter what was happening, he always gave a positive."

Floyd immediately began to focus on "keeping both hands joined to the club. I went a great number of holes (at the Open) without a bogey. I'd just come off winning the St. Paul Open, and I was really playing well (when) Jack made that observation. He was so spot-on. It was just a little flaw in a fundamental, but (the fix) got my rhythm going so good. The thing that impressed me a whole lot was the positive—no matter what you were doing, he would give you something positive."

His tremendous talent notwithstanding, Floyd showed more potential than solid results the next few years. He finally broke out with three wins in 1969, including the PGA Championship, then fell into another period of mediocre play. Finally in 1972, seven years after their brief encounter on the lesson tee in St. Louis, Floyd picked up the phone and reached out to my father, establishing a student-teacher relationship that would continue until Dad's death seventeen years later. "I called him and asked him would he look at me and (told him) that I was having nightmares with my swing," Floyd recalled. "He said, 'Come on over.' "

When Floyd first trudged onto the La Gorce lesson tee with my father that spring, his swing was, indeed, off kilter. "I had a very classic golf swing as a youngster," Floyd said. "If you see films of the '69 PGA that I won, you would say that's not Raymond Floyd as everyone knows him today. But I created some bad (swing) habits on tour, and I kept getting worse." Dad began working immediately on getting Floyd to move his golf club higher on the backswing. "I was having trouble getting the club to the top of the swing," Floyd said. "He started getting me to let my elbow move away from my body, which gets the club away from being flat ... and almost gave me a little second move at the top of my swing. But as soon as I got that club up there and got it set, I had it in position and I didn't get it hung up behind me. I was going so bad, and he said this will get that club up, and all of a sudden, I could see immediate results."

Floyd saw those first sessions with my dad as a turning point for his golf game—one of two turning points, actually, the other being his marriage in 1973 to Maria Fraietta, who would push him to be more disciplined in his life and begin living up to his golf potential. With Dad providing supportive coaching on the lesson tee and Maria providing tough love at home, Floyd rededicated himself to his career.

In a letter to me in 2004, Floyd wrote of working with my father at La Gorce in the fall of 1975. In that letter, Floyd focused sharply on Dad's low-key, always-positive approach to instruction. "I was hitting the ball very well," Floyd wrote, "and Jack was standing behind me not saying too much except to compliment me on occasion. He then said, 'You hit that fade great, now let me see you hit some draws.' I responded, 'I don't hit hooks, I don't ever want to hit another one.' He was very quiet for a few minutes, then he responded, 'So, you don't ever want to hook.' I responded, 'You got that right. I don't ever have to worry about the left side.' " Floyd wrote that Dad let that sink in for a few minutes, "Then came the question: 'Do you think you can be one of the best players in the world or beat the best players in the world by eliminating fifty percent of your options?' Now I was quiet for a while. It didn't take me too much longer to start working on the right-to-left part of my game."

It took some time and a lot of work on the lesson tee, but Ray Floyd would begin winning again. He was victorious by eight strokes in the 1976 Masters, then added nine more wins through 1982, the year he took his second PGA Championship. He won the Vardon Trophy in 1983 as the tour's leader in scoring average. And when he won the U.S. Open in 1986 at age forty-three, he was the oldest-ever winner of that tournament. In the wake of that victory, looking back at what by then had been fourteen years of coaching and encouragement from my father, Floyd wrote to Dad that "I want you to know that I could not have accomplished all that I have done without you. Your patience, your tutelage and your inspiration have been the formula for my success. I sincerely thank you."

Raymond Floyd would finish his PGA Tour career with twenty-two tournament wins, including four majors. He played on eight Ryder

Cup teams and captained the 1989 squad. He won an additional fourteen tournaments on the Senior Tour (for players fifty and over), plus a sprinkling of other events around the world. In 1989, he was inducted into the World Golf Hall of Fame. Looking back more than twenty years after Dad's death, Floyd returned over and over to the gentle, nurturing nature of my father as a golf instructor and as a friend. Always, Floyd said, my father focused on "telling you what you were doing right. If I went to him when I was playing well, when I came away from a session, man, I couldn't wait to get to the tee. I knew I was going to beat everybody."

Floyd talked of seeing Dad give Jack Nicklaus the same kind of encouragement, "Man, they can't beat you. Look how great you're hitting the ball." Remembering the occasional dark days when he felt he couldn't drive a golf ball "into a forty-acre field," Floyd said that Dad would just change the conversation, focusing on his pupil's strengths. "Jack would say, 'You know, Raymond, you still have the best short game of any man I've ever seen,' " Floyd recalled. "And I'd say, 'You're right, Jack, because if I didn't, I'd be selling cars right now.' He was always giving you the positive. He was a pure inspiration."

⁂

Lanny Wadkins, a World Golf Hall of Fame member who won twenty-one PGA Tour tournaments, including the 1977 PGA Championship, echoed Floyd's memories of practice-tee sessions with my father. Wadkins had built a successful tour career without regular help from a swing coach, his early instructor, J.G. Lumpkin, having died when Wadkins still was attending Wake Forest University. Wadkins won twelve PGA Tour titles, including that '77 PGA, in his first thirteen years as a pro, and he was in his fifteenth year before he finally took on Dick Harmon as his regular teacher in 1985.

"I knew my swing was a little different, so I was always leery of working with someone," said Wadkins, who talked of "a couple of" serious practice-tee sessions with Dad at Muirfield Village during The Memorial (where Wadkins posted five top-ten finishes in six years between 1979 and 1985). "When I spoke with Mr. Grout, the main thing I got was that he didn't want to make any wholesale changes. He just wanted to make things simpler for me, which I really liked ... I was struggling, and ... It seemed like everybody I ever talked to about what should I do, they wanted to make wholesale changes, and I just wasn't into wholesale changes. When my swing was on and worked, it worked extremely well. I won a lot of tournaments, and the swing held up under pressure. So it was more a matter of me getting 'my swing' right. I felt like Mr. Grout might have the ability to get 'my swing' right, not necessarily a 'system' right, and that's what I liked."

Wadkins recalled that Dad "had one of the same beliefs that I did, and that's that when you finish a lesson, you ought to have only one thing to key on, because I don't think you can work on more than one thing in your golf swing while you're playing. You might work on more than one thing on the practice range, but when you're playing you've got to have one key thought. This is something I felt that he really believed in, and he was with me in trying to find me a key thought that would make me comfortable and able to play. The key to that is to find something that you do that is positive, that you think about that and stress that, then the rest of your swing that you worked on and built your whole life will work around that one thing. That's what I was always looking for, and he was good at helping me find that."

Chapter 19
Almost Like Family

"What's so difficult about down-the-middle, on-the-green, two-putts, and go to the next hole?" —JACK GROUT

❋❋❋

One of the reasons Dad had given for leaving his secure position at Scioto Country Club in 1961 had been that the new club job in Miami would afford him a couple months off for travel during the summer, when the Florida heat scares away all but the heartiest golfers. A bonus for Dad, then, was that the men's major golf tournaments, except for the Masters, were held during the summer, a time when La Gorce had only light play. Dad thus attended numerous U.S. Open and PGA championships through his La Gorce years, although because of the travel distance involved, he never attended the British Open.

"Charlie's Gang" at Augusta in 1963. Standing in between Nicklaus and Grout are Mike Flesh (third from the right) and Charlie Nicklaus. (Bill Foley photo, used with permission)

My father took particular delight in attending the Masters during Jack Nicklaus' prime, regularly in the company of a group called "Charlie's Gang," made up of businessmen-friends of Nicklaus' father. Those Augusta outings always energized my dad, as he could let his hair down in the company of good friends, enjoying the food, the laughter, the companionship and, of course, the golf tournament on one of the world's most beautiful courses. Jack Nicklaus himself dropped by the Gang's rented house on the eve of the tournament the two years I accompanied Dad there and the year my brother John attended, chatting easily with the group even as he prepared for battle. Nicklaus recalled later being impressed that the drinks consumed by Charlie's Gang were "big as a milkshake."

My father also used his regular visits to Augusta National to renew his friendship with the legendary Bobby Jones, one of the founders of the Masters. Dad never played competitively against Jones, who dominated the golf world through the 1920s and won the "Grand Slam" of four major tournaments in 1930, then virtually retired from the game at age twenty-eight. But Dad did play occasional rounds with Jones beginning in the 1930s, and there was an autographed photo of the great amateur hanging in Dad's office at La Gorce.

It seems logical, in retrospect, that with Dad attending so many big tournaments in which Jack Nicklaus played, the pupil and teacher would have gone to the practice tee together at the various venues. But that wasn't the case, or at least not very often. At most of the major tournaments he attended, Dad would stand quietly near the practice range and simply watch Nicklaus warming up. My father didn't believe in pushing new ideas on his pupils on the eve of tournaments, nor did Nicklaus want new swing thoughts interfering with his careful major-tournament preparations.

Occasionally, though, Dad's from-a-distance observation of Nicklaus at the majors did turn into a bit of teaching. For example, I went with Dad to the U.S. Open at Merion in 1971, and after one of the tournament rounds, he, Jack and I made the short drive to Philadelphia Country Club so Dad and Nicklaus could work in peace. Dad later wrote in his book *Let Me Teach You Golf as I Taught Jack Nicklaus* that he had watched quietly as Nicklaus struggled with the direction of his shots on the practice range at the 1974 U.S. Open at Winged Foot, but finally he had felt compelled to speak up. "Jack, where are you aiming?" my father asked. "At that tree," Nicklaus answered, pointing down the center of the range. "See that fence over there on the right?" Dad asked. "Well, as far as I'm concerned that is out of bounds. And you are aiming your shoulders to the *right* of that

Student and coach at the practice tee, 1974 U.S. Open at Winged Foot Golf Club in Mamaroneck, New York. (Bill Foley photo, used with permission)

fence." Dad wrote that Nicklaus opted not to try to change his setup at that point, and he, in turn, decided to let things ride for the moment.

That story describes perfectly the student-teacher relationship between Jack Nicklaus and Jack Grout. From an early age, Nicklaus had been taught by his father, and by my dad, to think for himself on the golf course. You can't tote your instructor around in your golf bag, after all; when faced with technical glitches or mental lapses during a round of golf, the best players know how to figure things out and right the ship in mid-voyage. So, even though Dad watched Nicklaus on the range at many tournaments, their real time as teacher and pupil was reserved almost solely for nontournament weeks when they could get together in Florida or Ohio.

***

My father's willingness, even eagerness, to have Jack Nicklaus be independent from him and able to make his own decisions on the fly as a round of golf unfolded was typical of the way Dad operated. He respected Nicklaus and loved working with him, but he also wanted Jack to be well-rounded and confident enough in his golf skills that he could perform at the highest level of his sport without a coach's constant presence.

It was the same way Dad looked at his children, really; he cherished his family and was there for us when we needed him, but he didn't hover and wasn't overly demanding. Whether dealing with John's desire to finish high school back in Ohio or understanding Ronnie's motivation in hiding his hiring letter from La Gorce so that, maybe, she wouldn't have to move away from her friends in Columbus, Dad tried to be supportive and to let us experience life as it naturally occurs. As a consequence, my siblings and I developed at our own pace as individuals, with Dad and Mom tolerating our youthful ups and downs with a minimum of fuss.

Even in introducing us to his chosen sport, Dad encouraged us to enjoy the game at whatever level of intensity we found fitting; he never pushed us to reach proficiency as golfers. Over time, my brother and I both took golf quite seriously; John became a two-handicapper at one point, and I eventually became a club professional and touring pro capable enough to make it into the 1979 U.S. Open at the Inverness Club in Toledo. My sisters dabbled in the game and enjoyed it, but they never pursued it seriously. The game still gave them good memories, though, with one of Debbie's favorites involving receipt of a pair of "golf shoes" from the jockey Eddie Arcaro. The diminutive navy canvas shoes had a very thick sole of yellow rubber and spikes, and Debbie and I called them her "Swiss cheese shoes."

There were many occasions when our family simply enjoyed each other's accomplishments or reveled in experiencing together the range of activities available in South Florida. At home, my siblings and I had fun watching Mom and Dad in intense battles over their Chinese Checkers games or listening to their tales of La Gorce's lavish New Year's Eve dinner dances featuring entertainment such as Guy Lombardo and his orchestra. Even more enjoyable for the Grout children, although probably quite a bit less for Mom and Dad, was our normal teenage preoccupation with auto transport. Bowing to our desires more than any real needs, in 1968 Dad purchased a nifty brown Chevy Camaro with wire wheels, primarily for my use until I went away to college, then as transportation for Debbie. That car really was a good one, but it paled beside the used Datsun 240-Z my dad let me buy later that enhanced my social life immeasurably.

My father relished the many pleasant times we had during our Miami-based years. But as those years passed, he also would have his share of difficult days. His younger siblings Raymond and Jenny both died in 1967, in Oklahoma City, at the ages of fifty-six and fifty-one, respectively. Then, in July 1968, Dad's appendix ruptured, requiring emergency surgery in a North Miami hospital. And in February of 1970, Dad mourned when Charlie Nicklaus succumbed to cancer at the age of fifty-six. Jack Nicklaus, then only thirty, was deeply affected by the loss of his beloved father, and he would say later that in the absence of his dad, Jack Grout became, in effect, his second father, a guiding, kind and loving presence in his life.

Dad willingly embraced the role as Nicklaus' new father figure, and he and Jack would continue their player-instructor relationship until Dad's death in 1989. In the years following Charlie Nicklaus' death, however, his son would come to depend less on my father's coaching and more on his own sharp instincts for the game of golf. In the early '70s, Nicklaus, weary of being labeled "Fat Jack" by Arnold Palmer fans who resented him for supplanting their hero as golf's best player, slimmed down considerably and even grew his blond locks modishly long, rendering more accurate than ever the "Golden Bear" nickname that had been pinned on him in the early '60s. Nicklaus was becoming his own person, in a big way, and in the flush of tremendous successes on the professional circuit became increasingly self-reliant in maintaining his golf game. No question, Jack was being carried along on a wave of deep self-confidence. And given the record he was accumulating in his sport, who could question his high level of self-regard?

Nevertheless, Nicklaus faithfully continued his annual early-season tune-ups with my father and would see Dad for a quick review before the major championships. But in general, Nicklaus would rely more and more on his own knowledge and immense skills to maintain his game. Still, Nicklaus clearly respected my father's golf knowledge, valued his input and his friendship, and wanted to keep him close at hand. So as Dad approached retirement age in the mid-1970s, Nicklaus created a plan for helping both his old friend and himself by placing Jack Grout in new environments where he could thrive and, importantly, in which he always would be available to provide coaching when Jack William Nicklaus needed it.

Chapter 20
An Ideal Way to "Retire"

"My teaching has always been based on what I believe to be the time-proved fundamentals of the golf swing, even when such an approach has been unfashionable—as has been the case many times in my career."
—JACK GROUT

***

Looking back over his career from his Miami Beach perch in the mid-'70s, my father could enjoy many good memories. Truth was, he'd enjoyed the work and the members at each golf club where he'd plied his trade. Yet La Gorce had to be his all-time favorite spot. Given the high-profile membership there, and the ever-present celebrity visitors who brought special energy to the place, Dad felt he'd fallen into the perfect job. That his highest-profile pupil, Jack Nicklaus, would take up residence just up the highway from La Gorce in North Palm Beach was just icing on the proverbial cake.

Dad told me he received job offers during his thirteen-and-a-half years at La Gorce, but he always turned them down because they could not match what he already had in terms of stability, compensation and weather. With Jack Nicklaus having risen to the top in professional golf, Dad's stock as a teacher was high; he could afford to be discriminating about any future move. Still, Dad would reach age sixty-four in 1974, and he was beginning to think about retirement. The thought of just quitting altogether didn't appeal to him, but it would be good if he could ease up a bit.

Even before Dad began to ponder all this, Nicklaus was dreaming his own dreams—and not just about new golf conquests. As early as the mid-1960s, when he was only twenty-five, Nicklaus had been tinkering with the idea of building a world-class golf facility right in his hometown. In a conversation in the kitchen of his friend and neighbor Pandel Savic in 1965, Nicklaus talked of bringing a high-quality annual golf event to Columbus. Then the next year at the Masters, the companion idea of building a great golf course to host the event was discussed by Nicklaus and his long-time friend Ivor Young. Land for the project was purchased, in the Columbus suburb of Dublin, in 1966, and construction began on July 28, 1972. Named Muirfield Village Golf Club in honor of Scotland's Muirfield course—Nicklaus' favorite British Open venue—the new club was dedicated on Memorial

Day, 1974. An exhibition match between Nicklaus and his fellow Ohioan Tom Weiskopf was the feature of opening day.

Nicklaus, who designed his new course in collaboration with noted golf architect Desmond Muirhead, saw the golf course and a planned new annual tournament there as his gift back to a game that already had given him so much. Nicklaus launched the Memorial Tournament in 1976, and, as he had hoped, that annual event became one of the most anticipated by players on the PGA Tour.

At some point early in the '70s, Nicklaus talked with my dad about the new course, about his plan to launch the Memorial Tournament, and about his personal gratitude for the good work Dad had done with him. Then Nicklaus asked my father a question that was both generous and very smart: Would Dad consider coming to Muirfield Village in the summers as a teaching professional, in essence as the club's teacher-in-chief? Dad would set his own hours, teaching as much as he wanted, and he never would have to stick around for the cold and damp Ohio winters. "The intent was to always have a great teaching pro available for the members when they came in," said former Muirfield CEO John Hines. It was a generous offer, because my father was nearing retirement age, and this would be a wonderful opportunity for him to remain active without working fulltime. And while Hines said that Dad's hiring "was a service (to Muirfield members) rather than to attract business," it was also a smart business move. Having such a prominent golf teacher around the new club was likely to attract many good players, including professionals, who wanted to learn from such a man.

Jim Gerring, who was named head golf professional at Muirfield Village in late 1973, suggested that part of Nicklaus' strategy in bringing Dad on board the next year was to provide the new head pro with a seasoned mentor. Gerring had trained under head pro Walker Inman at Scioto Country Club but said modestly that "Jack Nicklaus knew what a rookie I was ... Jack knew I needed guidance, and Mr. Grout, without even knowing what he was doing, helped me tremendously. He spent countless hours with me, watching and helping."

Not surprisingly, Nicklaus talked of substantially broader and largely personal motives for his move to bring my father aboard at Muirfield. "I looked at it more as Jack Grout was my friend and teacher, and I just wanted to make sure that Jack Grout was happy doing what he wanted to do," Nicklaus said. "He said he was thinking about leaving La Gorce, and I said, 'J. Grout, why don't you think about coming up to Muirfield and teaching there in the summer,' and we ended up providing a position for Jack and he could work at whatever level he wanted to work and spend as much time as he wanted to ... " In terms of this being a good business move for Muirfield, Nicklaus said that "any time Jack Grout went anywhere for anybody, it was a good business decision."

Nicklaus believed that my father's acceptance of the offer had nothing to do with money and everything to do with his desire to be around good people. "I don't think Jack Grout was motivated by money in any way, shape or form," Nicklaus said, suggesting instead that Jack Grout "was a people person, and he wanted to be around people who enjoyed the game of golf and the people that I was associated with. He wanted to spend his time where I might be around, and where other people that he knew in the game of golf would be around."

The Muirfield offer had no downside for my father. He would be able to retire from full-time work but would get to return during the beautiful summer season to an Ohio city he had enjoyed a great deal. With the rest of the year free, he would be able to steal away to the milder climate of Florida. Jack Nicklaus had made an offer that could not be refused, so in the spring of 1974 Dad informed his colleagues at La Gorce that he was going to retire.

While never one to want a fuss made over him, my father was pleased to find that his friends and admirers at La Gorce weren't about to let him just walk quietly into the night. In late spring of 1974, Jack and Barbara Nicklaus, the noted golf instructor Bob Toski, 1941 PGA Championship winner Vic Ghezzi, New York Yankees owner Dan Topping and scores of other La Gorce members and guests—including the reigning world champion backgammon player, Tim Holland—gathered for a sendoff dinner for Dad and Mom in the main dining room of the La Gorce clubhouse, up the beautiful, broad staircase from the large sitting area on the club's main level. Guests could hear live music as they entered the front door and were greeted by a display of photos of my dad, including some from his childhood in Oklahoma City and others from his days on the early pro-golf circuit with Ben Hogan, Byron Nelson and other all-time greats. And there were, of course, photos of Dad with Jack Nicklaus.

With club president Harry Daumit as emcee, the evening was full of fun stories and tributes to my father, including warm statements by Nicklaus and Toski and some farewell remarks by the guest of honor. There was dancing after dinner, and Dad was in high spirits, with my mother vibrant and beautiful in a stylish sheath and with her hair pulled up in her signature style. At evening's end, honorees Jack and Bonnie Grout, basking in the afterglow of the loving and appreciative sendoff by their many friends at La Gorce, went home to prepare for their next adventure, one that would last for the final fifteen years of my father's life.

***

As he had done in his move from the quiet Scioto to the rollicking La Gorce in 1961, Dad now moved into an altogether different kind of environment, one considerably more sedate than that at the club in Miami Beach. Muirfield Village was the personal brainchild and the pride and joy of Dad's most prominent pupil, who also happened to be the world's best golfer. And the world-class Muirfield golf course and its beautiful clubhouse, practice range and guest cottages were home to a steady stream of top-flight professional and amateur golfers, many of whom over the next fifteen years would reach out for instruction from and friendship with this new teaching professional who was Nicklaus' personal golf mentor.

I think Dad probably pinched himself over his good fortune. Muirfield Village is one of those courses that golfers dream of playing, then after doing so, never stop telling their friends about. Think Augusta National or Pinehurst No. 2 or Pine Valley. Carved out of rolling, wooded terrain and with streams or ponds strategically located on numerous holes, the course is exhilarating to play. The clubhouse is perched on a slight rise, the first tee on one side, the eighteenth green on the other. Members and guests headed for the golf shop, the locker rooms or the grill pass through a lobby lined with Nicklaus photos and memorabilia.

There's also a handsome dark wood plaque in the main hallway—moved to that prominent location in 2009 at Nicklaus' personal direction—that is flanked by large photos of my father with the Golden Bear. Bearing a plate with the words "The Grout" beneath the club logo, it lists winners of an

The annual tournament honoring Dad that raises money for scholarships for caddies and other club employees. (Photo courtesy of Muirfield Village Golf Club)

annual club tournament formally called "The Grout Invitational" (but known as just "The Grout"). According to the 2009 tournament booklet, "The Grout Invitational is a special event in that we honor one of the true legends of the game, Jack Grout. 'The Grout' began in 1990, in honor of our friend and respected teacher, Jack Grout, to raise money for the Jack Grout Scholarship Fund. The Grout Scholarship money is used to help staff achieve their academic goals by providing funds for them to continue their education." Played over a Friday and Saturday usually in early October, the thirty-six-hole event began with fivesomes—four amateurs who were members and their guests, joined by a professional. The format eventually changed to two-man teams, a member and a guest, playing a scramble the first day and best-ball the second.

The club's Memorial Tournament, hosted personally by Nicklaus, annually draws the biggest names in golf. Winners through 2012 included Tiger Woods, Nicklaus, Greg Norman, Tom Watson, Hale Irwin, Ernie Els, Raymond Floyd, Paul Azinger, Jim Furyk, Curtis Strange, Kenny Perry, Hal Sutton and David Graham.

My parents rented a home and spent six weeks in Columbus in the summer of 1974, with Dad giving golf lessons and getting to know Muirfield's members and staff. By the next year, Dad had settled into his mid-May-through-September routine in Ohio, laboring on the lesson tee, working with the golf-shop crew, and mingling with members and guests. Clearly my father had found a satisfying and relatively pressure-free way to wind down his career. And Jack Nicklaus had discovered a substantial marketing tool for his new golf club: My father quickly became a favorite of Muirfield Village members, their guests, and visiting golf professionals.

Dad's life away from the practice tee unfolded in a similarly satisfying way, his happy home life with Bonnie complementing the professional satisfaction and monetary rewards he was getting from teaching. My mother had a strong personality and ran the household. Dad was fine with that. Mom always took care of the day-to-day household problems and family concerns such as preparing all the bills for payment, but she made sure Dad could have his cherished quiet time in the evening. She would baby him, and he liked that. He was totally devoted to my mom, whom he called "Heartsy." She likewise was totally devoted to him and fought fiercely for him.

Their return to Columbus sparked for my parents many good memories of their earlier days there, including my mom's newfound interest in golf. Having been bitten by the golf bug, Mother found pleasure in her regular Tuesday Ladies Day foursome during our years at Scioto. Reminiscent of the days when Dad, as a young boy, would sit around the dinner table in Oklahoma City and recount his experiences as a caddie, Mom would relive her round—in great detail—at our Tuesday dinner table, describing to our dad her play on each hole, stroke by stroke, usually about 110 of them. Dad always listened very patiently, and I recognized then how much he loved his Bonnie.

I remember one event in particular—the annual Ladies Day Tournament—during which the women would play golf in costumes. Mom dressed as a clown one year, and one of her friends picked her up at our house in a golf cart since we lived close to the second green. They headed down the second fairway, away from the green, and failed to see a bunker that loomed ahead. The two drove straight over the bunker's grassy side, sailing to a crash landing in the sand! Their cart had to be towed out, but luckily there were no injuries, just a couple of badly shaken lady golfers. Fortunately for the rest of us, by the time we moved to Miami Beach in the early '60s, Mom was able to break 100 and would spare us the hole-by-hole replay.

By the end of 1975, when Mom and Dad sold their Miami home and bought a seasonal residence on a spacious lot not far from Muirfield Village, my brother, John, was settled into a career as an airline pilot, and my sister Ronnie was married and living in Atlanta with her husband and two-month-old daughter. Sister Debbie and I stayed close to home, living with our parents off and on. Debbie was out of school, though, and I was pursuing my dream of a career in golf by practicing and playing in amateur tournaments, and after turning pro in 1977, playing on various mini-tours throughout the country.

While he enjoyed Columbus, my father embraced the opportunity for golf assignments back in Florida during the winters from 1976 through 1989. Typically from January through April he gave lessons at the Loxahatchee and Frenchman's Creek country clubs in the North Palm Beach area where Nicklaus lived, or at a Nicklaus-designed par-three course at the Cheeca Lodge in Islamorada, in the Florida Keys ninety minutes south of Miami. These jobs were arranged with Nicklaus' help, and all brought Dad numerous golf pupils ranging from rank beginners to, more often, talented amateurs and players from the PGA Tour. Now, as he moved through his seventh decade, my father had carved out what was for him the perfect world: winters teaching golf in sunny and warm Florida, summers teaching at beautiful Muirfield Village, and, in the margins, months when he and my mother could just enjoy their life together.

The common thread that tied all this together was that, in "retirement," my father was available to continue his most important work—maintenance of the golf swing of one Jack Nicklaus. Their annual first-of-the-year "swing checkup" sessions continued throughout the '70s and '80s, and Dad would work with Nicklaus at Muirfield Village or at one of the Palm Beach-area golf clubs, although not with great frequency during Nicklaus' prime golfing years. Nicklaus had learned the fundamentals of the swing early in life, and Dad's role through the '70s and '80s often was to be more of a cheerleader and mentor for Nicklaus than a golf-swing taskmaster. Certainly the early-year update sessions were serious efforts to ensure that Nicklaus could roll into the winter tour in January with his game running full bore. Other sessions through a given year, though, including those before the year's four major championships, in many cases tended to involve more talking as good friends than fixing any swing problems.

Nicklaus addressed those pre-majors working sessions in a 1998 interview with *Golf Magazine*, saying that he would "spend four or five days with Jack Grout, but three of those days we might not even talk about what I was doing." The two men long ago had established a working pattern, one that saw their personal friendship and mutual respect gradually become as important to each of them as their work on Nicklaus' golf game.

***

Jack Nicklaus was a prodigy who reached the zenith of his illustrious career in the 1970s when he won the PGA Tour money title five times in six years, was named player of the year four times in five years, and won eight of his eighteen majors (most in any decade). As he was achieving his status as golf's greatest champion around this time, I was arriving in adulthood, trailing him by a dozen years in that respect. The toughness, drive and competitiveness that had always been there came to the forefront of his personality, and he became more demanding. Inevitably, with that our relationship changed.

I got a firsthand dose of the demanding Nicklaus when I played Muirfield Village with him not long after the course opened. After crossing over a narrow footbridge at the third hole, Jack spotted a worn section—a "cow trail," as he called it. At the base of a hill where everyone had been walking, the grass had been trampled to death. When Jack saw the all-too-obvious bare spots, he was upset. I sensed that he might be looking for other things to get steamed about, and it turned out I didn't have long to wait. Once Jack reached the green and noticed the many dents in his beautiful putting surface from golfers not repairing their ball marks, he pivoted, looked at me and our two caddies, and said, "If I find out who's NOT fixing their ball marks, they're OUT of here!!!" Then he instructed all of us to search the green for blemishes and do our best to fix them. The construction of Muirfield Village was a cherished Nicklaus dream that almost had turned into a nightmare, nearly breaking him financially before its completion and eventual success. Understandably Nicklaus would tolerate no imperfections in his prized creation.

While I was bent over attending to a small crater I'd found, Jack stood next to me and asked if I knew "how to repair a ball mark properly." Knowing Jack, I realized the key in his question was the word "properly." I'd been repairing ball marks for more than a decade. I knew how to do it. Still, I hesitated before finally saying, "I think so." "Let me see," Nicklaus said. It was at that moment that I felt the real meaning of pressure. With the mighty Nicklaus peering over my shoulder, I began fixing that ball mark, even as I asked for divine guidance with a quick prayer: "Oh Lord, if I've ever done this properly, let it be now." My effort must have been adequate, because when I finished, Jack simply uttered a grunt and walked off toward the fourth tee.

Never one to lack self-confidence, Nicklaus could be open, warm and gracious, but he also could be brusque. Nicklaus has written about the day when a friend pulled him aside to chastise him for being rude to someone on the phone. Golf aficionados will recall that pretty much the same thing happened to the late Payne Stewart, who blew off a fan in a tournament parking lot one day and was chastised by his wife, Tracey. Just as Stewart began to ease off on his occasional brusqueness after his wife's admonition, so did Nicklaus take his friend's criticism to heart.

A passage from Arnold Palmer's autobiography, *A Golfer's Life*, also puts the Nicklaus persona in its proper perspective: "I had never seen anyone who could stay focused the way he did," Palmer wrote of the way Nicklaus handled the rowdy, rude Palmer partisans at Oakmont in 1962, "and I've never seen anyone with the same ability since. In my view, that's why Jack Nicklaus became the most accomplished player in the history of the game. You just couldn't crack that concentration. He had his own game plan, and he stuck to it, come hell or high water—or noisy hometown fans."

I've always felt that my father was the ideal teacher for Jack Nicklaus, not just because Dad was a highly skilled golf instructor, but also because he had spent a couple of decades on the PGA Tour dealing with tough, competitive and sometimes-curt men such as Ben Hogan, Byron Nelson and Sam Snead. Through his interactions with these great players, he grew to understand the drive and the

Sam Snead and Jack Grout: old friends together at Muirfield Village Golf Club in 1984. (Photo courtesy of Muirfield Village Golf Club)

Old "Masters": Jack Grout and Byron Nelson sit under "The Big Oak Tree" at Augusta National. (Photo approved for publication)

personalities of highly talented individuals who often were self-involved and insensitive to how their actions impacted others. Dad thus had an intuitive understanding of Nicklaus' strong and demanding personality, intense focus and occasional impatience with persons or issues that distracted him from the work at hand.

My father, with his relaxed way of dealing with people and his low-key approach to teaching golf, matched well with Nicklaus' personality for several reasons. First, Dad was consistent. Through exposure to accomplished professional golfers on the early tour and decades of working with good players, he had come to a set of golf-swing principles that he taught unwaveringly. He was not attracted to and did not confuse his pupils by advancing every new swing theory that came down the pike. Nor would Nicklaus have wanted him to. Second, Dad was by nature a highly supportive and encouraging person, and this characteristic won him great loyalty from Jack Nicklaus, Raymond Floyd and many other top-level golfers who were his students. And, third Dad was by nature a humble man. He drew great satisfaction from the success of those he taught, but he had no need to be the "star of the show." He was happy to stand in the background and let his golf students take full credit for their successes both on and off the course.

Jack Grout "was perfect for my dad," said Nicklaus' son, Jack Nicklaus II, himself a talented golfer and course designer. "Whether it was my dad's analytical mind trying to understand on his own accord what to do and how to make adjustments on the golf course, or Jack Grout's way of teaching that allowed him to do that ... it was probably a combination of both. Whatever buttons Jack Grout pushed, my dad responded very well to."

No question, Dad's relationship with Jack Nicklaus was multi-dimensional. Throughout their time together, however—and I believe that this is the primary reason the two men worked so well as a team through four decades—the core of their relationship remained consistent, and that core was the constant return to a set of golf fundamentals that my father preached from the first day they worked together to the last: the setup, the grip, body alignment, the critical role of proper foot action. The relationship between these two very different men—different, but beautifully complementary in their skills and personal styles—grew from their early focus on these and other fundamentals of golf, then deepened over time as they shared mutual learning regarding the fundamentals of life.

***

My father had a moderate estimation of his own talents and abilities, and he was attractive to other people, including Jack Nicklaus, largely because he never seemed to be trying to put them down or one-up their accomplishments. It was Dad's natural inclination to stay in the background and let Nicklaus occupy the spotlight which meshed perfectly with what the highly accomplished golfer needed from his instructor. Jack Grout and Jack Nicklaus simply did not have the kinds of clashes that Tiger Woods, for example, had with instructor Butch Harmon or caddie Mike "Fluff" Cowan, who made the mistake of sometimes seeming too eager to bask prominently in the reflected glory of Mr. Woods.

Dad considered his role with a mature Jack Nicklaus as that of the experienced jockey working with the thoroughbred racehorse. The powerful horse wins the race, but the jockey keeps him pointed in the right direction and supports his drive to the finish line. Dad gave all the credit to Jack for one simple reason: He felt Jack deserved it.

As far as I could see, there were no serious blemishes in their relationship. Yes, Jack Nicklaus, being the great athlete that he was, possessed an ego to match his talent and was known for speaking his mind. Sometimes the things he said probably didn't come out just as he meant for them to sound, and on occasion his words to my father

Book's author stands beside his two heros in 1978 on the practice tee at Muirfield Village Golf Club. (Photo courtesy of Tim Revelle)

struck me as insensitive. When I asked my father, "Dad, what about what Jack said when he said *blah, blah, blah*?" his answer was the same every time. He'd just shrug his shoulders, then say, "Dickie, you know Jack."

Looking back at their relationship, Dad told me, "Over the years, these instances may have resulted when he felt he had outgrown me and my brand of instruction. After all, from our earliest days together my message to him rarely changed. I never ever thought any of it was intentional. His conviction and belief in himself were so strong that things like that were bound to happen from time to time. I never forgot that it was his strong personality and ego which enabled him to achieve all those great victories. It's quite possible that if Jack hadn't been the great champion golfer he was, I would have written him off long beforehand. I was not inclined to do so, however, because you really couldn't argue with his tremendous success."

The bottom line on all this, really, is that my father and Jack Nicklaus stayed together and remained close friends through all of the normal bumps and bruises of a close professional and personal relationship. Nicklaus paid tribute to this when he wrote in his book *My Story* that "Much as I liked Jack, it never occurred to me ... how deep the relationship with my generous, modest, sweet-natured teacher would become, and how much of a contribution it would make both to my game and to my mental and emotional well-being for so many of my adult years. The truth is that we developed a friendship as close and warm and comfortable as two men can, and particularly after my dad's death in 1970, when Jack Grout became a second father to me."

Chapter 21
Tales from the Lesson Tee

"Sure, talent makes a difference. That's what the Good Lord gives us. But technique, now that's what we can learn, and technique can make up for a lack of talent." —JACK GROUT

***

As my father settled into his life at Muirfield Village and, during the winter months, at sun-bathed golf courses in Florida, he had reached a new plateau of comfort and happiness. He was accepted as a great teacher of golf. But maybe more important to him, he was accepted as a quality person. Dad was operating now as a gray eminence of sorts, celebrated for his work with Jack Nicklaus and other elite players but refusing to be treated as a celebrity.

"He was loved by everyone because of his temperament, for one, and for his way of life," said Pandel Savic, the one-time Ohio State football quarterback who, along with several other Columbus businessmen, helped Nicklaus transform the dream into the reality of Muirfield Village. "He made everyone happy. He always had a good word for everyone."

Former Muirfield CEO Hines remembered talking with Dad every morning at the club and being struck by his interest in and knowledge about the Civil War. "He used to talk about different battles, and then the Falkland Islands thing came up and we'd sit there in the morning and discuss the pros and cons of what was going on (there). He was a Midwestern conservative whose favorite event of the year was the Fourth of July parade. He couldn't wait to take the day off to watch the parade."

Boomer Byrum, a longtime clubhouse employee at Muirfield Village, recalled that Dad would come into the grill room every morning for breakfast and "kind of hold court. You know, he had his people that would come in and sit and talk with him every day, and it was kind of (an ongoing) deal." Byrum said that Dad would "talk about whoever he was teaching at the time, or he'd talk about ... when he and (Ben) Hogan were playing in tournaments in California, and he said they had an old Plymouth that they had to stop every time they got gas and fill up the radiator because the radiator was broken and they couldn't go very far because it would overheat. It was really cool to hear about that."

In an interview for this book, Byrum, who was particularly close to my father, talked of the golfers who flocked to Muirfield Village to take lessons from Dad. There was, for example, Muirfield member Kerry Packer, the ill-tempered Australian multibillionaire media magnate who became obsessively dedicated to improving his golf game under my father's direction. "He and Mr. Grout would stand out there and hit balls until Packer's hands would bleed," Byrum said. "He had us go to the store and buy him this stuff called New Skin. He'd put it on his hands and then he would come back and hit balls and hit balls ... Mr. Grout used to do very well off of Mr. Packer."

Just as intense in personal demeanor and just as committed to golf improvement under Dad's instruction was another Muirfield member, Dick Chapdelaine, or "Chappy" to his friends. Owner of a successful Wall Street brokerage firm, Chappy was a compact man with a commanding presence. He had a ruddy complexion and gave off vibes that, if provoked, he might be capable of real anger.

Chappy told me once of hearing about my father as "this guy ... who was Nicklaus' teacher and was giving lessons at Muirfield Village, where I was a new member. I had taken a lot of lessons from a number of pretty good golf pros, but my game was no good ... so I found out how to schedule a lesson from Grout and made an appointment with him."

As the lesson began, Chappy said, "I hit about ten or twelve shots, but he did not say anything. In all the other lessons I'd gotten, the teachers would have said a couple of volumes by now. But he was just watching me, sizing me up, and I was wondering what was going on.

"Then he asked me if I had any brothers and sisters," Chappy continued. Annoyed, he answered, "Yes Jack, I have one sister."

"I'll be honest with you," Chappy said. "At this point I thought that this fellow, Grout, might have a couple of loose screws! Then he asked if my sister ever played with dolls when she was little."

Chappy said he wheeled around and fumed, "Yes, Jack, as practically all kids who grew up in those days, my sister had a Raggedy Ann. And I had a Raggedy Andy. So what about it?'

"Needless to say, at this point, I was red-hot!" Chappy went on. "But it was your dad who enjoyed the gotcha' moment.

"He simply pointed his finger at me and said, 'Dick, that's who I want you to be. I want you to be Raggedy Andy.' You see, I'm really a tense person. Jack could see this right away and didn't want me to be so stiff and rigid. He wanted me to loosen up.

"Believe me," Chappy concluded, "I've had lessons from everybody, all of the best teaching pros. But when I'm playing my best, I'm Raggedy Andy. That Jack Grout was truly one of a kind."

Many of my father's best memories came from working with Muirfield members such as Packer and Chapdelaine, but even non-prominent nonmembers sometimes schemed their way onto Dad's lesson tee. A good example was Mick Dannin. Born in Denmark, Dannin moved to Sweden with his family at age six, then took up residence in the Canary Islands in 1975 with his new American bride. Introduced to golf there, he soon was hooked. No matter how hard he worked, though, he "hit the wall" at about a sixteen handicap. Then, Dannin said, "I heard more and more stories from my golf friends, and the name 'Jack Nicklaus' kept popping up, and I was told that he was the best player in the world. I thought, 'If Jack Nicklaus is that good, then he must have the best coach in the world and I want to meet that special man and work with him ... ' "

By coincidence, Dannin's wife's parents lived in Columbus, so he asked them to help find out who coached Jack Nicklaus and how to get in touch with this man. The in-laws laughed. But Dannin persisted, and soon the phone rang in the Muirfield Village golf shop, and the following conversation ensued between the teacher of the world's best golfer and a stranger with a sixteen handicap:

"Hello, this is Jack Grout."

"Oouuhhh, hello Mr. Grout, my name is Mick Dannin; thank you for taking my call."

"What can I do for you?"

"Well, I understand that you are one of the best golf instructors in the world, and I would love to come over and work with you for a month or so!!"

Dad calmly asked whether Mr. Dannin was a golf professional.

"No. I am a sixteen handicap. I have played one year, I love the game and I am determined to improve, so that's why I would love to come over and work with you."

Dad explained gently that he had a very busy schedule and that he generally had time to work only with professional golfers. But Dannin was insistent and wore Dad down.

"Well, I am very busy," Dad said, "but why don't you come out here and say hello when you get to Columbus."

Shortly thereafter, Dannin traveled to Columbus, called Dad again, and wound up getting a personal tour of Muirfield Village Golf Club from the distinguished teaching pro. "We hit it off right away," Dannin says, "and by the end of the tour, Jack said, 'Well, young man, why don't you come back tomorrow with your clubs and I'll take a look at your swing.' "

Dannin not only showed up the next day; he actually worked with my father almost every day of July 1975. That fall, he says, "my handicap came down to an eight, and I am forever thankful to Jack Grout for the amazing feeling of wonderful friendship he extended me."

While my father enjoyed helping average players who loved the game of golf and hungered to master its intricacies, I don't want to give the impression that he was driven solely by human compassion in allowing players of limited golf talent into his orbit along with pros and accomplished amateurs. He was, after all, charging them all $100 or more per hour of lesson time! "He usually had several players a week that would come in and spend several days with him, generally better players, amateurs and pros," remembered Dad's friend Boomer Byrum. "Mr. Grout used to take a guy out (to the practice area), and he would stay out as long as a guy wanted to. Of course, Mr. Grout charged by the hour, so it was no problem for him." Byrum added, "People didn't mind, even back in the '70s, paying a hundred dollars an hour, because Mr. Grout improved their game."

***

My father's teaching-pro assignments at Muirfield Village and during the winters at Cheeca Lodge, Frenchman's Creek and Loxahatchee in Florida brought countless opportunities for him to see struggling amateur golfers discover the secrets to better play and to observe talented pros sharpen their already formidable skills. I remember, in particular, the following stories:

Actor Sean Connery—the original "James Bond, 007"—played a charity match with Jack Nicklaus at Scotland's St. Andrews in 1978, joined Muirfield Village soon after, and eventually approached my father there for help on his game. "I was in the grill room here at Muirfield with Grout, and he asked me to stand up and show my stance," Connery told Kaye Kessler in 1983. "Well, sir, I did. First, he changed my stance. Then he changed my grip, my address, my head and shoulder turn and then my position at the ball. Then he wanted me to extend my thumb down the shaft. You know, your thumb is only so long. Otherwise, he thought I was fine." Armed with my father's initial advice, Connery said, "I next went to the practice range and hit probably six hundred balls. Psychologically, when you see golf balls in front of you, you're compelled to hit them. My arm's so sore now I don't think I can move it. My thumb hurts. But Grout was correct."

Fred Ridley, who later would rise through the ranks of the United States Golf Association and in 2004 become its president, was a member of the University of Florida golf team and certainly a better golfer than Sean Connery when he first sought my father's help. Ridley's Florida teammate, Brad Baldwin, had been a student of Dad's and arranged an introduction and first lesson at the La Gorce club in Miami Beach in 1974. Ridley said he was "amazed that a person of (Jack Grout's) stature would even have seen me," and the next year he traveled to Ohio to spend a week studying with Dad at Muirfield Village. "To be at one of the world's great facilities with one of the best golf instructors of all times was like dying and going to golfers' heaven," Ridley said. After Ridley won the U.S. Amateur championship in 1975 and realized that as the amateur champ he'd be paired with defending champion Jack Nicklaus in the next year's Masters, Dad helped ease the young player's nervousness by arranging for the two men to play practice rounds together at Muirfield and at Augusta National. "While playing with Jack was still intimidating," said Ridley, who became an attorney in Florida, "those preliminary rounds made it a lot easier."

Jim Palmer, the Hall of Fame baseball pitcher, arrived at the lesson tee at Cheeca Lodge in quite an impressive way. I was standing on the practice field one day when Palmer set down nearby in a helicopter, there for an appointment with Dad! On another day, Carl Navarre, then chairman of the board of the Miami Coca-Cola Bottling Company, arrived by helicopter and ferried my dad and me up the Florida coastline from the Keys to Jack Nicklaus' home course, Lost Tree Golf Club, in North Palm Beach. We landed on the practice tee, were met by Nicklaus, then practiced and hit balls under Dad's critical gaze before heading out for eighteen holes. I remember that on the flight back down the coast to Cheeca, we flew over a beached whale that was surrounded by a group of people.

My father delighted in all of these experiences—the new friendships, the teaching, the joy of seeing his amateur students get better at the game he loved. And he felt doubly fortunate to be able to move freely from helping eager amateurs to the very different world of working with the highly skilled professionals who sought him out right up to the end of his life. It was in this high-pressure world of elite professional golfers that Dad could feel the greatest challenge and achieve the most satisfaction. Here, an instructor's bad bit of advice, a careless word that leads a golfer down the wrong swing path, could mean real damage to a player's pocketbook and his career.

***

Through his so-called retirement, my father spent hundreds of days on the practice range with the world's best golfers, and he did it in a variety of quality venues. Perhaps no venue, though, had the sheer dynamism and amazing variety of star golfers, teachers and celebrity observers as the practice range at Frenchman's Creek. Just being there redefined the meaning of the term, "adrenaline rush." On a given day at the club, Dad would be working with one player or another while other first-rate teachers such as Bob Toski, Gardner Dickinson, Keith Marks, Toney Penna, Jim Flick, Jim McLean and Phil Rodgers worked with others or just dropped by from time to time to be part of the action. Some days, famed crooner Perry Como would slide by in his private golf cart, a scarf tied over his nose and mouth to protect his precious vocal cords as he eyed the ongoing teaching and learning.

Burly Raymond Floyd might be there, too, working on shaping shots. The great LPGA player JoAnne Carner also might be on hand, crushing drives as few female golfers ever have, while Olin Browne labored intensely to turn his modest natural talent into a quite successful golf career, and Jay and Lionel Hebert, Tommy Aaron and other fine players banged balls under the Palm Beach County sun. Then Jack Nicklaus would stroll in, and the energy level would skyrocket. Very serious work would be done by all, the mere presence of the Golden Bear sending new levels of competitive juices flowing through the assembled lineup of golfing heavyweights.

The scene at Frenchman's Creek "was a very unusual thing," said Flick, who was one of Nicklaus' instructors after my father's death. "We had a mix of all kinds of people who would come in there, and a lot of it happened because Gardner had designed the golf courses and they were marvelous, challenging golf courses and a place to learn how to play the game. I would see the best players in the country come in and get lessons from a number of people there, and it was a tremendous collection. I joined (Frenchman's Creek) so that I could watch Gardner, Mr. Grout and Toney Penna teach because it was three totally different concepts of how to teach the game."

Players who took instruction from my father at Frenchman's Creek or on other practice grounds in Florida, Ohio and elsewhere brought a range of swing problems to be worked on, but they found a common approach to their issues: Dad saw them all as people first, golfers second, and he never, ever tried to make golf seem a complex endeavor.

Pro Lee Rinker talked of my father's skills at allowing a golfer to "visualize" the problems in his swing. Rinker was only in his midteens when he first took a lesson from Dad, at Frenchman's Creek, not far from the Rinker family residence. "I told (Mr. Grout) that I was hooking the ball," Rinker recalled. "He said he could understand that because I had a 'ham sandwich' grip. I looked a little puzzled at him and said, 'What does that mean?' He then stuck his hand out at me with his palm facing to the sky and said, 'Give me a ham sandwich.' " Even at a young age, Rinker understood that Dad meant his grip was too "strong," the right hand rotated too far to the right. "I immediately started trying to get my right hand up on top of the club," Rinker said, "and then I couldn't hook it to save my life." Rinker later said "that one lesson was a major event in my career as a competitive golfer."

David Graham, the superb Australian player who had nearly forty professional wins worldwide, including two majors, worked with Dad at the Lost Tree Club. "I think the one single (most important) thing that Mr. Grout did for me was he gave me attention," Graham said. "He was primarily known as Jack Nicklaus' teacher, so when Jack Grout gave me time, he was either doing it because Jack asked him to ... or he was just genuinely interested in my career." Both at Lost Tree and at the Memorial Tournament at Muirfield Village, Graham said, "Mr. Grout would help me with my swing. He worked on my backswing a little bit, and I started doing stretching exercises and I started swinging a very heavy weighted club to lengthen my swing." Remembering steady improvement in his game at that point, Graham said that "obviously, his suggestions worked extremely well for me."

Graham also talked of my father being an icon of sorts on the practice range at the Memorial Tournament: "He would walk up and down the range and say hello to a lot of players on the range ... He had unbelievable respect because of what he had done for Nicklaus." Often, those players—the great South African champion Gary Player was one of them—would corral my dad as he passed by during his practice-range wanderings and solicit a quick look at their swings. "I truly appreciate the fact, Jack, that you took time to watch me 'swing a bit,' "Player wrote to my father after the Memorial in 1981. "It is rewarding to me to know that a man such as yourself, who has such a keen appreciation for the game of golf, is willing to help everybody."

Californian Jerry Heard, a five-time winner on the PGA Tour, found in my dad the most taciturn of approaches to golf instruction. Heard had a single lesson with Dad and said in a letter to me, "I was very anxious to hear what your father had to say about my golf swing. He said, 'Hit some balls and let me observe.' " Heard started with his short irons and worked through his entire bag. Dad said nothing. "I finally got to the driver ... and I hit four or five perfect drives and finally turned around and said, 'What do you think, Mr. Grout?' He gave me a look and said, 'If I were you, I'd move a half-inch closer to the ball.' And that was the end of the lesson. To this day, I've told that story many times and believe me, (Mr. Grout) was right."

Dad took a similar approach while working with Gibby Gilbert, a solid player who won three events on the PGA Tour and six more on the Champions Tour. "He came to me, and I saw immediately he was standing six inches too far from the ball," Dad told *Golf Digest* writer Larry Dennis in 1975. "This caused him to hit either duck hooks or pushes to the right. I had him assume my stance, and he immediately started hitting the ball straight. And he could fade it or draw it when he wanted to." Dad said he told Gilbert to "get to a phone and tell 'em he'd be at the next tournament, that he didn't need that much practice." Talking later about that lesson, Dad would note with satisfaction that Gilbert had been "playing better ever since."

Olin Browne, winner of seven professional events, including three PGA Tour tournaments, told a different kind of Jack Grout story, one that suggests that while my father may have had diplomatic skills, he also could be brutally honest in his practice-range assessments. Browne professed that he "couldn't play a lick" when he got out of Occidental College but called my father anyway and requested an audience on the lesson tee at Muirfield Village. My father agreed, and Browne was waiting there when Dad drove up in a golf cart, got out, and introduced himself. "Well, show me what you've got," Dad said, and Browne took out his seven-iron. "The adrenaline was just coursing through me—I could hardly keep my feet on the ground," Browne said, "and I hit three seven-irons, and all three of them went exactly where I was aiming them—they were perfect shots. I looked up and Jack just looked at the ground and shook his head, and he said, 'Nope, that's no good at all.' " That well-intentioned put-down notwithstanding, Dad spent time working with Browne at Muirfield and later at Frenchman's Creek, eventually advising the young player not to turn professional. "He said that I'd be better off having a nice amateur career and getting a nice job and having a family," Browne says. Browne respectfully ignored that advice, worked tirelessly on his game, and became a solid touring professional.

Browne looks back fondly at the excitement of the wintertime lesson tee at Frenchman's Creek. "There was a real mecca there ... where some of these great players with wonderful résumés and long, long, hugely successful careers were making an appearance," he said. "For those of us who were just learning the game, it was a real eye-opener." If Browne didn't have a lesson scheduled on a particular day, he would show up to watch Dad teach somebody else. He said, "There was certainly a bunch of us who would gather around whenever Jack Nicklaus came to hit balls, or Ray Floyd, or JoAnne Carner or somebody like that. It was an immersion for a neophyte, a crash course in golf, and it came from all different areas ... from all different people." The whole scene, Browne said, "was all very interactive. There were a lot of very knowledgeable and accomplished people—teachers, students and players. I did the best I could to keep my mouth shut and my ears open."

After his impressive victory in the 2011 U.S. Senior Open Championship at Toledo's Inverness Club, Browne lamented never getting to show Jack Grout the championship player he'd helped mold: "Unfortunately, Jack passed away before I had any real success, so he was never able to see my improvement."

Dad showed off his unique analytical ability with one rising star of the 1980s without even taking the player to the practice tee. That player, Fred Couples, was on the practice range during the 1982 Memorial Tournament at Muirfield Village when my dad joined a group of people who were watching the young pro hit balls. According to a magazine called *The Majors Series*, one of the men was turned off by Couples' unorthodox golf swing. "What a lousy-looking move," the man sniffed, adding that Couples would have a very difficult time on tour. My father offered a different opinion, though. "Don't bet too much," he said to Couples' critic, adding that Freddie's swinging motion "is about as pure as you'll ever see. And just look at the power it produces. Depending on what's in his head and his belly, I think he could have quite a future." Point well made. Couples took his first PGA Tour victory the next year and went on to be named PGA Player of the Year in both 1991 and in 1992, winning the Masters in the latter year and rising to the top of the world golf rankings.

Chapter 22
Turning Back the Clock

"Thrive on hard work. Yet have the patience to realize that everything will not come at once. This attitude will help anyone who aspires to play a decent game of golf." —JACK GROUT

❊❊❊

While my father welcomed the chance to teach so many talented players through his Muirfield and Florida years, he never ceased keeping a close eye on his protégé's results on the world golf scene. And, by the late 1970s Jack Nicklaus was having problems with his game. Problems so serious, in fact, that the Golden Bear actually was thinking about giving up the game, of hibernating permanently from his life as an active player. Nicklaus had had other stretches when his play had not lived up to his lofty personal standards—standards demanding that he be measured by his wins in the golf majors—but he'd been able to struggle back to championship form. After winning seven majors from 1962 through 1967, for example, Nicklaus did not win another until the British Open late in the 1970 season. Nicklaus came back with six additional major wins from 1971 through 1975 but tapered off again, winning only one more through 1979, the first year in his professional career in which he took no wins at all.

In an interview for *The New Yorker* magazine in 1983, Nicklaus told noted golf writer Herbert Warren Wind that by the late '70s he'd pretty much lost the swing that had carried him to the top of the golf world. "During the seventies, I wasn't a good striker of the ball at all," Nicklaus said. "My head would bob a bit. I started to see my hips bobble. I was doing something on my backswing that pushed me up in the air, and at the top of the backswing my hands would be directly over my head instead of behind it. On my downswing, my left leg would sag. This would throw me outside the proper line, and I would wipe across the ball from right to left. That's why I lost so much distance. For years, I couldn't identify what caused that hip bobble. No one could—not even (Jack) Grout."

Nicklaus wrote in his book *My Story* that Dad "watched the decline with increasing concern and repeated urging of me to go all the way back to the drawing board and, with his help, fix my full swing once and for all." As Nicklaus recalled, my father was blunt in his assessment, saying that Nicklaus had lost the depth formerly reached by his hands in the backswing, and that "If you don't do something about that, your career will be a lot shorter than both of us would like."

Nicklaus, though, was slow to take Dad's advice. In fact, he wrote in *My Story* that "... although I heard Jack, I never really listened to him" in this period. "Fearful of falling between an old method and a new one, fearful of losing whatever game I had left, I simply wasn't ready to make the commitment in time and effort necessary to, as I saw it, master a new golf swing. Instead, I continued to fiddle around and make do, basically applying one useless Band-Aid after another until the only alternative to quitting became starting over again."

Those comments reflected pretty closely what my father had told *Sports Illustrated* writer Dan Jenkins more than a decade earlier, after the 1967 Masters. After detailing a series of problems that had cropped up in Nicklaus' game, Dad said that Nicklaus "needs to take ninety days off and work and work. But he only half listens. All he says is, 'I'm laying it off at the top.'" No one suggested it at the time, but possibly Nicklaus was a victim of the very self-reliance his teacher had encouraged him to develop.

***

Faced with clear deterioration of his game in 1979, Nicklaus fretted about whether he could find the desire to make the needed changes. Eventually, though, he would follow my father's admonition of a decade earlier that he take a months-long leave from competition. Nicklaus didn't do that so that he could work on his game, however. Rather, he said, "When I finished playing the PGA Championship (in August), from then until about January 3rd I think I touched a golf club three times. I didn't qualify for the Ryder Cup ... I don't recall playing anything at all. I did that on purpose to get away from it."

Nicklaus would reach his fortieth birthday in 1980, the age when most professional golfers begin to see their games deteriorating as they lose their youthful flexibility and focus. He also had reduced his playing schedule substantially to allow for sharper focus on the four majors each year, and because he simply didn't have the enthusiasm to play as many tournaments as in his earlier days on tour. He was also spending more time with the modest empire of businesses he'd built, including the design of golf courses around the world, so it's easy to understand how his golf game might have declined. Nicklaus, though, wasn't just any other golfer whose skills were fading; most observers regarded him as the best player ever, and he didn't want to relinquish that status. Finally, at the end of 1979, he came down to two choices, neither of which greatly appealed to him: Retire from the game or dive into major reconstructive work on his swing.

Nicklaus chose the latter option, of course, and early in 1980 he launched an intensive effort to restore the golf swing that through two decades had carried him to scores of victories around the world, including fifteen majors. Nicklaus sought short-game advice from his friend and former pro player Phil Rodgers that spring, working particularly hard on pitching, chipping and bunker play. But for the toughest changes, for the intensive search for the swing that had been so reliable for so many years but that now seemed to have disappeared, Nicklaus turned again to my father. Dad was living near Nicklaus in Florida that winter, and the two dove into the effort to right the great man's listing ship. Nicklaus said he told Dad that he "wanted to get all my bad habits out of the way and forgotten so I could start fresh and start working on my golf game and make the changes in my swing that I needed to make ... We both agreed to that, and so when I started back up we worked pretty hard."

The two men focused sharply on taking Nicklaus back to the swing he'd been taught when he was ten years old, a movement in which, at the top of the backswing, his hands were more *behind* his head and upper back than *above* them. That change sounds simple, but it's not, and Nicklaus struggled mightily with it. "Time and again," he wrote later, "I would be convinced I had it all down pat, only to watch Grout and others who happened to be on hand and knew my game somberly shake their heads. It was *tough*." All in all, Nicklaus said, "it was the hardest I had worked at golf since my teen years."

The bulk of this work took place on the practice tee at Frenchman's Creek. I was working at the club then and was standing nearby on the January morning when Nicklaus and my father began the difficult swing-restoration project. As often occurred during his many sessions with Nicklaus, Dad would bounce his ideas off me and ask for my thoughts and mostly my eyesight, as his was not very good by this point. Dad would check with me after a swing to see what I thought of Jack's positioning. And Nicklaus would hit balls and hit balls and hit balls. It was as if the determined young Jackie Nicklaus from Dad's junior golf class at Scioto Country Club in the summer of 1950 had reappeared.

With my father watching, guiding and encouraging, Nicklaus poured himself into the work; he knew this could be his last shot at a return to his old form, and he wasn't about to blow it off. Looking back, Nicklaus said that during those marathon sessions, "I probably worked four or five days a week with Jack, as well as played, and tried to move my swing to where my plane was shallower. I moved my hands behind my head ... my hands at impact were too high, (and) I tried to work my hands lower at impact, tried to work on a complete release."

The work was intense, but as Nicklaus would discover, there were no magic solutions. He finished no better than eleventh in his first three tournaments in 1980, but then his spirits were lifted somewhat by a second-place finish at Doral, where he shot a fine 69 in the final round only to lose in a playoff to Raymond Floyd. Following that, though, were more mediocre finishes, including a thirty-third at the Masters and a particularly discouraging showing in Dallas, where he finished forty-third in the Byron Nelson Classic, fifteen strokes behind Tom Watson. Nicklaus was despondent. "The frustration at that point suddenly became overpowering, sinking me into as depressed a mood as I can recall suffering," Nicklaus said later. Barbara Nicklaus told her husband at that point, "Quit if you want to. I don't mind. You have so many other things to do. But golf is such a big part of your life. I don't think you can be happy without it."

Nicklaus mulled it over some more, decided to keep working, and within a couple of weeks began to feel his game coming around. In a practice round for his own Memorial Tournament at Muirfield Village, his overall game was sharp, flawed only by so-so putting. Then, Nicklaus recalled, on the Saturday evening of the tournament's third round, "Jack Grout came up with what proved to be the finishing touch. Typical of his great diagnostic eye and his minimalism, he watched me stroking (putts) for only a minute or two before saying, 'Stop dragging the putter through the ball, stop blocking the hit. Take the thing back inside and release it—*hit* the damn ball!' I rolled a few more putts and something clicked."

Clicked, indeed. Just three weeks later, on a Sunday evening at the revered old Baltusrol Golf Club in New Jersey, Jack Nicklaus celebrated his return to world-class form by accepting the winner's trophy for the 1980 U.S. Open Championship. Nicklaus had posted a spectacular 63 in the tourney's opening round and made clutch putts on the final two holes on Sunday to close out a tight victory over Isao Aoki of Japan. It was the sixteenth major-tournament victory of Nicklaus' career, and certainly one of the sweetest. Nicklaus said that, in his own view, he never had played a better nine holes than the back nine in that Open's final round.

As if to prove the Open victory was no fluke, Nicklaus won again in his very next tournament, the 1980 PGA Championship at Oak Hill in Rochester, New York. Clearly the hard work with my father and

Phil Rodgers had paid off. The Golden Bear was back, in command of his game, an intimidating presence again. Or at least that's how it seemed. But while he would play well enough in the next five years to finish third or better in twenty-one tournaments, Nicklaus would have only three victories in that period, none of them majors. For many professional golfers, that record would have been something to celebrate. For the mighty Nicklaus, it was severely disappointing. Maybe, just maybe, the Nicklaus magic was gone for good.

***

My father and Jack Nicklaus would see each other regularly through those years, at Muirfield Village during the summers and at the Loxahatchee Club near both mens' Florida residences during the winter. Occasionally they would work on Nicklaus' golf game. On other days they would just get together on the practice tee and talk, two good friends basking in the mild Florida winter, enjoying each other's company. My father, who turned seventy-five in the spring of 1985, still was giving numerous golf lessons at that point, both in Ohio and in Florida. But by the middle of that year, he was confronted with health issues much more serious than the bad back and weak eyesight that had long plagued him. In late July Dad had a "flare-up" of his heart, then just three days later he had another. An angioplasty was performed in early August, and while that procedure was successful, Dad was told that open-heart surgery would be needed eventually.

That day came sooner than expected. In late November my mother drove Dad south from North Palm Beach to Miami Beach where, on December 2, he had open-heart surgery at the Miami Heart Institute. Happily the operation went well. Dad was discharged within two weeks and surprised Mom on the way home by suggesting a quick stop at a Wendy's because he was craving a burger! By the time the two of them reached home, though, Dad's mood had darkened. He came in through the back door, walked to his desk, sat there for a minute, and then started crying. My father was not an emotional man, but his heart surgery had shaken him badly.

Before too long, Dad could look at his health more philosophically, even joke about it. When my sister Ronnie and her husband visited him in February 1986, Dad opened his shirt to show them his scar. "Look, they cut me open like a chicken," he said. Doctors had cautioned my father to take it easy, not to rush his recovery, but Dad was impatient; he just wasn't a man to sit around idle. By the middle of February, his cardiologist gave him the OK to begin light activities, and by early March Dad was back on the lesson tee at the Loxahatchee Club.

It was at this time that Jack Nicklaus reached out for the last significant coaching he ever would receive from my father. As recounted at the start of this book, Nicklaus was in despair over the state of his game in the spring of 1986, and he asked Dad if he felt well enough to venture down to the Doral Country Club in Miami and try to help him. Dad made the trip, and his simple but dead-on assessment that Nicklaus' swing was "way too handsy" struck a chord with Big Jack, led to needed modifications in his swing, and was a critical factor in his dramatic win at the Masters a month later.

Nicklaus was simply magnificent on the last day of that Masters. His final-round charge began with a birdie on the ninth, then birdies on the first two holes of the back nine. A disappointing bogey on the famed par-three twelfth provided a temporary setback, but Nicklaus charged back, a birdie at the thirteenth leaving him only two strokes behind tournament leader Seve Ballesteros. After a par at fourteen, Nicklaus brought his gallery roaring to its feet with a twelve-foot putt for eagle at the par-five fifteenth, then a birdie two at the sixteenth. With Ballesteros having hit into the water and taken a bogey at fifteen, Nicklaus moved into the lead momentarily with another birdie at the seventeenth. His closing par at eighteen left him in a tie for first with the rallying Greg Norman, but the Australian bogeyed the final hole and Tom Kite just missed a birdie putt that would have sent the tourney into a playoff. Jack Nicklaus, written off by most as old news on the PGA Tour, had staged one of the most dramatic final-nine rallies in major-tournament history to claim for the sixth time the green jacket that goes to the Masters winner.

The Golden Bear, a bit less fearsome in his forty-sixth year but ecstatic at having so unexpectedly turned back the clock one more time to his more intimidating days, was relaxed and forthcoming in his post-victory session with the media. For more than an hour, he replayed his round shot by shot. He talked about the loving support he'd gotten from his family, and he reported that just a month earlier he had turned to his old friend and instructor Jack Grout to help him with a golf swing that was confounding him with its faults.

Even as Nicklaus chatted on, my dad sat in his home in Tequesta, Florida, a few hours to the south of Augusta National, quietly celebrating his friend's most unlikely triumph. Over the course of thirty-six years, my father and Jack Nicklaus had journeyed together through the toughest challenges and the greatest rewards of the game of golf, and they had shared a lot of good days, a lot of high points. But in that decades-long collaboration, this may have been, for both, the proudest moment of all.

Chapter 23
Heart to Heart

"Dickie, you should feel sorry when the sun goes down. Because it'll be too dark to see the ball, and we'll have to quit and go home." —JACK GROUT

❊❊❊

My father was seventy-six years old when Jack Nicklaus recorded his amazing victory in the 1986 Masters, and by then Dad had been playing and teaching golf for more than six decades. Maybe, in the wake of his most famous pupil's greatest victory, many men in Dad's shoes would have felt it finally was time to quit, to leave the hard work of the practice tee to younger men. My father, though, opted to keep going, to teach as much as he could on Muirfield's magnificent practice range during the summers and to give as many lessons as possible during his winter months in Florida.

Not that Dad was a slave to his work. His Muirfield Village friend, Boomer Byrum, remembered the many days when Dad would arrive in the morning and say, "Boomie, we're going bang-tailing today," which meant that a day at the thoroughbred track was being planned. Byrum would ask Dad who was going to the track with him, and Dad would rattle off a series of names, then say, "We'd love for you to come, Boomie."

Dad and his group spent many pleasant afternoons at nearby Beulah Park, an undistinguished venue for little-known racehorses but still a place to have a good time watching the ponies. "It was an experience," Byrum said, "because Mr. Grout was an experienced bettor and he knew the races." Dad would ask Byrum, "Boomie, what do you think of that five horse?" Then, given a favorable review, he'd say, "Well I like that five horse. Here, go get a little something on that five horse for me." Dad would fork over some cash, and Byrum would place the bet and bring the tickets back to Dad's spot in front of the television. "But he couldn't see the TV very well either," Byrum said, "and he'd say, 'Boomie, how's our five horse doing up there?' "

Those afternoons at the little track in Grove City, a modest drive from Muirfield Village, took Dad back a half century to his days as a part-time betting-window worker at Arlington Downs in Fort Worth, and he loved the reminders of those days—the smell of the track, the beauty of the horses and the sound of their hooves pounding the dirt in the homestretch. "He loved the spirit of gambling," Byrum recalled, "but I would never say Mr. Grout was a big gambler. He loved the camaraderie of the four or five guys going and spending the afternoon at the racetrack and just being together, talking and hanging out. I saw that as one of Mr. Grout's personality traits, that he just loved to be around guys and he loved to talk golf and sports."

Dad found plenty of opportunities for such discussions in his closing years. During winter days at Frenchman's Creek and Loxahatchee from 1983 until 1989, Dad would hold gabfests with Nicklaus or more serious sessions with other pros such as Ray Floyd or with the amateurs who continued to reach out for his teaching. The routine was similar on summertime days at Muirfield, with Dad usually having breakfast in the grill room, surrounded by club staff, visitors who wanted to meet and get to know him, or whatever player might be about to head to the lesson tee with the man who taught Jack Nicklaus.

"He was a very animated storyteller," said Jack Nicklaus II, who spent a great deal of time with my dad at Muirfield Village. "I used to love that about him, and people just wanted to be around him." Jack II remembered, in particular, a story my father shared about playing in a tournament at the famed Medinah Course No. 3, and how my dad used the tale as a parable about the use of bad language on a golf course. "This guy, his playing partner, three-putted the first hole, and apparently this flurry of foul words came out as he walked off the green and it was loud enough for the gallery to hear it as well as the players, and Jack Grout could hear this," Nicklaus said. "Mr. Grout approached him on the second tee and said, 'I don't ever want to hear those words out of you again. It's embarrassing for you, it's embarrassing for us as professionals. It's not good for our sport, and it's not good for our fans. I don't want to hear you say that again. You're going to regret it if you do it again.' "

The second hole was a par three that required a precise tee shot over Lake Kadijah, and Nicklaus said that "apparently, on the second green the guy three-putted again and he again said a flurry of words, and the story goes ... that Mr. Grout calmly handed his putter to his caddie, walked over to the guy, says 'I warned you' and grabbed the guy and threw him right into the lake! Whether that story was completely accurate, or maybe it was just Jack Grout trying to tell a young boy a story on how strongly he felt about cussing on the golf course, that's the story he told me and it made a lasting impression."

The younger Nicklaus said that such stories were endearing and he came to have great admiration for my father as a role model and also, over time, as something of a low-key cut-up. "I would do anything that he told me to do," Nicklaus said. "I remember when I was about twelve years old ... he saw me eating a peach and he told me, 'Do you realize, young Jack, that you will have the best luck on the golf course if you play with that peach pit in your mouth?' I think he was giggling nonstop, but I played about five holes and about choked on that pit three times ... and he almost fell out of his cart laughing."

***

While Dad never lost his enthusiasm for teaching golf, the passing years finally began to take a serious toll on his body. Through 1987 and 1988, bouts with bad health forced a pullback in his work routine. He still got up and headed for work every morning, still gave many lessons, but those closest to him could see him making accommodations to his advancing age. "You could see in the mid-'80s that he was starting to leak oil a little bit, that he was declining," said Boomer Byrum. "You could see that he couldn't last on the range all day like he used to, that he didn't come in as early in the morning. He left earlier in the afternoon. He didn't have the stamina that he had before." The one time Dad seemed a bit rejuvenated was during the annual Memorial Tournament week, when a steady flow of talented players sought him out. "Raymond Floyd was one who always wanted (Grout) to take a peek at him ... and (there were) many others during the tournament," said Muirfield member and longtime Nicklaus friend Pandel Savic.

Dad's family sustained him through these years, showering him with love and admiration. My older siblings, John and Ronnie, were out on their own and had children; I had married in 1981, and my wife, Denise, and I had two children by 1986; and my younger sister, Debbie, was single and lived part of each year with my parents. My dad thus had children to help him, grandchildren to spoil, and many quiet evenings to spend watching television or challenging my mother to serious games of backgammon or Chinese checkers.

As time passes, so do lives, of course, and Dad suffered the loss of two more of his siblings during the '80s: Duane, his oldest brother, and Dick, the beloved sibling who had taught Dad to play golf and who took him to Texas as his assistant pro at the Glen Garden Club during the Great Depression, both died in 1982. Dad's health issues in the succeeding years drained his energy, even if not his zest for life. He was hospitalized in Columbus in the late fall of 1986, suffering from anemia, and two months later in Florida for treatment of an E. coli infection apparently caused by bad or improperly cooked oysters my mom had prepared.

Weakened a bit but still eager to work, Dad returned to giving lessons during the winter of 1987. The truth was, Dad simply loved golf. He loved the smell of the grass, the blue skies under which he labored, the sound of club striking ball, and the lovely arc of a shot well struck. Most importantly, he loved helping golfers play better. That he could charge hefty fees for his instruction had little to do with it. In fact, Dad's little secret was that sometimes he charged nothing at all!

Dad had a real soft spot for young players with ambition and a high degree of empathy for those who were struggling financially as they chased their dreams of playing golf professionally. One such player was Maria Marino, who toiled on the LPGA Tour for four years in the late 1980s before shifting her energies to golf teaching and a business career. Marino first went to see Dad at Frenchman's Creek. She wrote to me later that "people had told me how truthful your Dad was ... and I was fearful that he would tell me I wasn't good enough to play on the LPGA Tour. He was great. He told me that with a little practice I would be just as good and hit it just as long as the girls on tour." Maria said that when she tried to pay my father for that first lesson, "he told me to keep the money and go eat a steak so I could put some weight on."

There is an echo in that story of my father's earliest work with Jack Nicklaus, when Dad didn't want to bill Charlie Nicklaus for the young man's frequent lessons. It's clear that my father didn't set out to find riches in professional golf. He fell in love with the game at his first glimpse of a golf course back in Oklahoma City in 1918, and he played it professionally, then taught it for decades, much more for the camaraderie involved and the many chances it gave him to help people, than for the remuneration. Dad charged a buck an hour for his lessons in 1925 and $100 an hour or more in his later years, and while it pleased him a great deal to know that he could command that kind of money for doing what he dearly loved, it also gave him pause. "Dickie, I feel kinda bad about charging these nice people who come to me for lessons a hundred dollars," he once told me. "But when I see what other people charge me for things, then I don't feel so bad."

***

Mom and Dad returned to Columbus in May 1987, and in late June I enjoyed one of my best moments in our father-son relationship. Dad and Mom came to our house, and Denise and I gave him a Father's Day card with a check for the amount we'd borrowed from my parents to help us buy our first house. "Dickie, what the hell is this?" Dad demanded. "Can you afford to do this?" It was a nice moment, nice to be able to pay him back for yet another kindness.

That summer was a good one for my father, although he and mom were distressed at the June death of E.W. Bradley—mom's brother-in-law, who had introduced her to Dad back in December 1940. Uncle Ed was eighty-seven, and my parents drove to Florida for the funeral, which was on my mom's sixty-sixth birthday.

The rest of the summer was much happier, with Mom and Dad in Ohio and Dad eagerly awaiting the holding of the twenty-seventh Ryder Cup matches at Muirfield Village Golf Club. I was standing immediately behind the eighteenth green, with him to my left and my wife to my right, during the Cup's opening ceremonies on September 24. The two teams were introduced, and there was lots of excitement with bagpipes playing and people being stirred by the pageantry. But it all came together in a single wonderful moment for my father as the Ohio State University band came marching up the eighteenth fairway. Dad's love of Muirfield Village, Jack Nicklaus, the game of golf and, yes, marching bands, was almost too much for him. I thought all the buttons on his shirt and jacket were going to pop off. As the band erupted in a raucous drumroll, Dad said, "Dickie, what the hell is that?" Then the entire band marched right up to the front of the eighteenth green. Wow!

Less spectacular that week was the play of the American squad. With Jack Nicklaus captaining the U.S. team and Tony Jacklin the Europeans, the visitors posted their first Ryder Cup win on American soil, fifteen points to thirteen. A few days later, Mom and Dad departed Columbus for another winter in Florida, the start of a year that would bring very bad news for my father.

***

My parents were back at their home in Tequesta, Florida, in March 1988 when I called to wish Dad a happy seventy-eighth birthday. I didn't call early enough, though; by the time I tried to reach him, he already had left for his teaching job at the Loxahatchee Club. "He took off for the club like he was shot out of a cannon," my mother said. When I left for my job back in Ohio that morning, I smiled at the thought that here Dad was, seventy-eight and with health issues, and he still couldn't wait to get to the golf course!

Dad continued to give a lot of lessons even into his seventy-ninth year and, particularly, to spend as much time as possible with Jack Nicklaus. The two spent dozens of hours on the practice range but, as Nicklaus noted, not necessarily working on golf technique. "Jack would call me in the morning and say, 'What are you doing today, Jackie buck?'" Nicklaus recalled. "And I would say, 'Well, Jack, what do you want to do?' And he said, 'Well, I thought maybe we would go out to the golf course today and hit some golf balls.'" Nicklaus admitted that, by this time in his golf career, he "had no desire to go out and hit golf balls," but that "I had a lot of desire to go out and spend time with Jack Grout. He was a wonderful man. We would go out on the driving range, go down there and hit balls ... and ... talk about everything but golf and my golf swing."

Looking back at those sessions in an interview for this book, Nicklaus said the discussions wandered from topic to topic, just comfortable communication between two old friends. "Most of the conversation might be about me, or about Dickie (Grout), or my kids and their golf games. We very rarely got into anything about our personal lives," Nicklaus said. "He was a big horse guy. He might talk occasionally about a horse, but not too often because he knew I didn't really pay too much attention to that. We might talk about sports or a football game or, I don't know, we just talked."

The two men "did that, day after day," Nicklaus said, "and finally maybe after four or five days, we would be hitting balls and he would finally say, 'Hey, you know, I would like to see your hands in a little different position at the top.' Oh, really? What do you think that would do? 'It will make you hit it better.' OK, we'll do that." The infrequency of those golf-instruction exchanges was the norm in those late days of their relationship. "We weren't talking about golf," Nicklaus said. "We were talking about being friends and the relationship between two people."

***

At Muirfield Village in the summer of 1988, Dad would make his way to the club most days, even when feeling his lowest; he wanted to see his friends and give a golf lesson or two. Dad's eyesight was very poor by this point. Sometimes through his later years I would stand on the lesson tee with him as he watched Nicklaus hit balls, and Dad would turn to me from time to time to ask what I thought. What I really thought was that Dad just couldn't see where Big Jack's shots were going.

Former LPGA Tour player Marino remembered that when she sought Dad's help with her game in the late 1980s, "His eyesight wasn't so good ... but he could tell me where the shot went just from the sound it made off the club head." Pandel Savic picked up on the same thing as he watched Dad and Nicklaus on the Muirfield Village practice range, observing that my father "could tell by the sound of the ball whether (Nicklaus) was hitting it properly or not."

At that time, I was working in Columbus as a golf professional at Winding Hollow Country Club and staying pretty busy Tuesday through Sunday. Most Monday evenings Denise and I and our children would meet NaNa and PaPa for dinner somewhere in Columbus, and I have many good memories of those dinners. Dad always looked forward to seeing each of his grandchildren—at that time, six total. In the summer of '88 our Natalie was four years old and Tony was nearly two. They made Dad laugh with their carryings-on and he made them laugh with his antics. Dad said, "Dickie, this whole babysitting situation is backward if you ask me. (Babysitters) should pay you to (let them) look after these kids, not the other way around." That really was the way Dad felt about kids. The well-behaved kids, that is. Truth is, he didn't much care for the out-of-control ones.

Our times at the dinner table throughout that summer reflected Jack Grout at his best. He always wanted to know how things were going for me at Winding Hollow. How were my lessons going? How were the members treating me? Was I making any money? Anything that I possibly was going through at my golf club, he had been through many times. So he always had an answer for my troubles. As wonderful as those family dinners were, though, there was one problem: Dad wouldn't eat. His appetite was gone. No matter how thin he was becoming and how much he needed to eat in order to keep his weight up, he shunned food. And soon we found out why. In early June, Dad's doctors told him of some "health" concerns they'd discovered. A CAT scan followed a week later, then after another three days, the diagnosis: Dad had lymphoma. Within days, radiation treatments for the cancer were started.

***

By the summer of 1988, my father and Jack Nicklaus had traveled together for thirty-eight years through a golfing adventure they never could have imagined when they first met. Nicklaus had become one of the most famous and honored athletes in the world, and Dad, while never seeking accolades, had drawn his share of attention for being the great golfer's instructor. "Obviously," mused Muirfield's Boomer Byrum, "(Jack Grout's) ticket to life was that he taught Jack Nicklaus how to play golf ... People wanted to go to Jack Grout (to learn) to be the next Jack Nicklaus." But Byrum also noted, accurately, that my father never reached for the spotlight. He preferred to linger in the shadows as Nicklaus and other famous pupils took the glory.

There was nothing Jack Nicklaus would have loved more than for my father to have been able to join him and his party of friends and the Memorial Tournament staff at the *Golf Magazine* "Golfer of the Century" award celebration in New York that June, and perhaps share in the glory of Jack's award. But it was out of the question; Dad was just too ill to travel. Even if Dad had been feeling well, I doubt that he would have enjoyed going to the Big Apple. Too much hassle. He was delighted for Nicklaus but content to stay home and read about the awards event.

Shortly after returning from New York, Nicklaus called my dad, something he'd been doing regularly just to shoot the breeze and try to cheer up his faltering teacher. Dad was touched by the thoughtfulness of the call and the fill-in on the awards event, and he quickly expressed his appreciation in a letter to his famous friend:

> Dear Jack:
>
> I appreciated your call more than I can tell you. As you might have guessed from my voice, I don't have a lot of pep these days. If I had had a little more energy, I would have told you a couple of things. Since I didn't, or couldn't, I have asked Bonnie to help me write this letter.
>
> What I wanted to tell you is this. I know you have had so many honors over the years that they are becoming old hat. I think, nevertheless, that you ought to pay some attention to this latest "Player of the Century" honor. Don't go get a big head or anything like that, but at the same time don't shrug it off either. Those people must have given a lot of thought about it. I can tell you from personal experience that you won over a bunch of real good players. I haven't lived the entire hundred years, so I haven't known them all. But for you to have placed ahead of Jones, Hogan, Nelson, Hagen, Snead and Sarazen—to mention a few I did know—was some kind of accomplishment.
>
> I think I know how you did it, Jack. I used to think that the greatest thing in the world was high achievement in sport. Now that I have more time to sit around and think about things, I have decided that even greater than high achievement in sport is high achievement in sportsmanship. Your dad and your mother taught you about the second one, and I think that's why you won.
>
> Whether I taught you anything about golf or not is not for me to say. In your own heart you know whether I did or not, and I'll take my chances on that. If your development had stopped with your understanding of the mechanics of the game, Jack, it is possible that some of those other great

players would have beat you out. I can tell you that several of them know just about all there is to know about golf.

What you have going for you, however, was born into you and then nurtured by your home life. When Charlie told you you couldn't play anymore if you threw another club he did you a great favor, Jack.

Don't get me wrong. You wouldn't be the 'Player of the Century' if you weren't a heckuva player. But so is Arnold a heckuva player, and Byron, and the rest of them. And they are all great sports. After the judges gave it a lot of thought, though, they gave the honor to the guy who is a great sport and a great sportsman. As far as I am concerned you are the greatest golfer who ever swung a club in the entire history of the game.

I wish you the very best in the coming years. Needless to say, I'd like to be some thirty years younger, so I could share some more of the good times.

All things considered, however, I don't think I have any reason to complain.

Sincerely, Jack

***

That July, all of our family got together for the first time since my wedding in 1981, and all of us were struck by how thin Dad was. Whatever appetite he'd had was stripped away by the radiation. Still, Dad was up and around and was able to give a reduced schedule of lessons at Muirfield. He also found the energy to come by Winding Hollow to check up on how I was doing. Always a stylish man in manner and dress, Dad arrived in a Chevrolet Corvette convertible, the top down, with his good friend Chuck Conrad. Dad looked quite the bon vivant with a classy scarf tied around his neck; he and Chuck had the look of two "with-it" older dudes just out for a cruise on a beautiful autumn day.

After lunch, Dad came into the pro shop to have a look around. I don't know whether he just couldn't see because of his fading eyesight or the place really was dark, but Dad said, "Dickie, you need to do something with this place. Get some light in here; it looks like a goddamn cave!"

Dad departed Columbus for the last time early that October of 1988. Three days after he and Mom made the two-day drive down to Tequesta, Dad was feeling so weak that he had to be hospitalized, this time for twelve days. The radiation treatments in Columbus had slowed the cancer somewhat but had sapped his energy. Once back in the soothing warmth of Florida's late fall, though, Dad tried to rally. Even when feeling his lowest physically in the following months, he would drag himself out to the Loxahatchee Club to give a lesson or two and have lunch with his friends. Dad also would muster up whatever energy it took to see Jack Nicklaus whenever Big Jack was at the club. Dad wanted to watch Jack hit balls or simply to say hello and talk a bit. Nicklaus recalled Dad's frailty during those meetings, saying, "Frequently I had such a lump in my throat I could hardly respond adequately."

For my father, every visit to a golf course, whether one at which he worked or the scores on which he played as a touring professional against the early legends of the game, provided a jolt of sheer joy. Dad just loved the sights and sounds of a golf course, the smell of just-cut grass, the flowers, the lakes, the civility of the game itself, and he cherished his times with Nicklaus and other good friends at Loxahatchee in his final months. By the end of March 1989, though, his cancer had left him gravely ill and debilitated. With Mom and my sister Debbie there to see after him, he settled into his final months at home.

Mom and Debbie doted on Dad through his final weeks as he rested in the guest room just off the kitchen. It was a beautiful room, with sand-colored carpet, white rattan furniture and twin beds with white bedspreads with a blue and green flower-bud design. The bed ruffles, valance and an upholstered club chair matched the bedspreads, and Dad had only a few steps to walk to a private bath. Dad liked the room because it was a lot smaller than the master bedroom and closer to the kitchen and Florida Room that were the nerve centers of this little health-care enterprise.

Eventually hospice would begin coming in daily to check Dad's vitals and give him his medication. Dad napped during the day, seldom watched TV, ate little, and occasionally made it to the den, but only with assistance. His nights were rough. Mom would be with him in his room, trying to make him comfortable, but comfort now was beyond reach. His body was just shutting down.

In early April, I flew from Ohio down to Florida to surprise my family, and my visit to see Dad just happened to be during the week of the Masters Tournament. As a family, we watched the tournament together, but it was my special duty to report the results back to Dad as he lay in bed. Not only could he not get out of bed at this point, he couldn't even raise his head from the pillow. While I was there, I spent as much time with him as possible, cherishing the opportunity to talk with him, express my sentiments, and remember everything I could about the experience. Throughout, I clung to my conviction that, somehow, he and Mom would return for the 1989 summer golf season in Ohio.

During our talks that spring, Dad and I exchanged a lot of memories. We talked about golf, our personal aspirations for and feelings about life, and our own relationship. Looking back at his career, Dad talked with quiet passion about the profession he'd chosen. "From the very beginning," he said one day, "the enthusiasm and excitement I felt for the game of golf never left me. All my life I just couldn't wait to get to the club in the morning. Going to work was pure joy for me and working continually at something I loved was easy. It was around golf where I seemed to feel the most comfortable and relaxed. I enjoyed that atmosphere above anything else I ever came across. Golf always gave me the same feeling I got that very first day back in Oklahoma City. It made me feel young to be around the game."

One day, I summoned the strength to talk with Dad about some of the shadows that had crossed my path. I guess that, without knowing it at the time, I was in the midst of taking "a last lesson" from my father. During that heart-to-heart, I said to him, "Dad, we both tried so hard to bring out my best as a player, and it didn't work out the way we wanted. I just want to say I'm sorry I never became the player you wanted me to be." Dad listened closely as I talked. Then he looked up from his pillow and calmly said, "Dickie, it's OK. You were a good player, and even more importantly, you were a good boy, and that's just fine with me."

Dad's simple response lifted what felt like the weight of the world off my shoulders. I knew that my father never tossed words around in a careless way, and especially not at a moment like that when both of us were speaking to each other so intimately. I'm certain he meant what he said to me. For that one small statement he uttered, and for so much more, I will always be grateful. My father was a gentle man with a loving heart, and in that fact resides the full measure of his greatness.

I wanted to stay a few more days, but Dad knew it would be best for me to head back home; the old pro knew I needed to get back to my job. Though I protested, he said it was time for me to leave. As I prepared to depart the next morning, I was unusually strong emotionally because I'd convinced myself that Dad would return to Muirfield Village for the summer. I went into his room to say good-bye; we talked, and he began crying. I had rarely seen my father lose his emotions in that way, so it confused me. I looked at my mother for some help, but she just smiled and motioned for me to take off.

As I reluctantly pulled away from their house, I still felt pretty good about everything, and I drove what must have been a hundred miles north of the Palm Beach area before it finally hit me. I suddenly realized that my father was crying because he knew that he'd never see me again. At that realization, I completely lost it and broke down sobbing. It took many miles until I regained my composure and felt better.

Chapter 24
Last Will and Testament

"Hit it hard and long, and worry about direction later." —JACK GROUT

***

My father and Jack Nicklaus had their final visit at the Grout home two weeks before Dad's death, and it was a visit to which Nicklaus had not looked forward. "I've always hated that kind of stuff, to walk in when you know it's probably the last time you're going to see somebody," Nicklaus said. "Nobody wants to be seen just before they go." Both men grew emotional as Nicklaus entered the bedroom where Dad awaited the end. "He cried," Nicklaus recalled, "and I knew that he knew that it was probably the last time (for me) to see him, and I cried when I walked out. I shared a bond with somebody for so many years that was now coming to an end. We both felt very strong about that, emotional."

Barbara Nicklaus and my mom shared memories nearby as Nicklaus and my father talked, and Nicklaus would say later that even in his weakened condition, Dad could be impish: "Behind their back," Nicklaus said, "Jack was making faces." In recalling that day, Nicklaus also has told of a remarkable gesture made by my dad, even as he lay so near death. "It was just after the Masters, and he's asking me, 'Why did you hit it right of the hole at eighteen? What changes do you have to make?' " Nicklaus said. "His mind was still very sharp ... (and he) made me stand up, take a stance and a swing. He told me why I hit the ball to the right. He was still teaching, and he couldn't even get out of bed!"

It was an appropriate ending to the story of two men whose lives and careers had been so tightly entwined. My father, on his deathbed, giving a final lesson to his star pupil, the man who under his decades-long tutelage had become the greatest champion in the history of golf.

Almost from their first meeting, Jack Grout and Jack Nicklaus had become more than simply teacher and student. Their relationship had grown into a deep, fast friendship—the trim, soft-spoken Oklahoman and the husky golf prodigy from Ohio, pursuing their dreams together. Now, with thoughts quietly expressed and loving respect wordlessly exchanged, the two men had said their final good-bye.

***

At 7:50 in the morning on May 13, 1989, Mom called with the news I had been dreading: "We lost your father."

I had known this was coming but still was stunned. I wrote in my calendar that day, "My Hero Has Fallen."

Debbie had been up early that morning and had seen that Mother and Dad were awake. Mom said they'd had a rough night and she was trying to get Dad to drink a little juice, so Debbie helped with things in Dad's room. A bit later, Mom entered Debbie's room and said, "I think Daddy's gone." They returned to his bedside, and Debbie, leaning close to Dad's face, actually felt him take his last breath.

I was there with my family two nights later when Jack and Barbara Nicklaus and other friends came to offer their condolences. Then there was a viewing for the family the next day at Aycock Funeral Home in Jupiter. Dad was dressed in his pajamas and robe—the pajamas with drawstring pants and the bathrobe with a navy, light blue, fine check on a white background. "He looked so nice and comfortable, just like he was sleeping," Debbie said. "No stuffy suit, tie. Just totally comfy."

The funeral Mass on the 18th was at Dad and Mom's parish church, St. Clare's, in North Palm Beach, with internment at Riverside Memorial Park in Tequesta. Dad was cremated, and his remains were placed in one of a twin set of bronze urns, the other eventually occupied by my mother's ashes after her death on September 26, 2006. The nameplate on Dad's urn said: "Jack F. Grout."

***

Given their relationship, it was no surprise that my father remembered Jack Nicklaus in his last will and testament. Nor was it a surprise that Dad showed in that last message to his friend a character trait that, perhaps as much as his playing and teaching talents, enabled him to be a success in the golf profession. That is, while dealing with so many of the key figures at the top of the game of golf for more than half a century, my father somehow had been able to maintain his most effective and endearing characteristic: a steadfast refusal to take himself too seriously or to take too much credit for the successes of his friends and students.

In that final declaration, to be read after his life's end, he wrote:

"In all honesty, I don't think I ever hurt Jack's golf game in any way. To put it another way, if he had not come under my tutelage in the early 1950s, I don't see how he could have turned out much better than he did.

"From the outset of our relationship, I recognized that the thunder in his stroke and the courage in his heart were gifts that clearly had been bestowed upon him, and that there was very little I could do to take them away from him.

"I do not mean to suggest that I made no contribution whatsoever to his game. For one thing, I worked him hard (and he seemed to enjoy every minute of it). I made him stand away from the ball with his arms fully extended, and I insisted that he swing hard. Within a few months you could hear the swish of his club head all over the practice range when he took one of his legendary cuts at the ball ...

"I always tried to encourage him; and in the very early days of his development I made a special effort to explain how extraordinary I thought his talents were, and for that matter still are ...

"There is not the slightest doubt in my mind that Jack Nicklaus is the finest golfer ever to swing a club in the entire history of the game. It has been a distinct honor and great pleasure for me to have played some part in his career. And that brings me to my final bequest.

"To you, Jack Nicklaus, I give my thanks."

Jack Nicklaus first read those words just hours after my father's death. At his home at Muirfield Village, awaiting his tee time in his own Memorial Tournament, Nicklaus was told of Dad's message and asked whether he wanted to read it before his round. He said he did.

When he was finished, the Golden Bear ... the toughest competitor and greatest champion any man ever faced across the first tee of a golf course anywhere in the world ... a man who ground his opponents down and broke their will not only with his talent and his sheer determination but also with self-confidence and self-possession that were as impenetrable as a slab of cold, hard granite ... that extraordinarily accomplished and very tough man ... broke down and cried.

Raymond Floyd Remembers Jack Grout

"You'll never know everything there is about this game because the deeper you scratch there'll always be more."—JACK GROUT

***

It was such a familiar scene on the practice range at big golf tournaments in my day. Players would be lined up hitting balls, working on their swings. And here would come this tall, slender, classy-looking man, quietly saying "hello" and "how you doing?" to this player, then the next and the next.

Occasionally one of the players—it could be a major-tournament winner such as David Graham or Gary Player, or it might be a young pro just starting his life on the PGA Tour—would stop the man and ask, "Would you mind checking out my swing?" And Jack Grout, this great golf teacher and fine gentleman, would just smile and say, "Sure. Show me what you've got."

And more often than not, after the player had made a few swings or maybe even a few dozen, Jack would say a word or two, ask a quiet question, make a respectful suggestion. The player would absorb every word this highly accomplished man said, then go back to work, and likely find that whatever swing flaw Jack had pointed out soon would become a distant memory.

Through most of my prime years on the PGA Tour, from the early 1970s through the 1980s, I had the real privilege of getting regular golf instruction from Jack Grout, and I watched as the scene I described above played out again and again. Jack Grout was like a magnet; this, after all, was the man who had taught the great Jack Nicklaus how to play golf, and player after player sought him out, hoping that the magic he and Nicklaus had created might rub off on them.

I can say proudly that in my case some of it did rub off. Under Jack's gentle but persistent coaxing, I was able in the mid-1970s to modify a golf swing that somehow had gone badly off course in the preceding years. And I began to win again, including three more major tournaments to go with the PGA Championship that I won before beginning serious work with Jack. As I wrote in a letter to him after perhaps my most cherished victory at the U.S. Open in 1986, I never could have achieved what I did on the golf course without his instruction, and certainly not without the constant encouragement he gave me.

They don't hand out advanced academic degrees for knowledge of the golf swing, but if they did, Jack Grout would have been one of the first to earn a Ph.D. in the subject. Yet while he certainly possessed a vast storehouse of knowledge about how to play the game of golf, perhaps his greatest asset as a teacher was that he understood human nature so well. Simply put, Jack Grout was a master in the field of personal motivation. No matter how badly you felt about your game, no matter how poorly you were playing, Jack would find something within the accumulated gloom to pick out as a positive, and he would hammer that into your brain: "Boy, you do that well, Raymond. You're looking great when you do that, Raymond. Just keep doing that!"

Raymond Floyd standing beside Jack Grout on the practice tee at Frenchman's Creek in 1980. (Grout family photo)

Jack's enthusiasm was energizing, no matter how bad your swing might be at that time, and you would begin to focus on the few little things you were doing well rather than the mass of things you were fouling up. Soon, with the proper amount of work, you would find the positives taking over and your game coming around. They really were inspiring experiences for me, these sessions with Jack on the practice tees at a series of clubs where he taught in Florida and at Muirfield Village in Ohio during Jack Nicklaus' annual Memorial Tournament. I always knew I would come away from a session with Jack Grout feeling the one thing that is most important for any highly competitive athlete: I felt—no, I *knew*—that I could win.

Sometimes after the Florida work sessions I would head to the golf course with Dick Grout, and we would share thoughts about his father, about Jack Grout the teacher, and Jack Grout the man. I could see reflected in Dick the same passion for the game of golf and for life that always characterized his father. It's fitting that Dick now has shared with us the full story of his beloved father's journey from the fledgling town of Oklahoma City, through the windswept golf venues of Texas and on to his serendipitous meeting with the young Jack Nicklaus, and their journey together into golf's history books. It's really quite a story.

His Rightful Place ...

"If you love this game as I do, your work will be a labor of love."
—JACK GROUT

❊❊❊

One measure of any man's life is how well and how often he is remembered once he's gone. In Jack Grout's case, there is ample evidence that he is remembered fondly and often.

Yes, by his closest friends and family. But also by the hundreds, perhaps thousands, of men and women he touched in his life as a golf professional.

Jack Nicklaus remembers.

Asked during an interview for this book whether he still thinks about Jack Grout, Nicklaus had a quick and firm reply:

"Oh yeah, I do that all the time. I'll go out on the practice range and I'll say to one of my kids or even to one of my grandkids, 'You know, J. Grout used to say to me ... ' I think of Jack a lot. As a matter of fact, there are a lot of times I'll be places, and—my kids all were taught by Jack, too—and sometimes they'll turn around and say, 'J. Grout, what would he have said about this?' "

As countless stories throughout this book document, the world's best professional golfers and the most-talented amateur players—even real hackers who were invited to his lesson tee and marveled at the insights and the kindness they found there—all are part of the chorus praising one of golf's greatest teachers.

The recognition, however, stalls there. Because thus far, Jack Grout's well-earned place in the World Golf Hall of Fame sits empty, the Hall having failed to act on the compelling case for his induction. This despite the words of golfing legend Arnold Palmer, words echoed by so many: "I had the greatest respect for (Jack Grout's) talents as a teacher and the way he dealt with people... He was a great man who had a very positive impact on the game we all love."

Why is Jack Grout overlooked by the golf establishment?

Maybe it's because, in our modern world, he who wants attention had best be an ambitious seeker of that attention.

And Jack Grout was not.

Olin Browne was one of many who attested to that. Winner of eight pro tournaments, including the 2011 Senior U.S. Open and three events on the PGA Tour, Browne was a student of Grout's at Muirfield Village and in Florida. And throughout their work together, Browne was struck by his famed instructor's lack of ego. In Browne's view, Jack Grout's noninclusion in golf's halls of honor "speaks volumes about what kind of person he was. He didn't toot his own horn; that is not what motivated him."

Then Browne added something that summarizes perfectly the essence of Jack Grout and perhaps the real reason he has been denied golf's ultimate honor.

"I know he greatly loved his wife and his kids, and he was just a kind and gentle man. He wasn't a complicated person. He was simple. He enjoyed his life; he lived his life the way he wanted to live it and on his terms. He didn't look for accolades or recognition of any kind ... I think that's one of the reasons why he's not talked about a great deal."

Testimonials abound:

"There is a void because he is not there (in the Hall of Fame)," said Raymond Floyd.

"A gross oversight," said David Graham.

"His inclusion should have happened years ago," said twenty-two-year LPGA veteran Beth Stone.

"(Jack Grout's) impact was very, very high," said Lanny Wadkins. "Number 1, consider that he was essentially the only instructor that the greatest player of all time had."

Wadkins, who upon his World Golf Hall of Fame induction in 2009 candidly expressed disappointment that he had not been selected a bit sooner, was candid again in assessing Jack Grout's overdue selection. "Seeing that we keep putting a lot of former (U.S.) presidents in," he said, "then we ought to look at some people who *really* had an impact on the game."

Bruce Devlin and Jo Ann Prentiss used slightly varying words but echoed Gary Player, who said Jack Grout "deserves his rightful place in the annals of golf."

That day still may come, in the view of Golf Teachers Hall of Fame inductee Bob Toski.

Jack Grout's effectiveness as a teacher, said Toski, "has never been realized because teachers were not marketed (in his day) the way they are today. Jack Grout never got the exposure that a teacher gets today."

But, Toski said, "Time will prove his greatness."

Author's Note

The phone rang in the pro shop at Muirfield Village Golf Club one afternoon in March 1995.

When assistant pro Tim Krapfel answered, he was surprised and suspicious when the caller identified himself as Byron Nelson and asked to speak to me. Krapfel—affectionately known as "Krappy" within the golf shop—thought it surely was a prank, the latest stunt by a club member and jokester buddy of his named Frank Stavroff.

"Hey, Stavs, quit fooling around," Tim replied.

Never much for shenanigans, the eighty-three-year-old Nelson responded sternly, "Young man, this is Byron Nelson. Do you know who I am?"

Tim's jaw dropped. Flustered and embarrassed, he apologized profusely and explained that "Dickie" wasn't available, but that he would surely pass along Mr. Nelson's message.

The next day Tim incredulously asked me, "Do you know Byron Nelson? And is there any reason he might have called the pro shop yesterday, asking to speak with you?"

The answer was that I had begun work on a book about my dad, Jack Grout. Thinking how interesting his story would be to golfers and non-golfers alike, I had started contacting some of the golfing greats from my dad's time on tour, including Nelson, just to collect their memories and thoughts on my father. All along I'd been categorizing any remembrances and stories about my dad as they popped into my head. I also collected newspaper articles and magazine stories about him, thinking that maybe someday I'd do something with them.

I could not have hoped for a better glimpse into the distant past than Byron Nelson provided, or a more candid assessment of my father, who was his good friend and touring companion for many years. When we spoke, Lord Byron (as he became known in the 1930s) was excited because it was the fiftieth anniversary of his amazing 1945 season, when he won eighteen of the thirty-one tournaments he played, including eleven in a row. I asked him why my father didn't have a better record on the pro circuit, especially considering his classic swing and later success as a golf teacher. "He had everything he needed except toughness," Nelson replied, then added, "Don't get me wrong. I was a nice guy, too. It's just that when the tournament started, I put the nice guy in me aside until it was over."

The truth is that the name Jack Grout had been lost a bit in the pages of golf history by 1995, even though he was the revered head professional at venerable Scioto Country Club in Columbus, Ohio, and always will be remembered as the man who took the young Jack Nicklaus under his wing and helped him become the greatest golf champion that ever lived. Lasting fame in golf, it seems, goes to players who win numerous tournaments, and especially major championships.

My dad would not have felt that a book about him was merited; he never was one to talk about his professional accomplishments or launch into stories about himself or his family. A person could go many years and travel great distances before they'd come across a more "private" man than Jack Grout.

It's for these reasons that working on this book has been so rewarding. My research, including scores of interviews, letters, email exchanges and telephone calls with my father's contemporaries and associates, led me to wonderful anecdotes about big-name golfers of Dad's day such as Hagen, Sarazen, Hogan, Snead and, of course, Byron Nelson, and about excellent but lesser-known players such as Henry Picard, Ky Laffoon, Martin Pose and Rod Munday. And I learned much more about my father's work with his prized pupils Jack Nicklaus and Raymond Floyd, and with many other leading tour pros.

Like these wonderful players, my dad lived a memorable life on the golf course and off. He competed with and succeeded against some of the world's most talented golfers, and later welcomed to his lesson tee a generation of the game's best players. Yet he was so humble that more than two decades after his death, his own inspiring story had yet to be fully told. At last, that's no longer the case.

I hope the various golf halls of fame are taking note, and they act soon to honor a man who defined what it means to be a class act, both in sport and in life.

Dick Grout

***

Co-Author's Note

It was a typically beautiful spring day on a practice green at the Cliffs Resort golf complex in South Carolina. My wife strolled over, pointed at a tall, slender man across the green, and said, "You should talk with him."

"Why?"

"Because he's a golf pro here, his father apparently was a famous golf instructor, and he's planning to write a book about him and is looking for a journalist to help write it."

"And his dad's name?"

"I didn't recognize the name. Something like 'Grout,' maybe?"

Now she had my attention. "Rosanne, do you mean 'Jack Grout'?"

"Yeah, I think that may be it."

"Here, hold my putter."

"Hello," I said to Dick Grout a moment later. "I understand your father was Jack Grout and you're looking for a journalist to help you write a book about him."

"Why, yes, I am."

"Actually, no, you're not," I said, pointing to my own chest. "Because here he is."

Then we talked. And what became obvious very quickly was, first, that Dick Grout was as devoted to honoring his father's memory as a son could be, and second, that Jack Grout not only deserved to have a book written about him, but that the book could be a wonderful contribution to the literature of golf.

Dick and I soon set off together on a four-year journey through nearly a century of golf history, beginning with the U.S. pro-golf circuit's hardscrabble days and that time when caddies were fixtures at every course. We tracked Jack Grout's up-and-down decades as a player on that early tour, where he was surrounded by some of the game's toughest-ever competitors. We followed him through his awkward, long-distance, letter-filled courtship of his beloved Bonnie. And we delighted in the story of his serendipitous meeting with a Columbus, Ohio, druggist named Charlie Nicklaus, a proud father who soon would deliver his young son to Jack Grout's golf lesson tee—the launching pad from which Jack William Nicklaus soared into the ranks of the game's legendary players.

I thank Dick Grout for allowing me along on a fascinating ride.

And I thank Rosanne for holding that putter.

Bill Winter

Acknowledgments

Many people in and around golf provided valuable information and encouragement for this book. My warmest thanks go to those who knew my father and are mentioned in the pages of this book and to those whose contributions the book reflects indirectly, including: Steve Auch, curator of the Jack Nicklaus Museum; Sally Becker, daughter of Jean and Rod Munday; Andy Coats, dean emeritus, University of Oklahoma School of Law; Peter T. Eagle, president of Eagle International; Maureen Feeley and Adam Wallace, PGA Tour communications department; Anita Franco, Arlington, Texas, Public Library; Brett Folkes, Illinois Section PGA Headquarters; my cousins Regina Gallus, from Texas, and Bert Grout, from Chicago; Dave Lancer, PGA Tour Headquarters; Sidney L. Matthew, P.A., author and Bobby Jones historian; Patty Moran, USGA Library; Larry Oberman, member/historian, Green Acres Country Club; Woodgie Reich, member/historian, Northmoor Country Club; Corbett (Mark) Thigpen, MD; Pete Trenham, historian, PGA Philadelphia Section; Adrian Whited, historian, Los Angeles Country Club; retired sports writer Kaye Kessler; Rosanne L. Winter, Ph.D., Winter Associates LLC; Jeffrey Franco, PGA Southern Ohio Section; Jimmy Headrick, PGA Gulf States Section; Keith Marks, PGA Carolinas Section; and Patrick Kenny, also PGA Carolinas Section, a wonderful man and one of my greatest supporters.

I would like to convey my great fortune in having Bill Winter as the book's co-author. His experience as a journalist gave organization and guidance to the story. He understood the importance of telling my father's story and relating it in a way that would both preserve and honor my father's memory. In addition to contributing further research and interviews for the project, Bill also brought Denny Dressman to the team. Denny, our talented editor and fast friend, cast his eagle eye over the manuscript and contributed numerous facts and perspectives that were vital to the completion of the book. Denny's advice and judgment were invaluable to both of us throughout this project. I appreciate him not only for understanding our vision for the book, but for helping make that vision a reality.

I also would like to credit my good friend Bob Grossi for his role as our literary agent. A longtime avid golfer who knows and appreciates the game, Bob displayed steady and shrewd acumen while navigating our manuscript through the challenges facing traditional book publishing. His absolute professionalism coupled with his patient, kind and respectful manner made him a pleasure to work with. Bob's admiration for my father's life story and his energy for promotion were, undoubtedly, important elements in Blue River Press deciding to publish the book. My gratitude also to Tom Doherty of Cardinal Publishing and Blue River Press, who saw the possibilities in my father's life story.

Special thanks go to my brother, John Grout. Throughout the process, he offered encouragement and was an active promoter of my efforts. He provided some great recollections, undoubtedly making the story even better. I appreciate his never-ending support and his desire to see this project succeed.

Finally, I'd like to thank Denise, my wife of thirty years. She was, and is, a great inspiration. Honorable mention goes to our two children, Natalie and Tony. They continuously offer me a fresh outlook on life and are fiercely protective of their father. To be sure, I have been blessed with loving and supportive family members who deserve my deepest gratitude.

Dick Grout

***

Numerous professional golfers and other friends of Jack Grout provided personal memories of the man for this book. Special thanks go to Jack Nicklaus and Raymond Floyd, whose vivid and appreciative recollections brought the Grout story to life. Golfers Arnold Palmer, Gary Player, David Graham, Olin Browne, Ben Crenshaw, Beth Stone, Jo Ann Prentiss, Lanny Wadkins, Bruce Devlin, Lee Rinker and Jerry Heard; noted golf instructors Jim Flick and Bob Toski; and course designer Jackie Nicklaus and former USGA President Fred Ridley all shared personal memories of Jack Grout or of the Nicklaus-Grout team. Retired Scioto pro shop employee Dom Lepore provided helpful insights into Jack Grout's early days in Columbus, and Muirfield Village clubhouse veteran Rick "Boomer" Byrum told warm stories of Mr. Grout's impact through his later years as an instructional guru. Others shedding light on Jack Grout's teaching techniques and unshakable personal values were friends of Jack Nicklaus including John Bishop, Pandel Savic, Muirfield Village executive John Hines and former Grout assistants Jay Weitzel, Mike Mollis and John Scheffler. Finally, head golf professionals Bill Stines at Scioto Country Club and Larry Dornisch at Muirfield Village, and their staffs, were cheerful facilitators as I poked around their respective clubs in search of information and, of course, good golf!

Scott Tolley of the Nicklaus organization and golfers/broadcast commentators Dottie Pepper and Brandel Chamblee, GolfChannel.com writer/editor Bailey Mosier, Champions Tour media official Phil

Stambaugh and journalists, authors and educators including Dean Mills, Norm Clarke, Ken Bowden, Roger Fidler, Ev Dennis, Jae Bryson, Alan Deutschman, Warren Lerude, Charles Pittman, Alecia Swasy and Kay Mills all offered comments, encouragement and guidance as the book took shape. Thank you.

Finally, my good friend Denny Dressman provided much-needed encouragement plus editing expertise that sharpened the manuscript immeasurably, and my beautiful spouse, Rosanne, was a constant source of encouragement and advice.

Jack Grout had much to be proud of, including his ability to inspire in his progeny great loyalty to their father. His children John, Debbie and Ronnie all contributed personal memories for this book. For his part, Dick Grout truly exemplifies the loving son and has worked tirelessly and admirably to ensure that his father's memory is justly honored. For Dick, this book truly is a life's mission accomplished.

Bill Winter

*Nine linksmen at the 1948 Reading Open: Lew Worsham, George Payton, Ellsworth Vines, Ed Furgol, Spec Hammond, Jim Ferrier, Jimmy Demaret, Skip Alexander and Jack Grout. (*Times *staff photo, used with permission)*

Appendix

JACK GROUT'S CLUBS

Between 1918 and 1989, Jack Grout utilized his unique gift for imparting an exceptional knowledge of the golf swing at seventeen golf and country clubs in the Southwest, Midwest, East and South, including:

Oklahoma City Golf & Country Club, 1918-24
Edgemere Country Club, Oklahoma City, OK, 1925-29
Glen Garden Country Club, Fort Worth, TX, 1930-36
Hershey Country Club, Hershey, PA, 1937-39
Northmoor Country Club, Highland Park, IL, Summer 1938
Irem Temple Country Club, Dallas, PA, 1940
Fox Hill Country Club, West Pittston, PA, 1941-42
Twin Hills Country Club, Oklahoma City, OK, 1943
Green Acres Country Club, Northbrook, IL, 1944
Butterfield Country Club, Hinsdale, IL, 1945
Harrisburg Country Club, Harrisburg, PA, 1946-49
Scioto Country Club, Columbus, OH, 1950-61
La Gorce Country Club, Miami Beach, FL, 1961-74
Muirfield Village Golf Club, Dublin, OH, 1974-89
Cheeca Lodge, Islamorada, FL, Winter 1976-78
Frenchman's Creek Golf Club, Juno Beach, FL, Winter 1979-82
Loxahatchee Club, Tequesta, FL, Winter 1983-89

INSTRUCTION BY JACK GROUT

Among Jack Grout's numerous contributions to the game of golf were three instructional books he wrote to help players improve their games, and one videotape:

Books

Let Me Teach You Golf As I Taught Jack Nicklaus, by Jack Grout, 1974, Atheneum.

On the Lesson Tee, Basic Golf Fundamentals, by Jack Grout, 1982, The Athletic Institute.

Jack Grout's Golf Clinic: Jack Nicklaus' Teacher and Coach, by Jack Grout, 1985, The Athletic Institute.

Videotape

"Keys to Consistency," by Jack Grout—Jack Nicklaus' coach and teacher, 1986, Ardent Video Publishing, Inc.

JACK GROUT'S TOURNAMENT HIGHLIGHTS

In addition to achieving renown for decades of work as a teaching pro, Jack Grout competed against almost two dozen future members of the World Golf Hall of Fame, including Walter Hagen, Byron Nelson, Ben Hogan, Sam Snead, Jimmy Demaret, Henry Picard, Gene Sarazen, Horton Smith, Paul Runyan and Harry Cooper. He played on the fledgling professional golf tour for nineteen consecutive years, from 1931 through 1949, twice in 1953 and in the U.S. Open of 1956. Here are some highlights of his playing career:

Nassau Open (1937), Bahamas C.C., Grand Bahamas Island; tied for fourth with Paul Runyan, four strokes behind Sam Snead

Pasadena Open (1938), Brookside Park G.C., Pasadena, CA; tied for sixth with Horton Smith, six strokes behind Henry Picard

Mid-South Professional Four-Ball (1938), Pinehurst No. 2, Pinehurst, NC; co-champion team with Henry Picard, tying Tommy Armour and Bobby Cruickshank

Thomasville Open (1941), Glen Arvin C.C., Thomasville, GA; fifth, one shot behind Ben Hogan and one shot ahead of Byron Nelson and Jimmy Demaret

St. Augustine Pro-Amateur (1941), St Augustine Links, St. Augustine, FL; runner-up, lost final match one-up to Sam Snead and amateur partner

Hershey Open (1941), Hershey C.C., Hershey, PA; tied for third behind Ben Hogan and Lloyd Mangrum

Atlantic City Open (1941), Seaview C.C., Atlantic City, NJ; tied for fourth behind Lloyd Mangrum (seven strokes), Vic Ghezzi and Ben Hogan (one stroke)

Radio City Invitational (1941), Pelham G.C., Pelham, NY; winner

Miami International Four-Ball (1942), Biltmore G.C., Coral Gables, FL; runner-up with partner Ben Loving in match play to Herman Keiser and partner, 1950 PGA Champion Chandler Harper

All-American Open (1943), Tam O'Shanter C.C., Niles, IL; tied for sixth by four strokes

Illinois PGA Championship (1945), Skokie C.C., Glencoe, IL; winner by one stroke over Errie Ball, by two over Johnny Revolta

Spring Lake Invitational (1948), Spring Lake G.C., Spring Lake Heights, NJ; winner by two strokes over group including Gene Sarazen and Claude Harmon

People Index

Books, Places, Tournaments Index

About the Authors

Dick Grout is a second-generation PGA golf professional who has followed closely in his famous father's footsteps. He is an accomplished player and teacher who specializes in the history and traditions of the game. As well as having some of his own golfing exploits documented, Grout has assisted a number of journalists in their writings about the extraordinary life of Jack Grout. He also maintains a website through which those wanting more information about the Grout brand of golf can find it: GroutGolf.com. Dick Grout lives in Taylors, South Carolina, with his wife Denise.

Jack Grout's story was written with the assistance of **Bill Winter**, a career wire service and newspaper reporter and editor who also served for sixteen years as president and executive director of the Reston, Virginia-based American Press Institute, the newspaper industry's leadership-development center. Dr. Winter splits his time between northern Ohio and southwest Florida, in both locales exercising with limited success his passion for golf.

Praise for *Jack Grout: A Legacy in Golf*

"Wonderfully entertaining." —*Cleveland Plain Dealer*

"Fascinating." —*Fort Worth Star-Telegram*

"… a valuable contribution to the history of golf." —*Coastal Life*

"(Jack Grout) developed the greatest golfer that the world has ever known." —*Daily Oklahoman*

"If Jack Grout was teaching the best player on the planet in an era of ESPN and the Golf Channel, his name would be everywhere …" —*Tulsa World*

"… a decidedly homespun tale." —theaposition.com

"… many colorful stories..." —golfdigest.com

The Experts on Jack Grout

"I'm delighted that now, through this book, a wide range of people, golfers and non-golfers alike, will come to know the warm, often funny and always eventful story of this good man's life." — Jack Nicklaus, golf's all-time leading major-championship winner

"Jack Grout was a terrific man. He taught without ego. He didn't have to be right about everything, he was just trying to help people." — Olin Browne, 2011 U.S. Senior Open Champion

"Jack Grout was a very encouraging type teacher; not discouraging, nor was he all about himself... He could teach anyone from the beginner to Jack Nicklaus." — Jack Burke, member, World Golf Hall of Fame

"(Jack Grout) had an uncanny ability to read people and get the best out of their athleticism, whether they were professional's or amateurs." — Bob Toski, golf coach and author

"Simply put, Jack Grout is one of the great unsung heroes of American golf...you won't be disappointed by time spent with this delightful tribute." — James Dodson, biographer of Ben Hogan